I0799863

IMAGES
*of America*

# ST. CHARLES

AN ALBUM FROM THE COLLECTION OF THE
ST. CHARLES HERITAGE CENTER

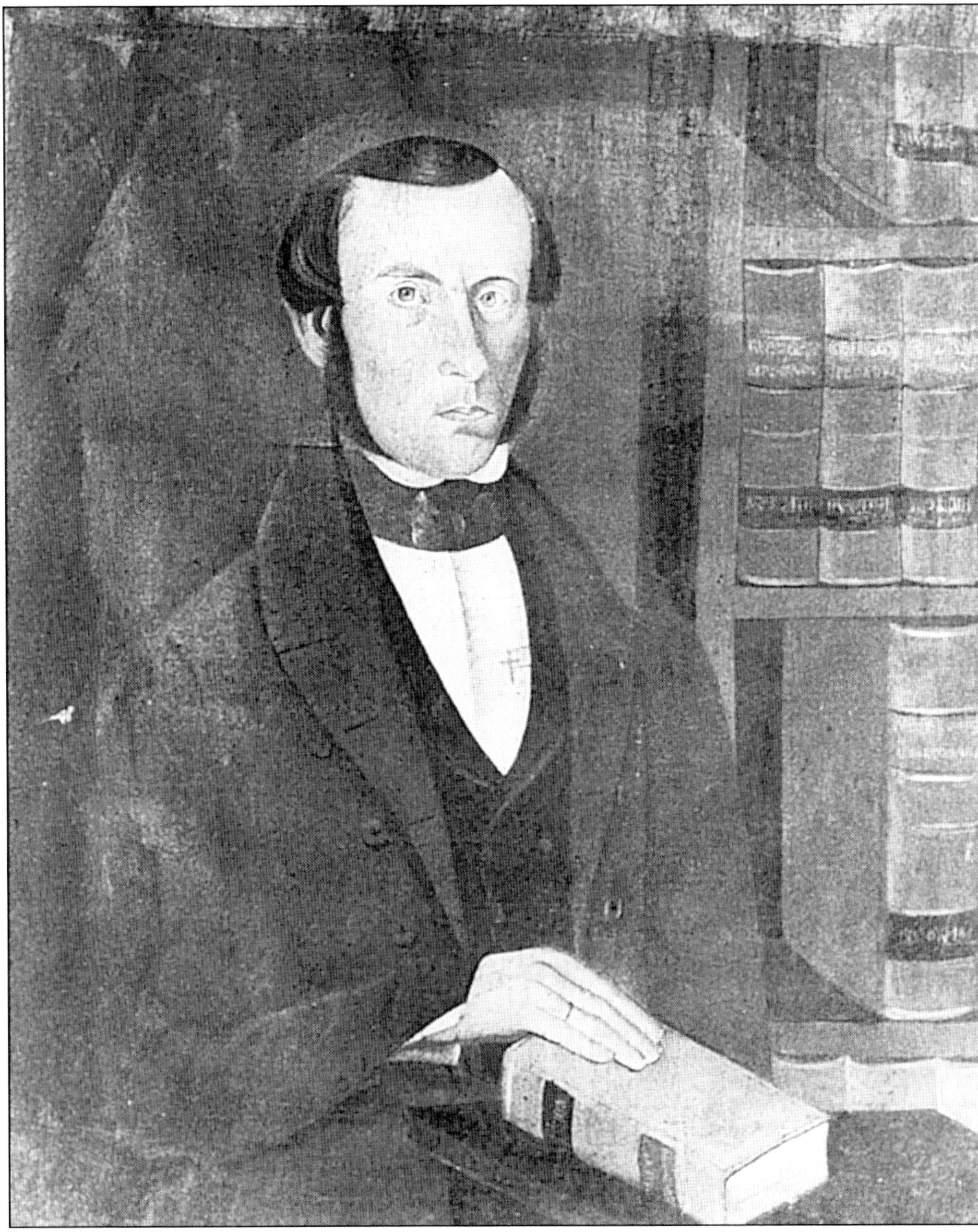

This portrait is attributed to Sheldon Peck, internationally recognized, early-American portrait artist. Inscribed on the back of the portrait is "S.S. Jones Aged 28, July 22, 1841." Peck was an itinerant portrait painter who worked in the folk art tradition. Peck is thought to be self-taught as an artist, and his work spanned the years between the 1820s to his death in 1868. He spent his last years in Illinois, farming and painting.

Stevens S. Jones (1813–1877) and his wife moved to St. Charles from Vermont in June of 1838. He was a lawyer, publisher, and judge. Jones has been credited with suggesting the name St. Charles for the village in 1839 when it was found that the previously adopted name, Charleston, was already in use in Coles County, Illinois.

IMAGES
*of America*

# ST. CHARLES

## AN ALBUM FROM THE COLLECTION OF THE ST. CHARLES HERITAGE CENTER

Wynette Edwards

ARCADIA
PUBLISHING

ISBN 978-0-7385-0125-3

Published by Arcadia Publishing
Charleston, South Carolina

Printed in the United States of America

Library of Congress Catalog Card Number: 99-62771

For all general information contact Arcadia Publishing at:
Telephone 843-853-2070
Fax 843-853-0044
E-mail sales@arcadiapublishing.com
For customer service and orders:
Toll-Free 1-888-313-2665

Visit us on the Internet at www.arcadiapublishing.com

# Contents

#  ACKNOWLEDGMENTS

The St. Charles Heritage Center was formed in 1933, and the photographs, paintings, sculptures, furniture, firearms, manuscripts, books, and everyday objects in the archives have been collected since that time. Much appreciation goes to those who thought enough about the history of the community to donate their personal momentos and antiques to the Center, for without them, looking at daily life in an earlier time would not be possible. Without these visual and written reminders, most people would not be able to visualize life before modern conveniences.

The Center is a repository for the history of St. Charles. The archives for Scholes School, one of the last one-room schools in Kane County, are here. The Dunham-Hunt Museum and Jane Dunham's archives are part of the St. Charles Heritage Center, and the Center is on the National Civil War Discovery Trail.

The photographs in the collection are not from only a few donors but are instead from people from all walks of life. They provide a good look back at what was important to those at all social and economic levels who lived in St. Charles during the first 100 years.

The staff at the St. Charles Heritage Center has been a delight to work with. Thanks so much to Director Jeanne Schultz Angel and Registrar John Costerisan for their enthusiasm, encouragement, and support. People such as these make projects like this one a joy on which to work.

Special thanks are due to Harris Wesson, the Earl Shuman family, Linda Goll, and Nicole Fedorow for their help and assistance. And to my husband, Jim Edwards, with his American History book and red pencil, I give my deepest gratitude.

# INTRODUCTION

*St. Charles: An Album from the Collection of the St. Charles Heritage Center* provides the reader with an interesting piece-by-piece look at the heritage of our town through the medium of photography. The book does not attempt to tell the whole story of St. Charles history, nor does it follow chronological boundaries. Rather, it views the past in snapshots, hoping that the reader will be intrigued by individual people, places, events, and ideas.

There is no doubt that every community's story is unique, but perhaps, what binds us together is that the events and actions in our town reflect the nation's history as a whole. Like every community, St. Charles experienced growth and decline throughout its existence. These patterns of change also serve to reflect the history of the region, nation, and, sometimes, the world.

When asked to define which events or people defined St. Charles, I was struck at the difficulty of the question. I found myself searching my memory for one or two things that illustrate the past. Was it the early entrepreneur's spirit, the incredible generosity from local philanthropists, or the hard-working factory laborers that inspires the pride in St. Charles? I eventually came to the conclusion that the significance is best defined by every citizen who ever resided here, every home that has been constructed, every street paved, and every building built. The answer to that question spans the boundaries of St. Charles and beyond.

The chronicle of the people who occupied this area extends for thousands of years. The Potawatomi were the last American Indian group to reside along the Fox, eventually cohabitating with some early settlers. By the end of the Black Hawk War in 1833, the United States Army began to force the native populations west of the Mississippi, clearing the way for European expansion. In 1833, Evan Shelby became the first settler by staking the first claim on a plot of land near the river. He returned to Indiana shortly thereafter.

Shelby brought back family members William and Lydia Franklin to his settlement in 1834, establishing the town of Charleston (later St. Charles). Over the next few years, many pioneers began flooding the Fox Valley seeking new homes. The town became an important stopover for settlers, boasting of 17 hotels by the mid-1800s.

Notable events such as the Richards Riot (see page 80), the Underground Railroad activity (see page 58), and the participation in the Civil War (see page 60) all highlight the 19th century. In addition, the railroad construction in the 1870s changed the town dramatically, adding new industries and new people and cultures.

By the early 20th century, the philanthropic families of Norris and Baker set the pace for the town by constructing impressive buildings to draw visitors. The Hotel Baker and Arcada Theatre, along with the scenic river views, cool summer cabins along the Fox, and the ample outdoor activities, provided the tourists with a multitude of things to do on a lazy afternoon.

The first 100 years of St. Charles are characterized best by the people, events, stories, and buildings that make St. Charles the "Pride of the Fox." If you would like to know more about St. Charles history, please visit the history archive web site at *www.stchistory.org*.

I hope the reader enjoys the pictorial journey that the author has provided. Hopefully, the snapshots will provide long hours of imagining and reminiscing for all to enjoy.

Jeanne Schultz Angel<br>Director, St. Charles Heritage Center

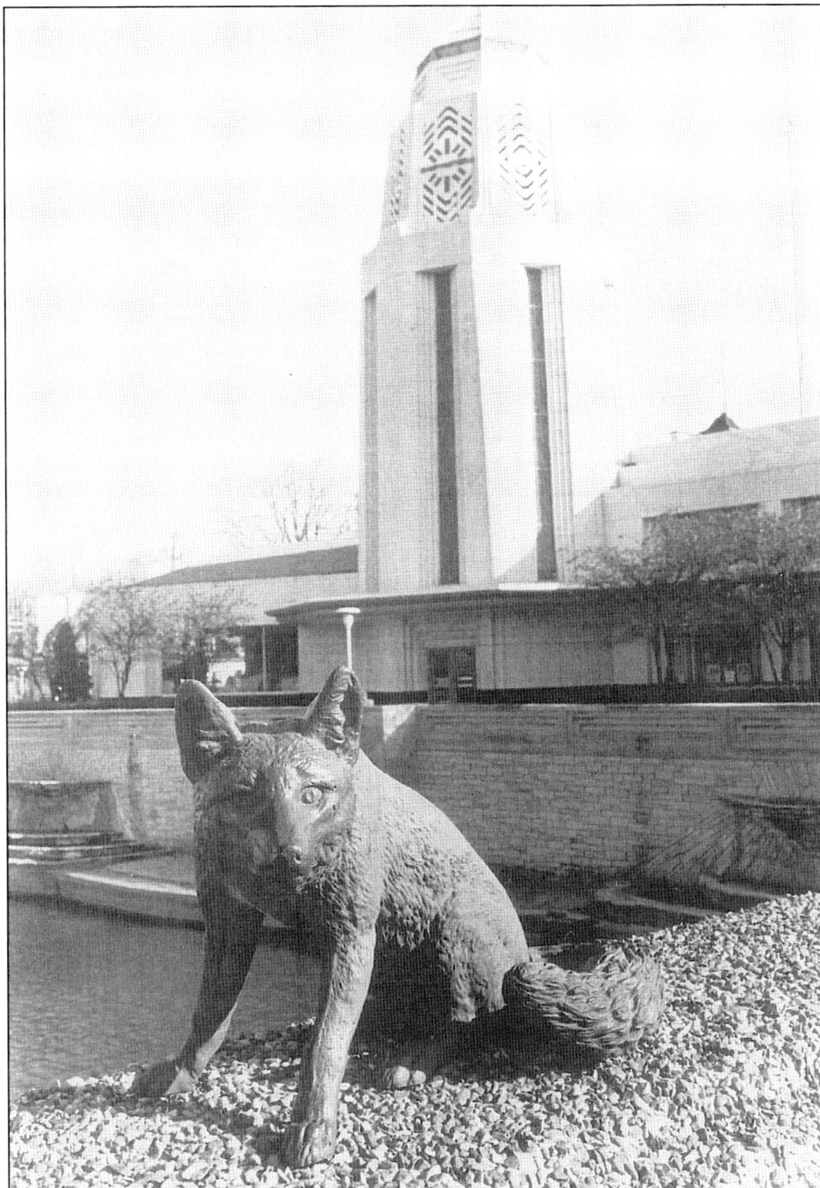

The St. Charles Heritage Center is located in the municipal building pictured here. The Center occupies the wing on the left side of the tower. Colonel Baker donated the funds for the building, and Lester Norris designed the fox that has become the symbol of St. Charles. This view is from the bridge shown on page 127.

# One

# Tales of Early Families
## *Farms, Mills, and Shops*

The Ferson brothers, Read and Dean, arrived in the Fox valley in 1834, and the Minard brothers, Ira and George, arrived in 1835. These four men traveled together from Vermont to Chicago and then to a village along Lake Michigan. The Fersons pushed on to the Fox Valley, and the Minards followed later.

About 1835 Ira Minard and Read Ferson entered into partnership to harness the water power and to found a town. Evan Shelby, the founder of Charleston, donated land for the town with the condition that they erect a dam across the river, build a sawmill, and open a trading house. In 1836 Bela T. Hunt became an equal partner with Minard and Ferson. Minard, Ferson, and Hunt formed a company in 1836 and laid the foundation for the new village of Charleston (later St. Charles). They built a store in the spring of the year. Later the same year, the company built a dam across the river and erected a sawmill on the east side. Charleston's first entrepreneurs were off to a running start with the first of their many enterprises.

Their can-do spirit blossomed. Main street was filling up with stores. Farmers formed regional dairies and were soon sending their butter and cheese east, thus laying the foundation for one of St. Charles' major industries of the 1800s. By the end of the century, the area was also known internationally for Mark Dunham's Percheron horse farm.

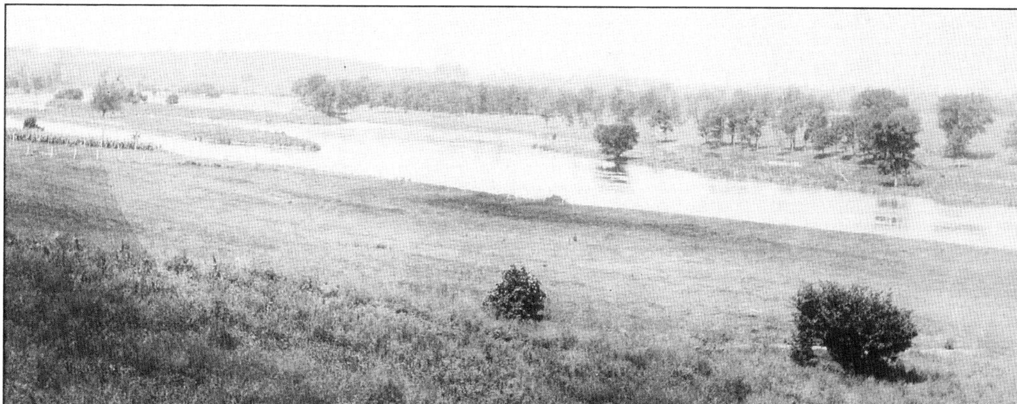

Evan Shelby is said to have first explored the St. Charles region in 1833. He saw that the river offered great potential for water power and that timber for building was close by. After staking his claim, he traveled back to Warren County, Indiana, and persuaded his brother-in-law, William Franklin, and his family to return with him to Illinois.

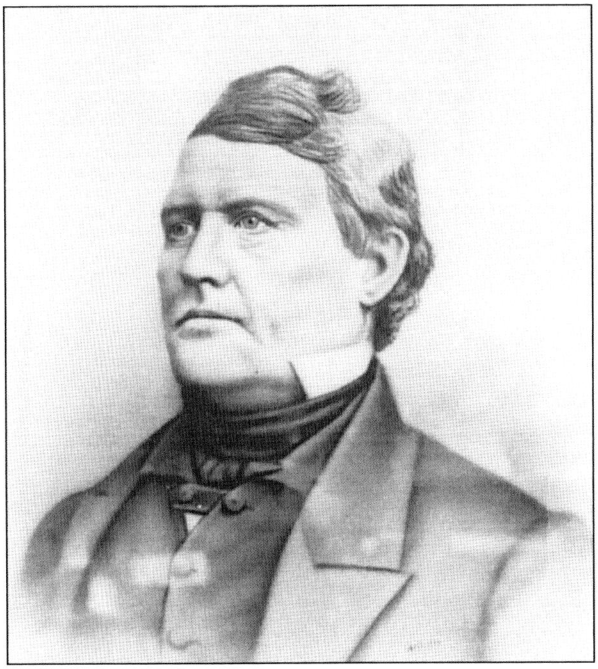

When Read Ferson and his brother Dean settled in what is now St. Charles in the Fall of 1833, they claimed land on the west side of the river and built a log cabin. Dean Ferson and Prudence Ward were married in her father's log house in 1836, the first such ceremony in the settlement. Read was a member of the company of "town proprietors."

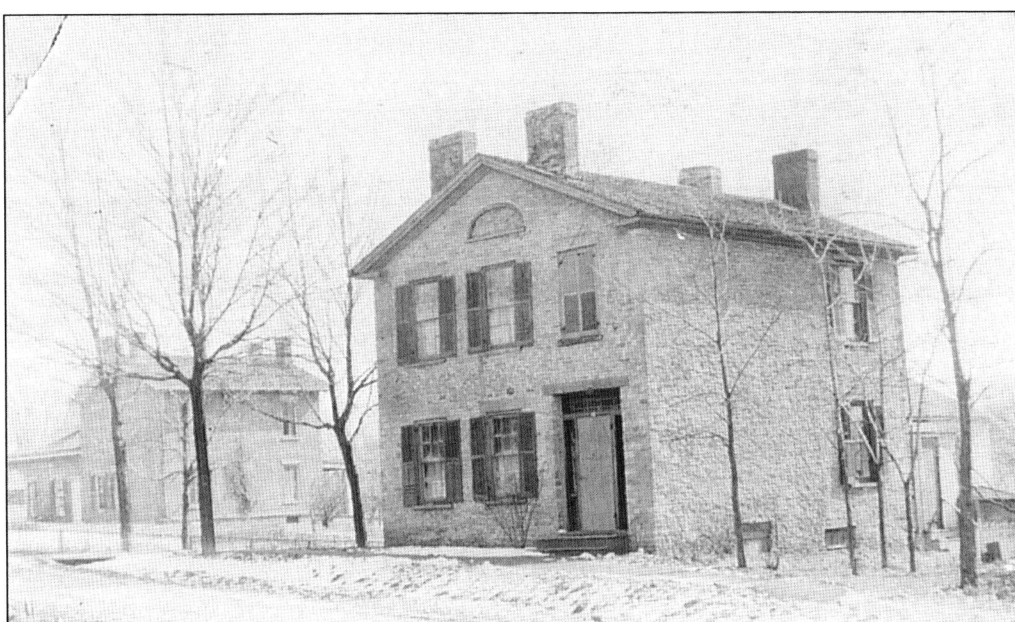

By early 1838, John Penny operated a brick yard at the corner of what is now Baker Park, on the corner of Fifth Avenue and East Main Street. Read Ferson built the house pictured above on the corner of Cedar and Third Avenues. It was later the home of Judge Barry after Ferson built a more elaborate house on Fourth Avenue in 1852.

Ira Minard was elected one of the area's first justices of the peace in 1836. When Minard was elected to the senate in 1842, there was considerable discussion about moving the county seat to St. Charles. This wild west tactic had been tried in 1838 with an alleged attempted theft of the county records.

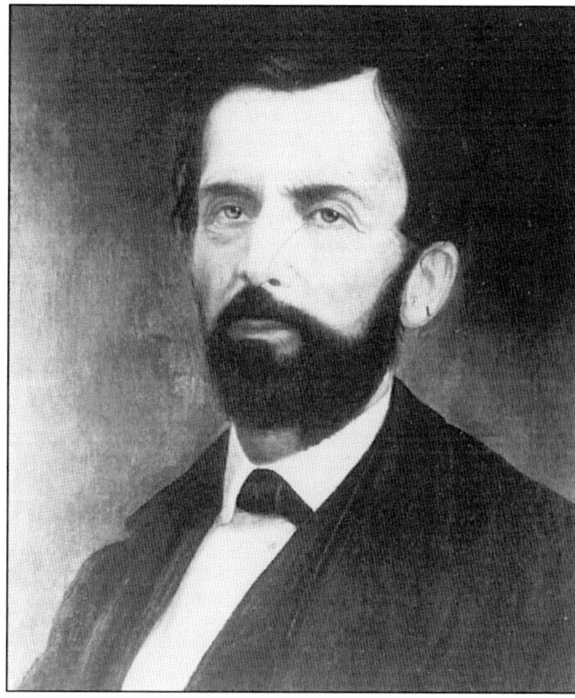

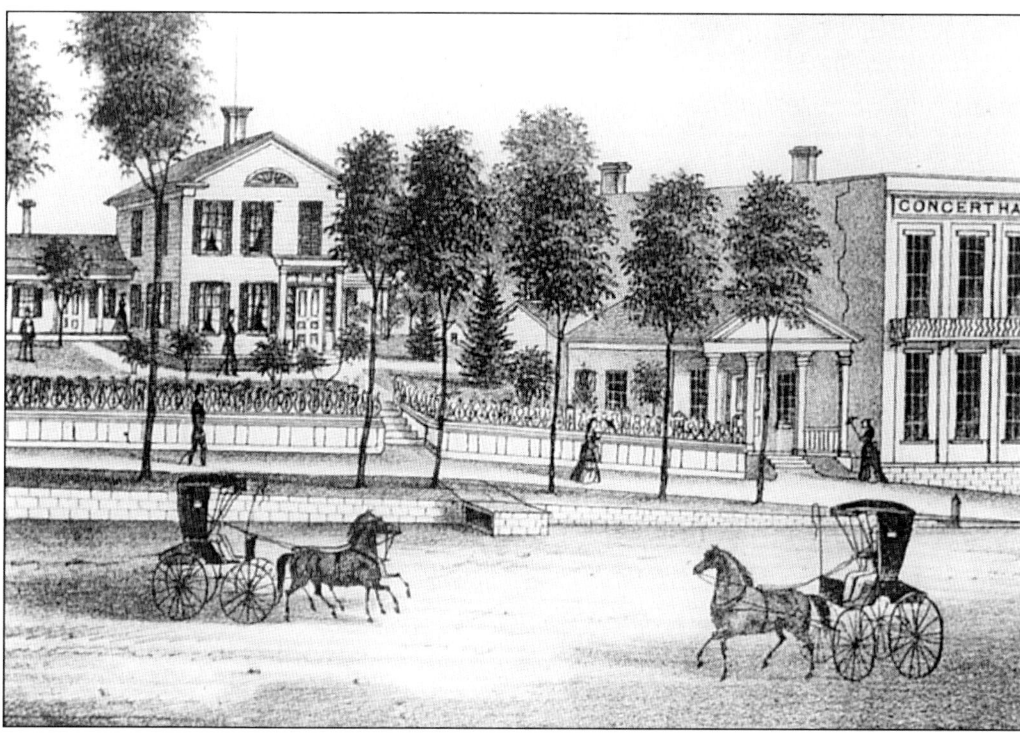


Ira Minard became a permanent settler in Charleston in the fall of 1834 when he built a log cabin, which was later owned by Calvin Ward, father of Prudence. This drawing is of a latter residence of Ira Minard. At the time of his death, he was the wealthiest resident of Kane County.

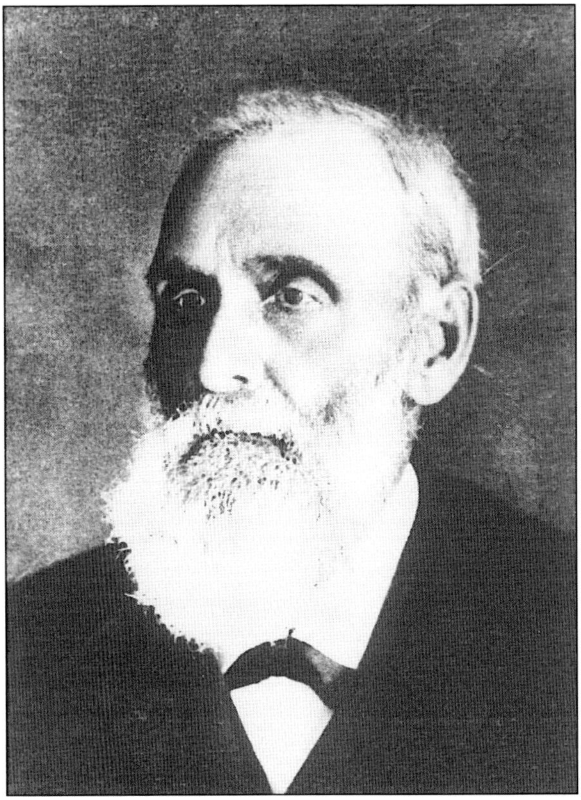

The third member of the town proprietors, Bela T. Hunt, settled in St. Charles in September of 1836. At one time or another, Hunt operated a general store, a tannery, a paper mill, and a hardware business. To these accomplishments, he finished a partially built hotel and added to it, opening the hotel with a grand independence ball on July 4, 1838.

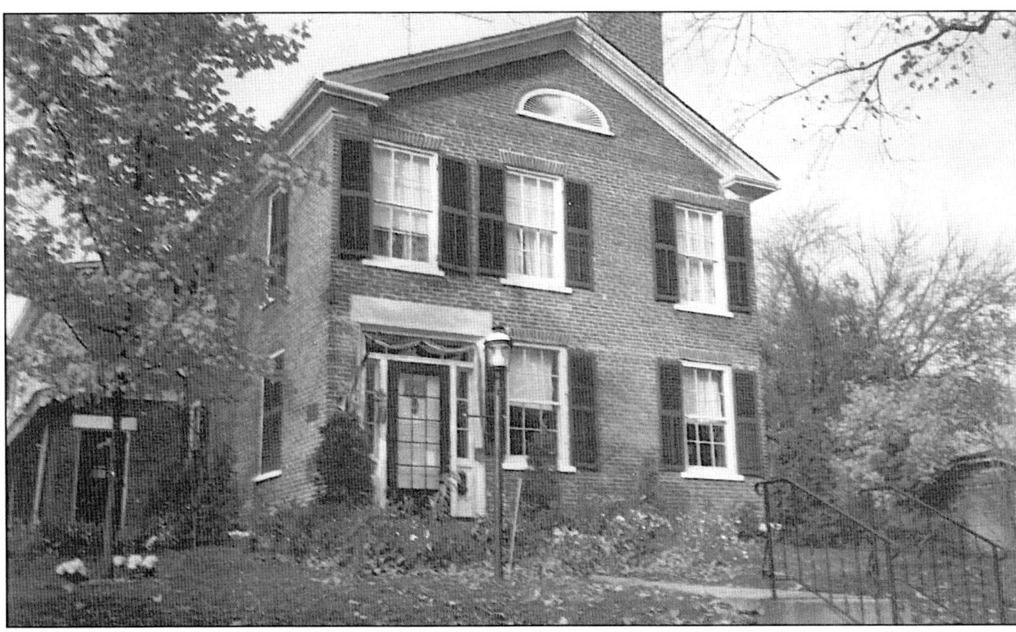

The Hunt house was the first brick dwelling built in St. Charles by brick from John Penny's kiln. This house was home to Hunts for six generations. Today it is known as the Dunham-Hunt Museum, a part of the St. Charles Heritage Center, and is located at 304 Cedar Avenue.

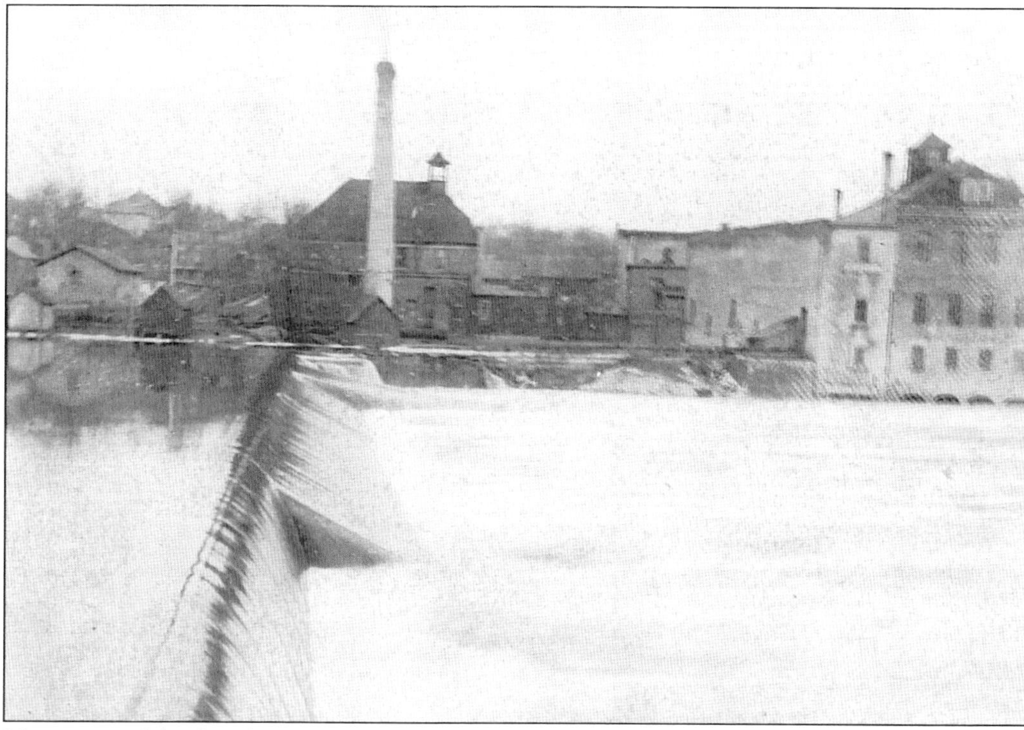

Placement of the first dam was determined by the natural course of the Fox River. The dam was built from felled trees, which had been trimmed into logs, floated down the river, and put into place. The mill race was a necessary part of the dam, for it was the racing of the water through a channel that powered the machinery in the mills. This picture of the dam shows Stewart Mill in 1905.

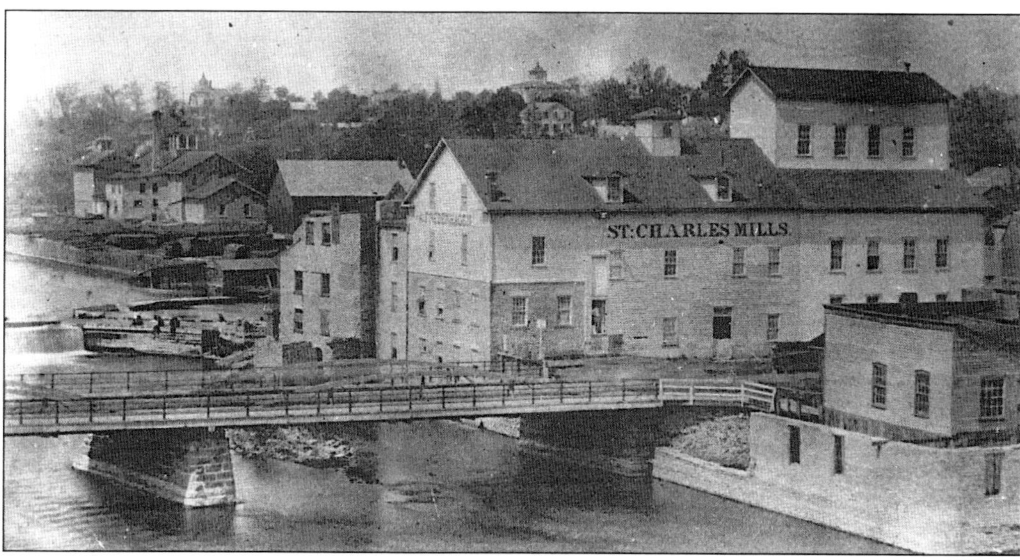


Freedenhagen Mill, shown here about 1885, was built on the site of the original sawmill built by Minard and the "town proprietors." The original mill had two upright saws as well as a machine to cut shingles. Logs were delivered to the mill, and rough sawed lumber was often bartered for flour, hides, and tallow. Asa Haseltine was employed to operate the first mill.

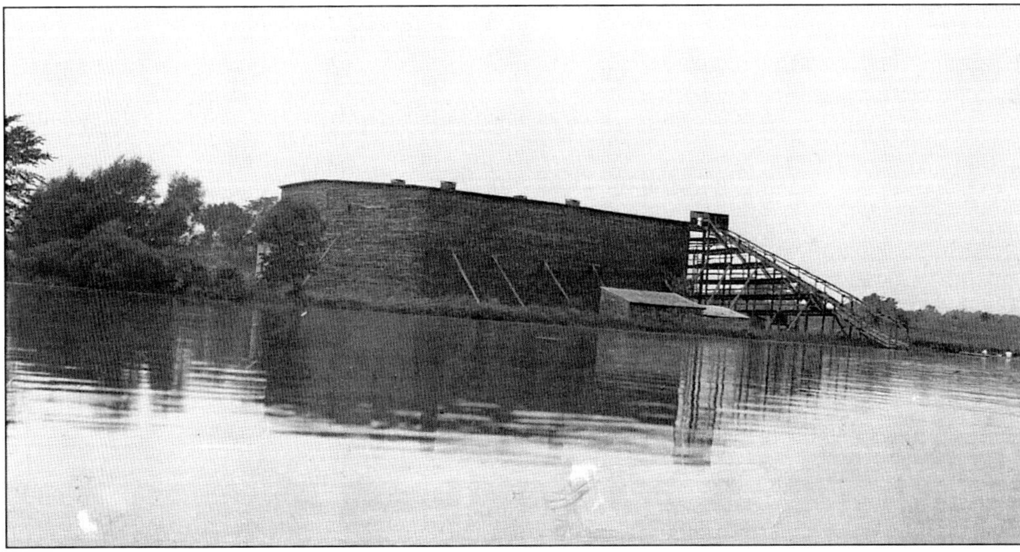

Ice was harvested from frozen rivers using teams of horses that pulled ice-scoring plows. After the frozen surface had been scored, men would cut the ice with saws. The cut blocks would then be moved into nearby icehouses where they would be packed with sawdust to keep them cold. Horse-drawn wagons delivered ice to businesses and families.

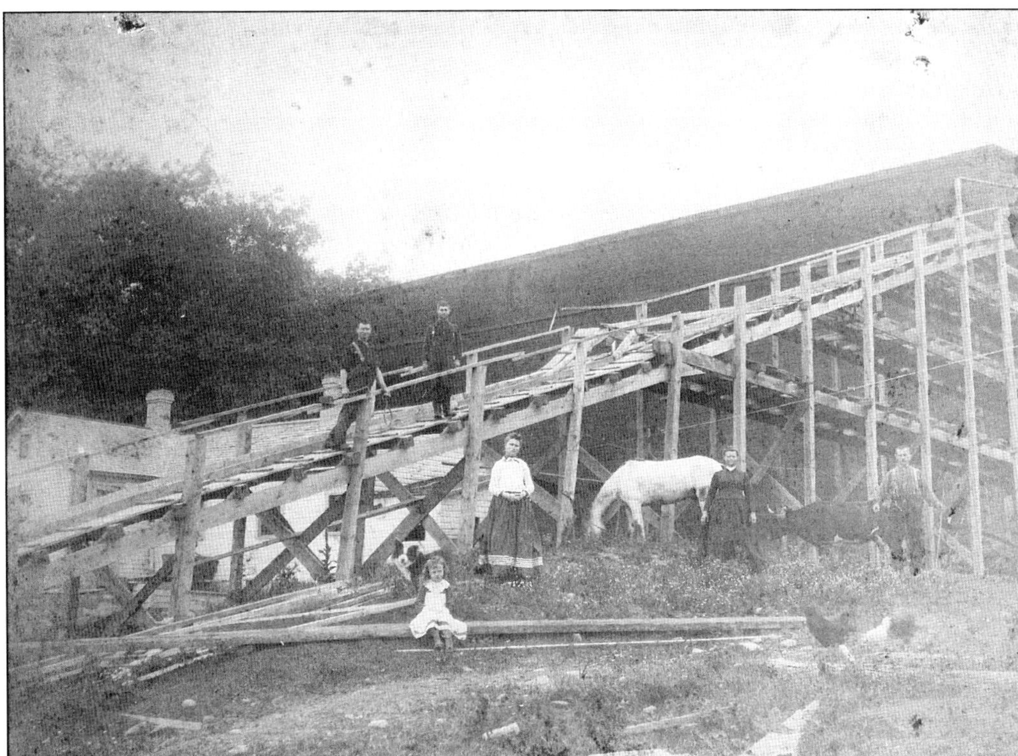

McBride Brothers of Chicago had an icehouse on the west side of the Fox River to hold ice cut from the river during the winter. Their ice was used to manufacture and store ice cream before the use of electric refrigeration in the 1920s.

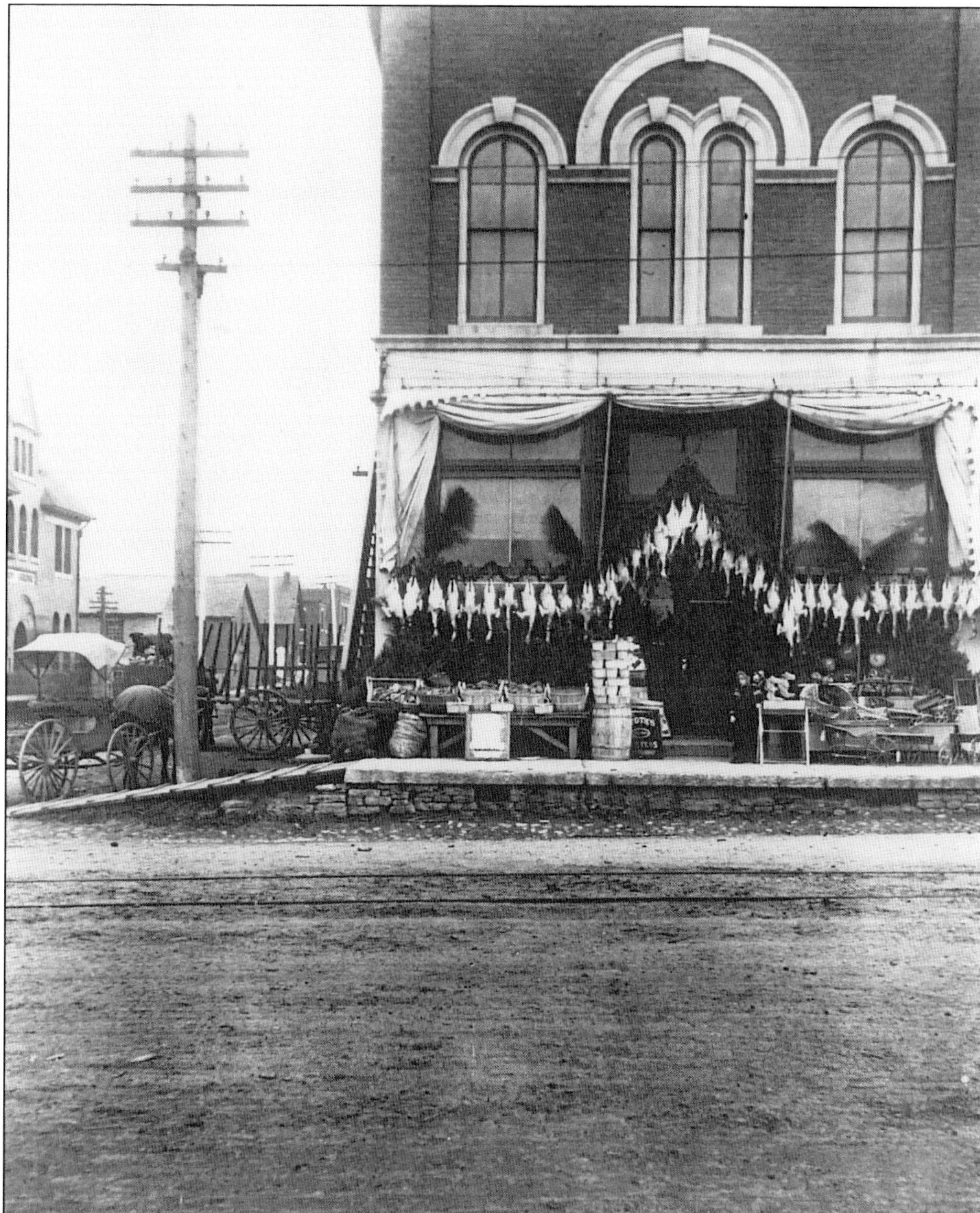

As part of the new town agreement, Ira Minard opened a sawmill along with a company store from which he sold dry goods to the town's early inhabitants. This store was located on the northeast corner of First Avenue and Main Street. The new frame building, built in 1836, was two stories high. By 1842 the store was the site of the Franklin Medical Institute. Eventually it became the site of Wilcox and Munn Grocery Store pictured above. This is one of St. Charles' oldest commercial buildings still standing. Before electric refrigeration was common, people shopped daily for produce and meat because ice was relatively costly at this time. It looks as if fresh turkeys were on sale the day this photograph was taken.

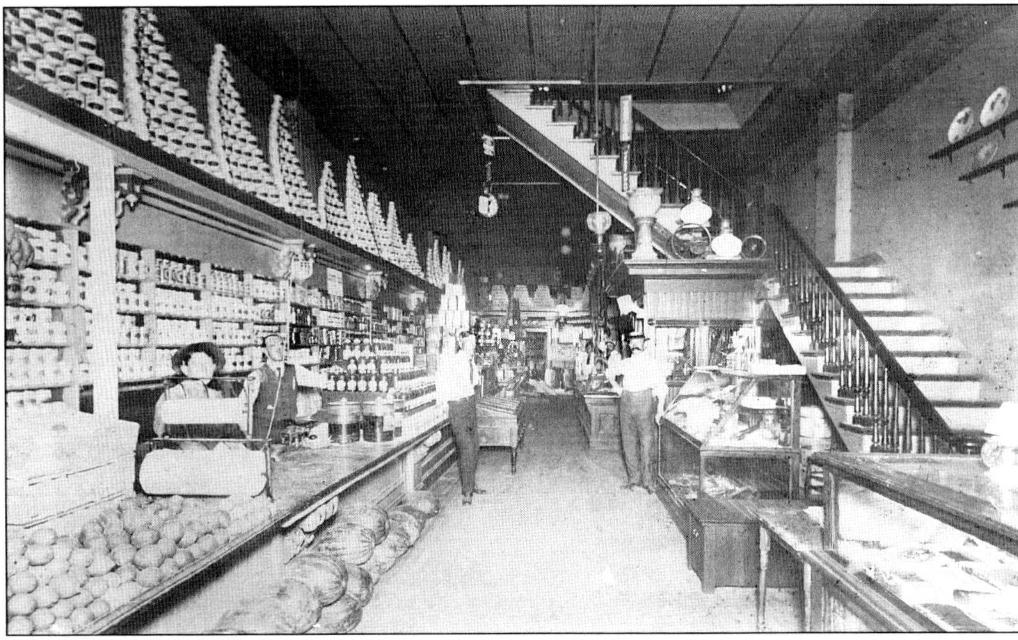

This interior of Wilcox and Munn Grocery Store is full of fresh summer produce as well as canned goods and cigars. Pictured from left to right are as follows: De Clark, unidentified, Robert Munn, and Jesse Munn. It is believed that in the days of Minard, men from his mill were housed upstairs.

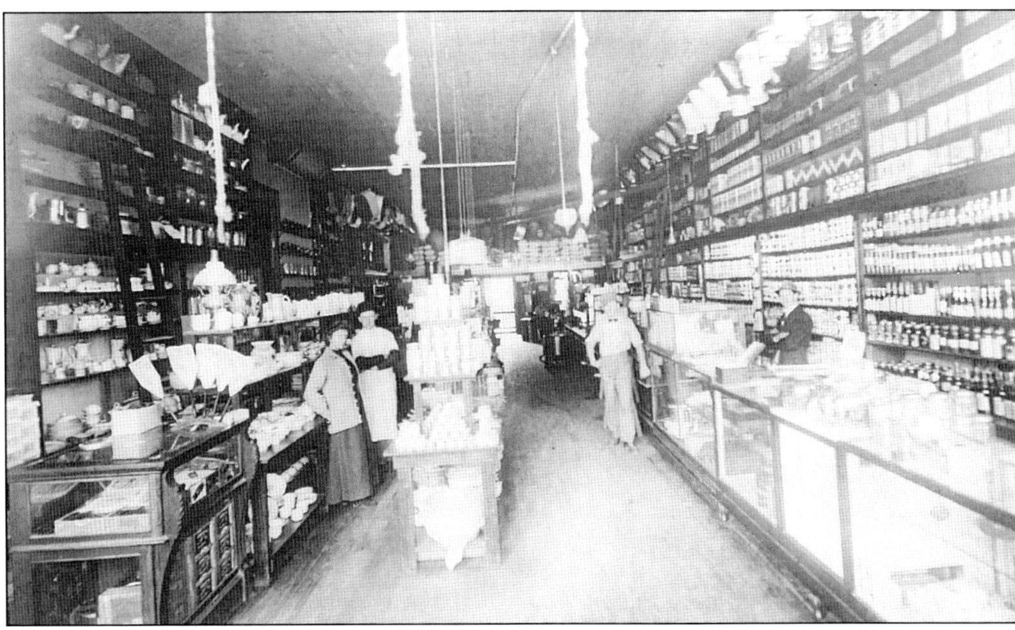

By mid-century, Main Street was lined with stores carrying merchandise of every description. Some stores specialized but more of them carried a general stock, such as dry goods, boots and shoes, groceries, crockery, and glassware. The tea kettles in the upper left corner sold for approximately $1 each, and steel pails sold for 50¢ to $1. Farther west, these supplies would cost a fortune.

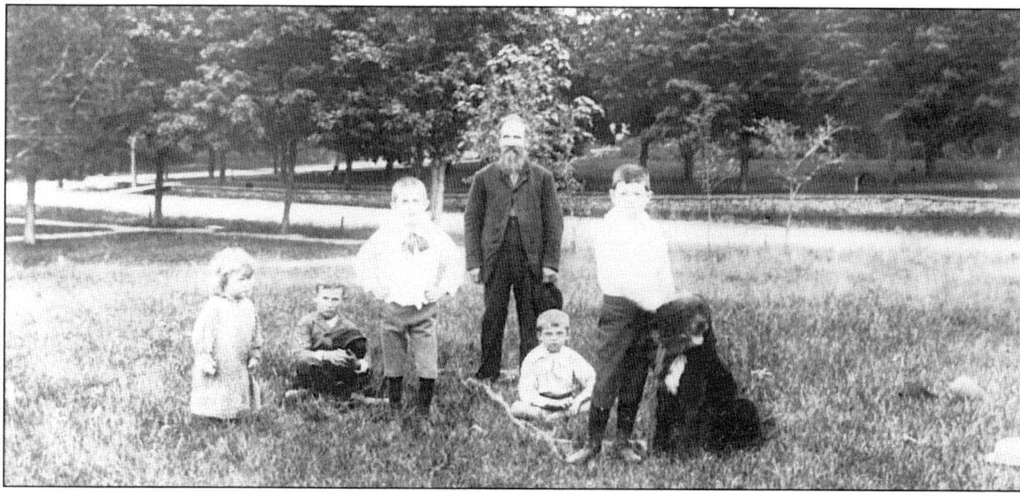

J.F. Colson was born in Sweden, but his family relocated in St. Charles in the summer of 1853. He began his business career as a clerk, and in 1885 he and business partner Charles A. Anderson began the dry goods store that was to become Colson & Company, a store that survived for over 100 years. Two of his children, Harold and Roy, are pictured above along with others. They are, from left to right, as follows: Harold Colson, Fred Gordier, Dwight Millington, Arthur Millington, Roy Colson, and Frank Ryan with a dog.

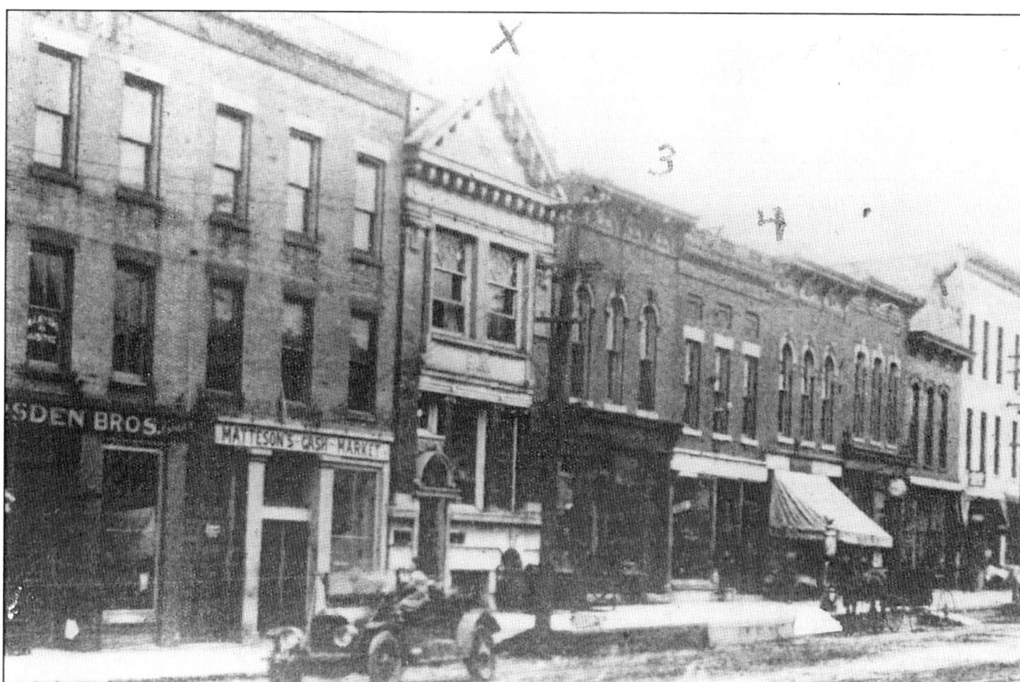


In the late 1800s, Colson operated his dry goods store at 24 W. Main Street. From left to right are as follows: Marsden Brothers, St. Charles National Bank, McWilliams Harness Shop, Egbert Cook Grocery, Colsons, unidentified, and VanPatten Drug Store. The Colsons always tried to employ clerks who could speak to the Belgians, Swedes, and Lithuanians who later immigrated to St. Charles.

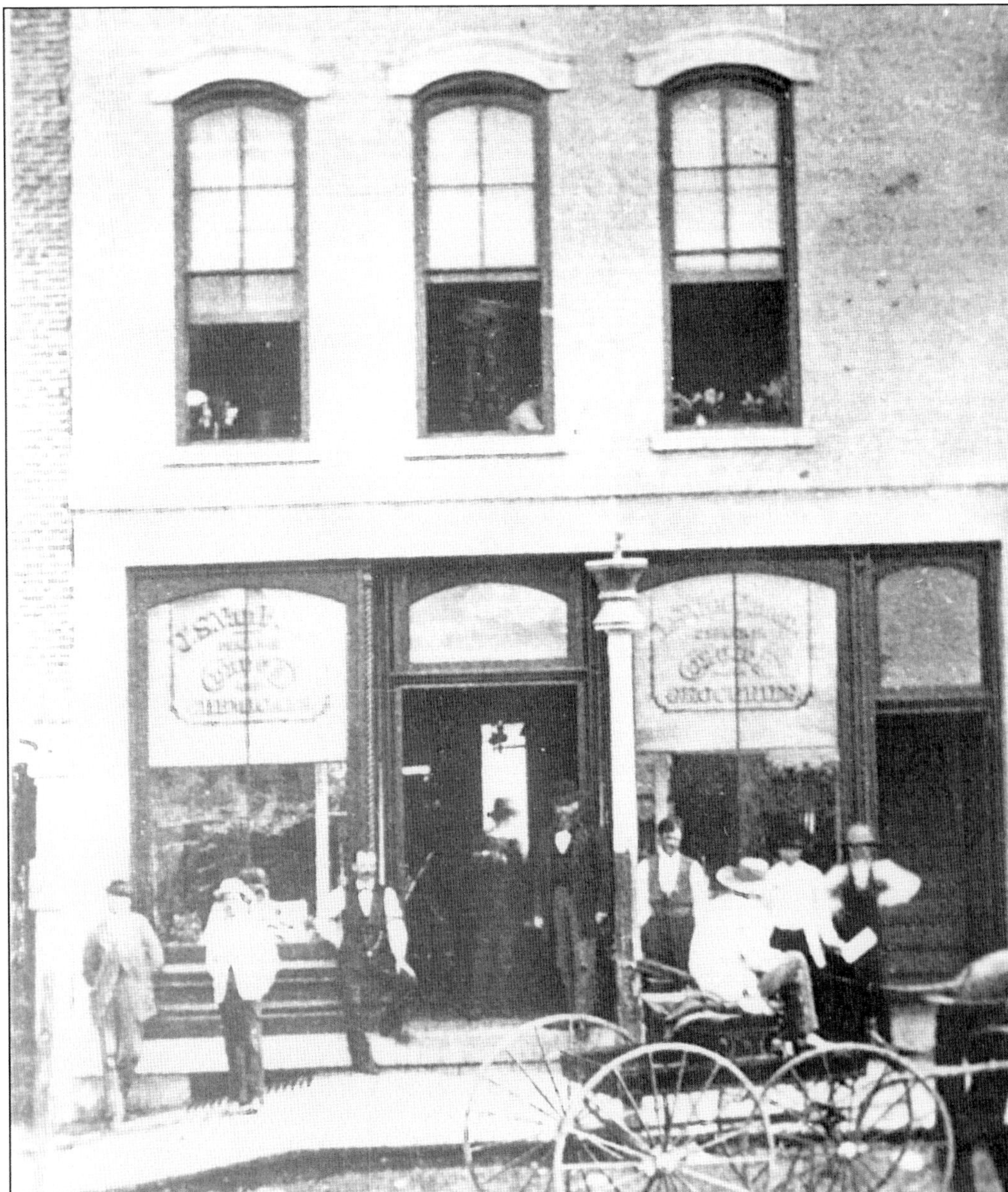

In the later 1800s, there was a great demand for patent medicine. J.S. VanPatten came to St. Charles in 1854 and purchased the drug business established in 1842 by Elisha Freeman. This photograph is of the store in the 1870s. In 1989 Michael R. Hoge, a mason, was involved in a restoration of this building and some adjoining buildings. He is a druggist bottle collector and was looking for bottles from VanPatten's day. When the trench for a water main was being dug, he found an old aqua-colored bottle. He reported in *Treasure* magazine: "Shovel in hand, I jumped into the trench and began frantically digging into its side. Sure enough, we had hit the mother lode [sic]—VanPatten's drug store dump site, the glory hole I have been hoping to find right from the start. Bottles, mostly broken, and crockery began rolling out during the brief 15 to 20 minutes I was allowed to work the site. Among these were two beautiful medicine bottles and a crockery master ink. I also found half of a J.S. VanPatten druggist bottle."

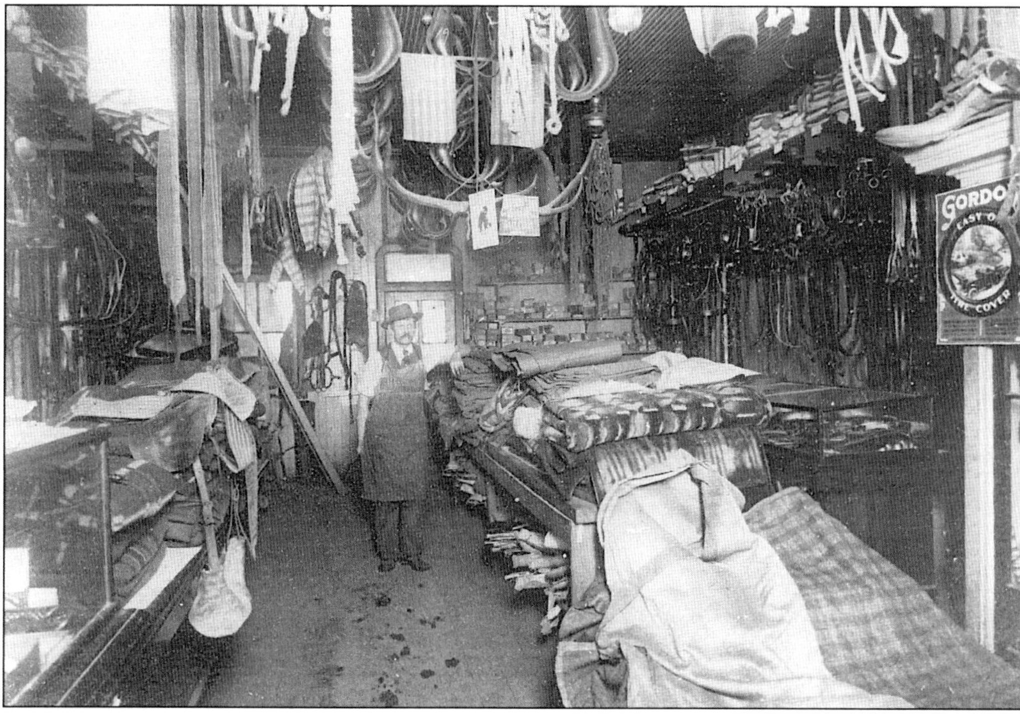

David McWilliams is proudly standing in his Harness Shop in 1877. He bought and built the shop of oak with two rooms downstairs and two rooms upstairs. In an interview for the St. Charles Heritage Center, Mae McWilliams recalled that she was born on the second floor in the Harness Shop building.

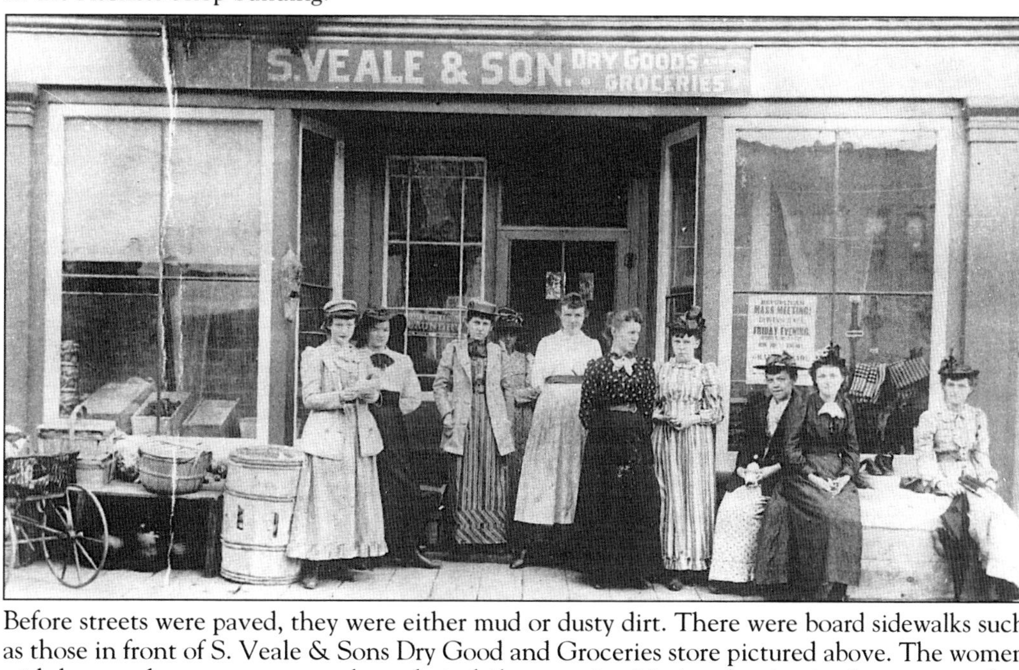


Before streets were paved, they were either mud or dusty dirt. There were board sidewalks such as those in front of S. Veale & Sons Dry Good and Groceries store pictured above. The women with hats on have come to purchase their daily groceries. Notice the sign in the store window advertising a Republican mass meeting.

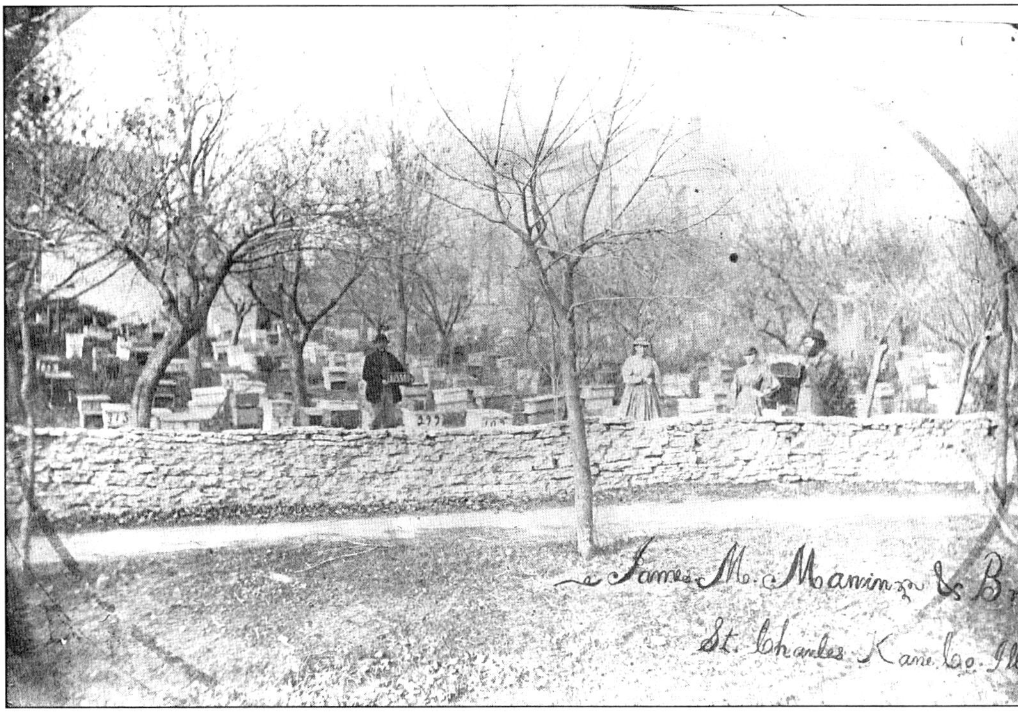


In the early 1860s, Jack and Jim Marvin went into the beekeeping business on their West Main Street property. The brothers produced half a ton of honey a season and kept over 300 hives buzzing for over 25 years. Their father, Seth, bought the entire block in 1852. St. Patrick Catholic Church is barely visible behind the trees.

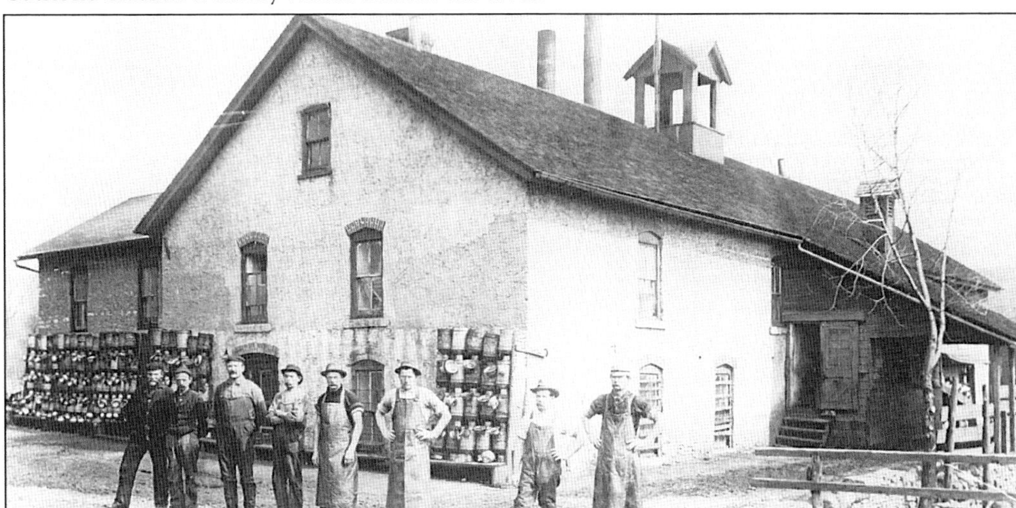

In 1877 Martin Switzer erected a stone cheese factory near a spring just north of St. Patrick Catholic Church. It was later called the Co-operative Creamery. The St. Charles Directory of 1885 stated that this Co-operative Creamery was "the largest and most complete in the United States, having a capacity for handling 50,000 pounds of milk daily." Some 1902 workers pictured from left to right are as follows: Charles Eckstrom, Frank Dixon, Hurd, Jim Heay, Charles Atkinson, Henry Spiker, and unidentified.

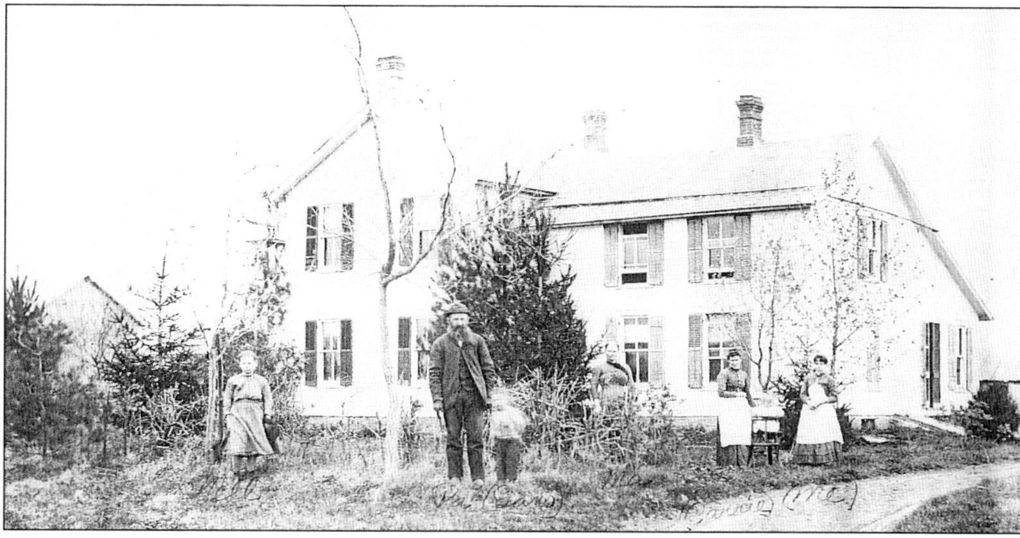

Martin Switzer, grandfather of Martin and Samuel, bought the old Foley farm about 1838 from Melvin Marsh. Pictured above is the old Switzer farm house with members of a household identified as follows: Nell, Pa, unidentified, Ma, Carrie, and me.

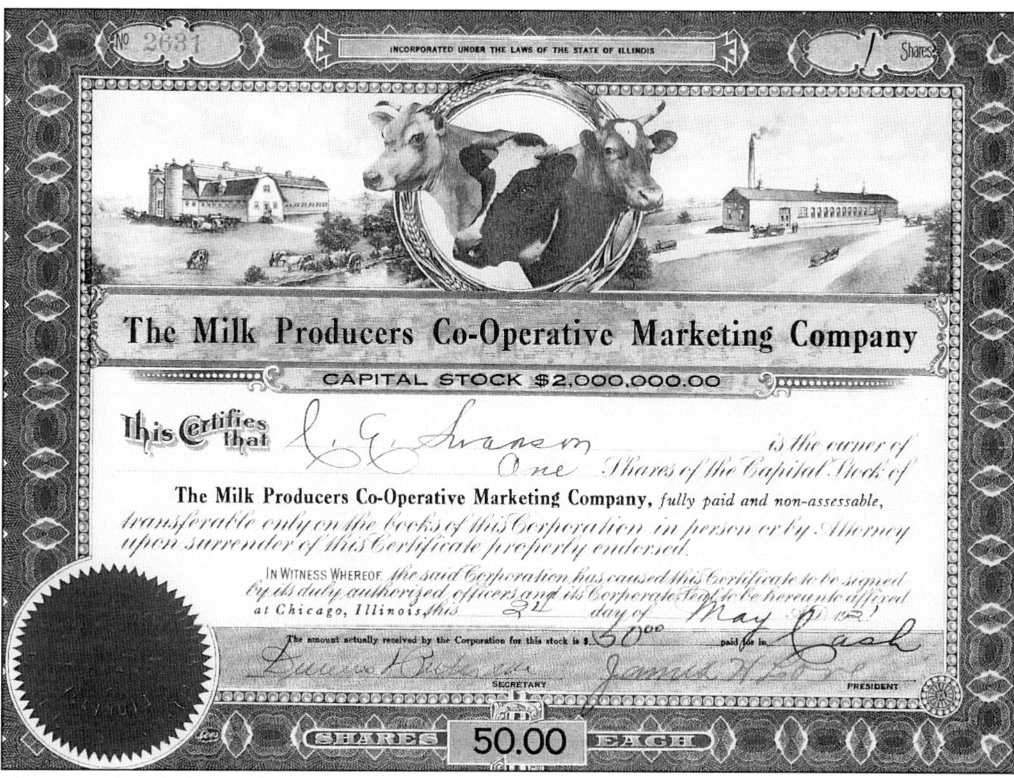


Dairymen banded together in associations to produce better butter and cheese. They also set standards of cleanliness and later marketed their milk cooperatively. The St. Charles Dairymen's Association was formed in 1872. The Milk Producers Co-Operative Marketing Company was a later association. Principle breeds used for dairy cattle were Holsteins, which gave the most milk, Gernsey, and Jersey, which gave the richest milk.

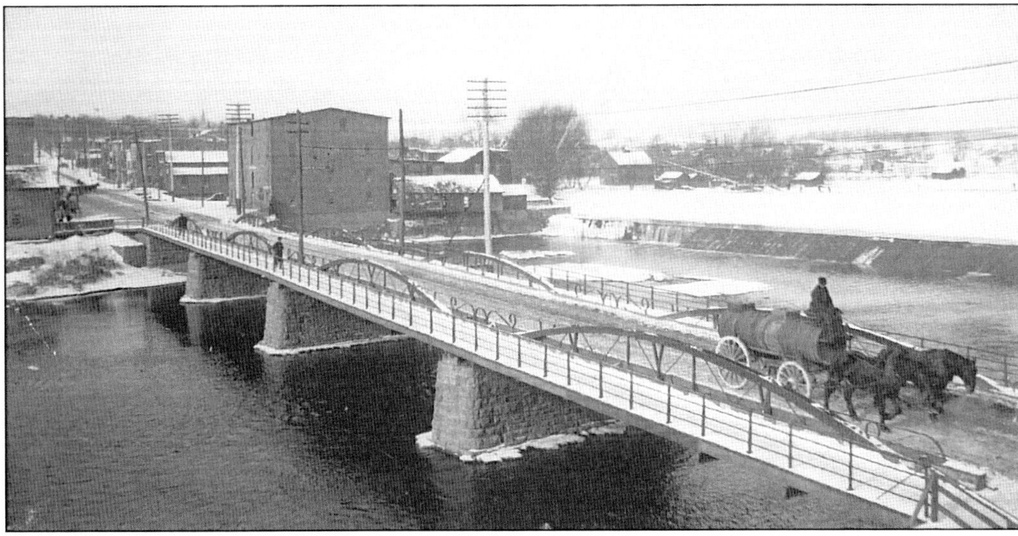

Prior to 1836, ferries carried early settlers across the Fox River. The first bridge, built in the autumn of that year, was 18 feet wide and stood 8 feet above the water at the water's lowest level. In March 1839, every bridge in Kane County was wiped out by an ice flow, and again, ferry service was used. Twice more, the St. Charles Bridge was built and destroyed. In 1874 the bridge was rebuilt with iron.

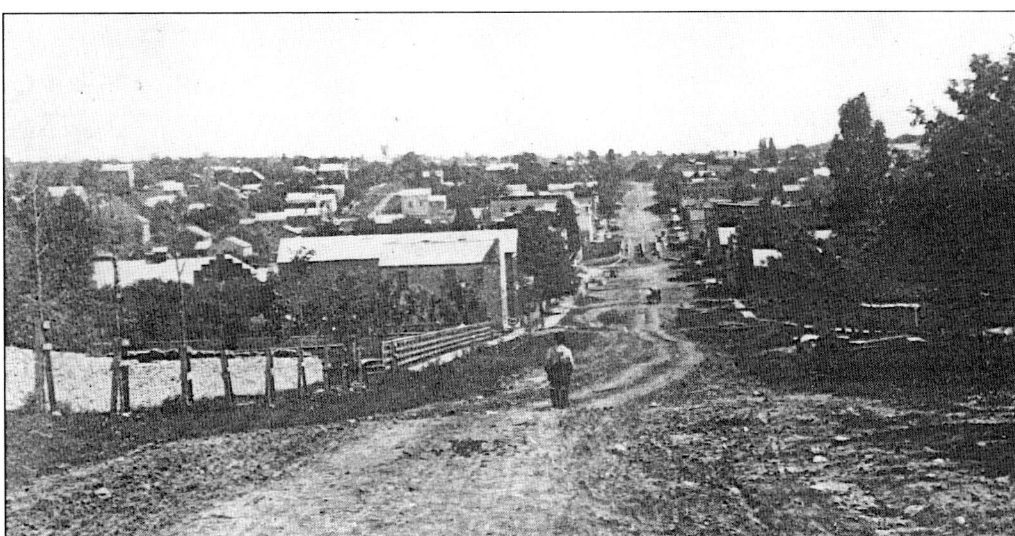

St. Charles had its share of mansions, millwrights, and builders as well as doctors, lawyers, and potters by the end of 1850. Industries such as a paper mill, oil mill, and an iron factory were all here. This is a view of Main Street looking east from the top of the hill. The village was on its way.

# *Two*

# Later Arrivals
## *Churches, Schools, and Cookbooks*

As the Native Americans were moved from lands west of the Mississippi, settlers headed west. For Illinois, the frontier was a thing of the past by 1840. St. Charles grew into a populous village by 1850.

There were several waves of Americans and foreigners into the peaceful valley. The land was, for the most part, the reason for settling in this area. The first settlers were from Indiana and New England, but the next groups made their way from Europe by way of Canada or the eastern states.

The largest two groups of foreign immigrants to settle in St. Charles were the Irish and the Swedes. Irish settlers migrated north from the Illinois and Michigan canal project in the 1840s looking for work on railroads or in factories. The Swedes began arriving in the 1850s looking for good farm land. By 1885 there were African Americans as well as several families from England, Germany, Scotland, Wales, Norway, Denmark, and France. The last two large groups of immigrants, from Belgium and Lithuania, arrived at the turn of the century.

These hard-working settlers built their churches, cleared the land, or set up shops much as those of every new town on the frontiers did. They were concerned about the education and safety of their children, fitting in with their neighbors, and preserving their native speech and customs.

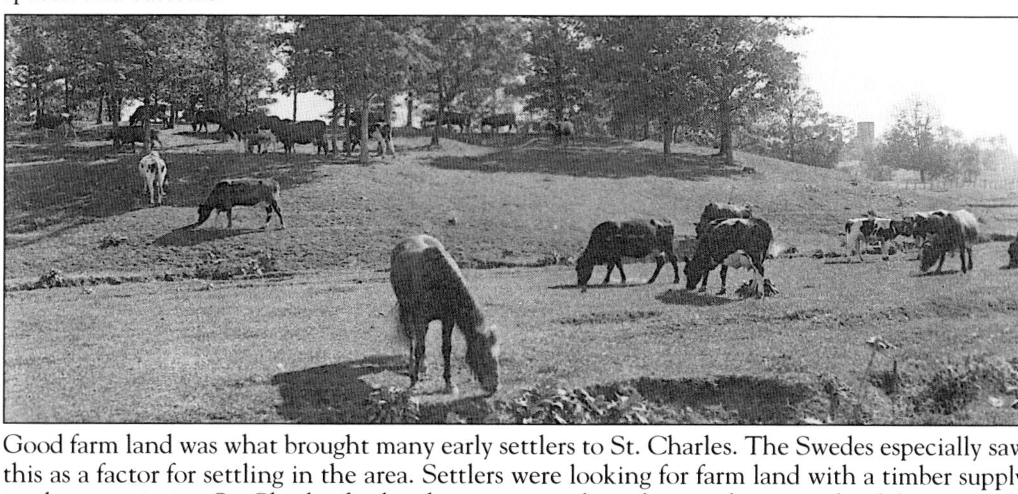

Good farm land was what brought many early settlers to St. Charles. The Swedes especially saw this as a factor for settling in the area. Settlers were looking for farm land with a timber supply in close proximity. St. Charles fit this description with timber on the east side of the river and prairie on the west.

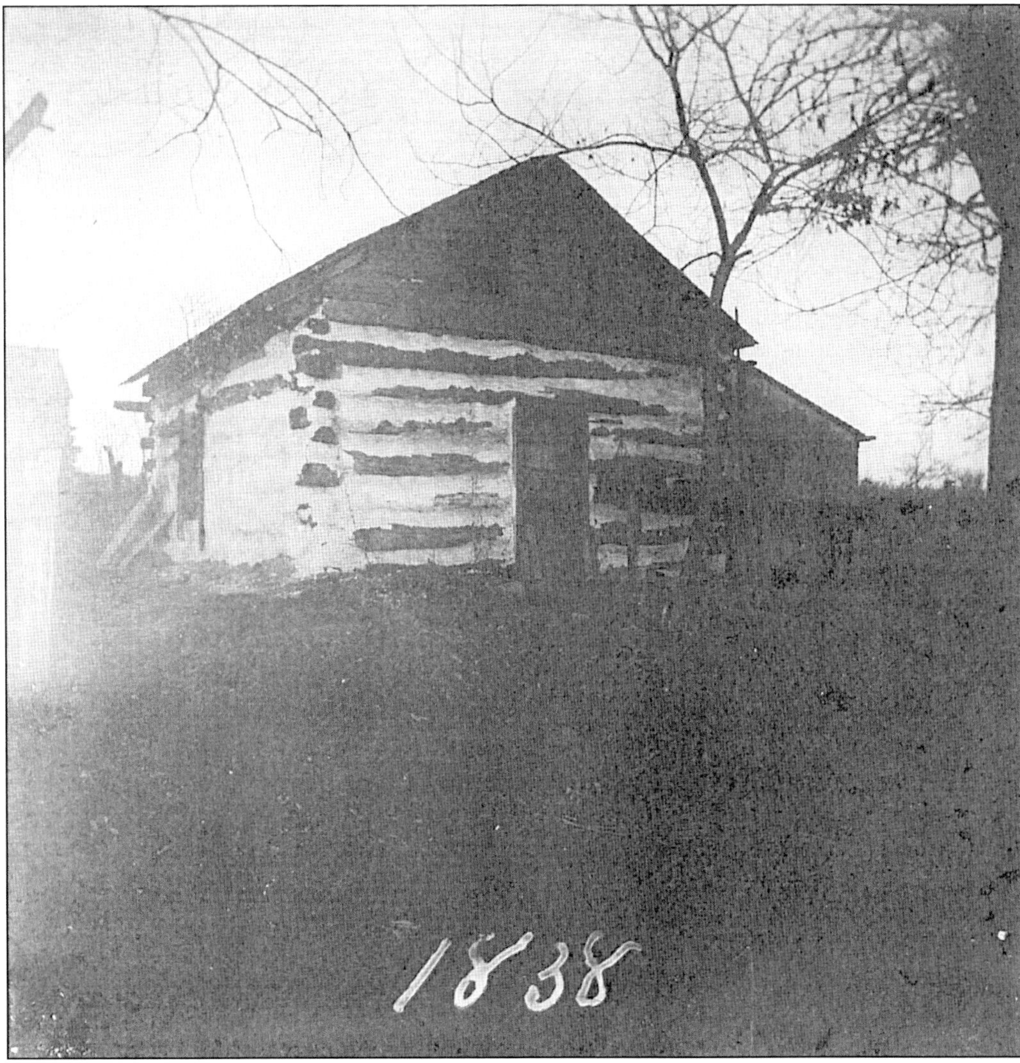


Shelter was the first item of business for new settlers. Trees were plentiful, but many had to be cleared before farming could begin. Just as other pioneers did in forested areas, Dean and Read Ferson built a log cabin when they settled beside the Fox. Theirs was one of six cabins fully or partially completed about that time. Of these, three were started by pioneers who left before their cabins were completed. Ephriam Perkins and William Franklin built the other two completed cabins. Franklin's cabin is considered the first permanent residence in St. Charles. Early settlers reminisced about when they used one or another of these cabins while their new houses were being built in the town's early history.

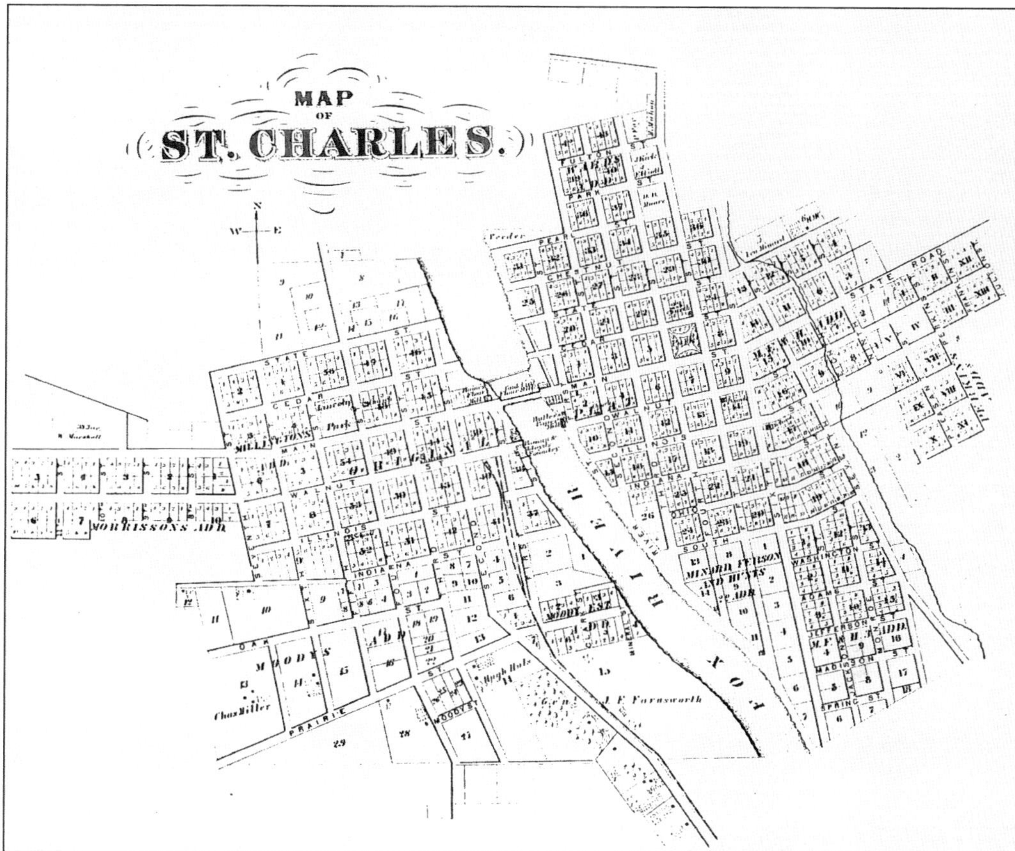


Mark W. Fletcher surveyed 56 blocks of the village in 1837, the east side for Ira Minard, Reed Ferson, and Calvin Ward and the west side for Gideon Young. Fletcher noted that the city is evenly laid out. At this point in the river, the banks slope up with an easy ascent on each side of the river, which promotes good drainage.

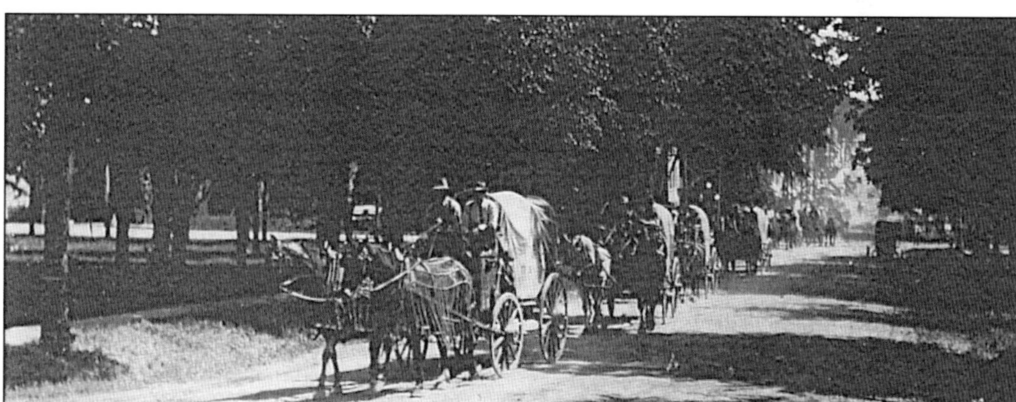

Settlers from the eastern states began to travel to Illinois after the end of the Black Hawk War in 1832. People traveled by horseback, covered wagon, boat, or on foot. Settlers carried no more than necessary. In the 1830s, a trip from St. Charles to Chicago typically took three days. This photograph is of later pioneers traveling through St. Charles.

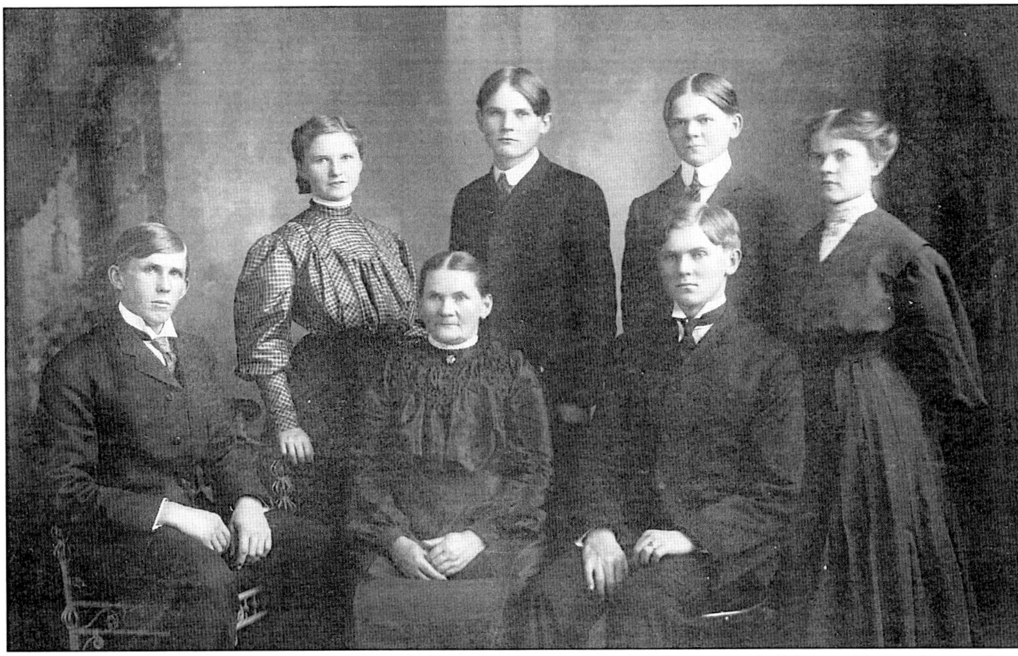

When Simon Anderson was 12, his father died. To support her six children, Simon's mother, Anna, took in laundry. In 1901 Simon purchased milk routes with horses and wagons and was in the milk delivery business. Anna Anderson is pictured above seated with Simon (left) and William (right) and surrounded, left to right, by Julia, Art, Carl, and Emma.

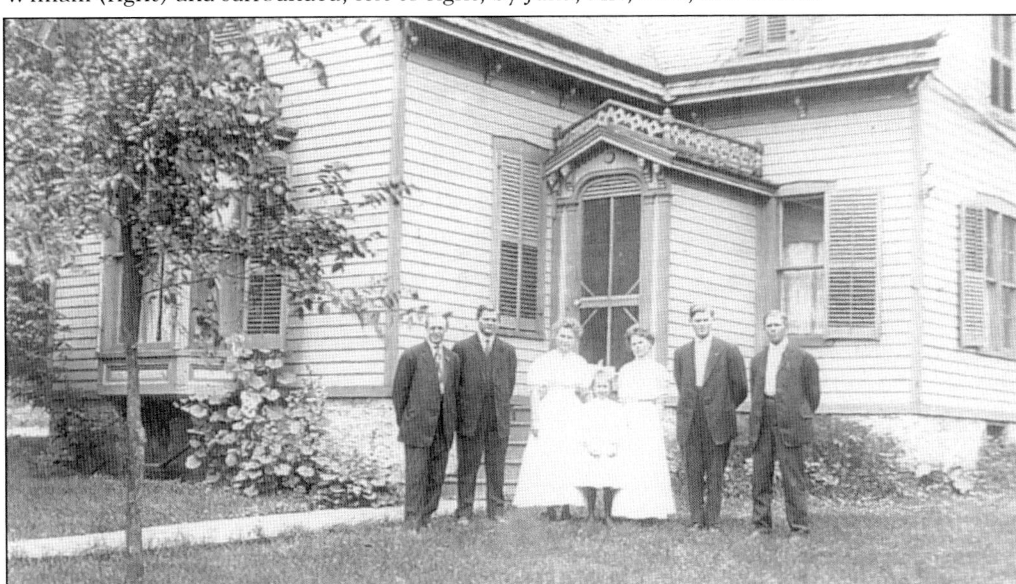

In 1902 Anna Anderson moved to this house at Second and Indiana Avenue where Simon set up the milk business in a barn and milk house behind the house. The business was first called Anderson Dairy, later Colonial Dairies. Colonial has been family owned and operated since its beginning. In 1917 the Anderson Dairy made the bold move of making ice cream. Pictured left to right are Gust Anderson (fiancee of Emma), Carl, Julia, Francis Paschal (neighbor), Emma, William, and Simon.

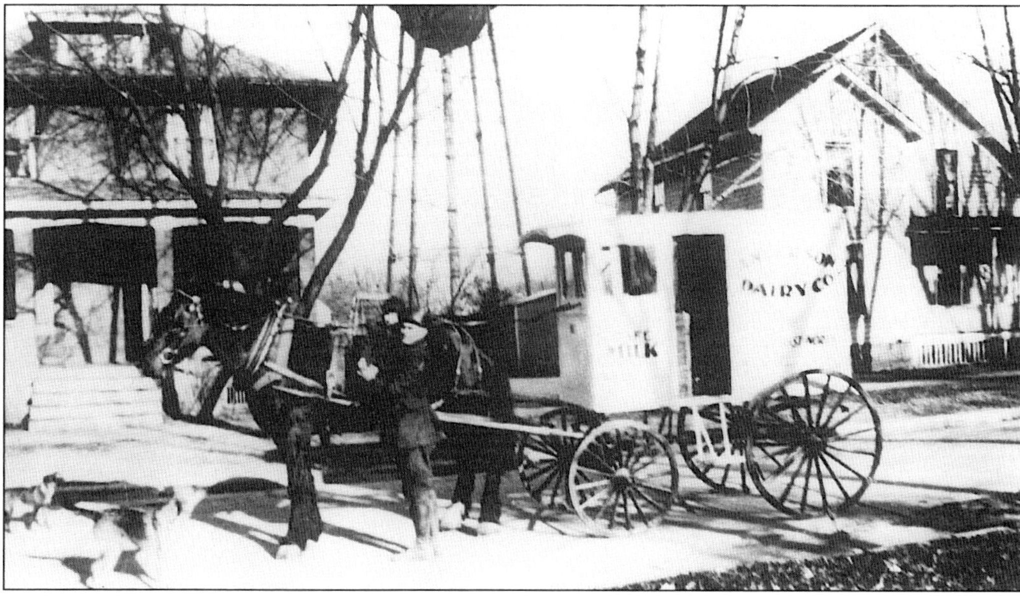


Horse-drawn delivery carts were used by Anderson's Dairy until the early 1930s. At first, the milk was hauled to town in 10-gallon cans. The horses had been taught exactly where to stop, so milk could be ladled out to the housewives, who would bring their own containers to the wagon for fill-ups.

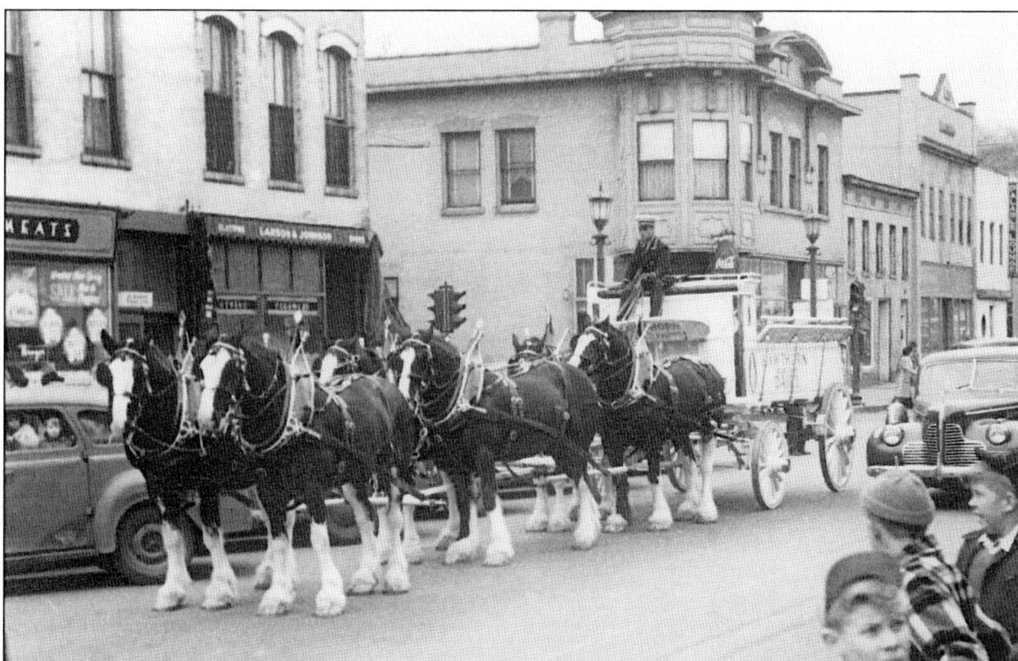


This Hawthorn Dairy wagon is pulled by six Clydesdale horses in what may be a parade through downtown St. Charles. Although it hasn't been verified, it is thought that these horses were bred on a farm west of St. Charles.

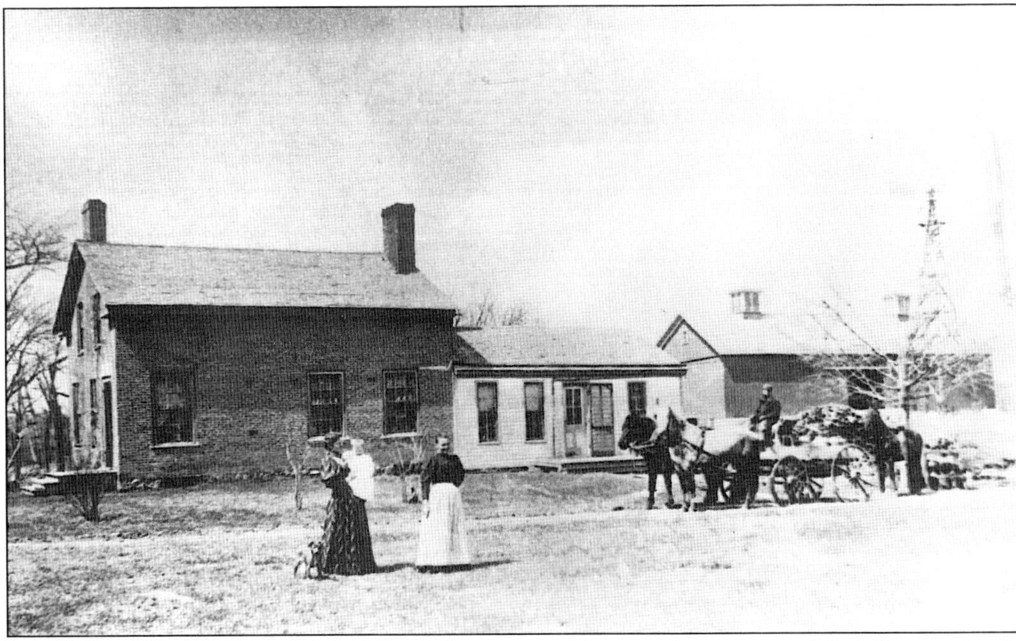

When James T. Durant migrated from Boston to Chicago, he purchased 1,000 acres in the Fox Valley from Dean Ferson. Durant opened a general store in St. Charles in 1842 with Louis M. Blaisdell. He sold out in 1856 and went back to work in Chicago, but his family continued to live in St. Charles while he commuted to work by train. This was a glimpse of things to come.

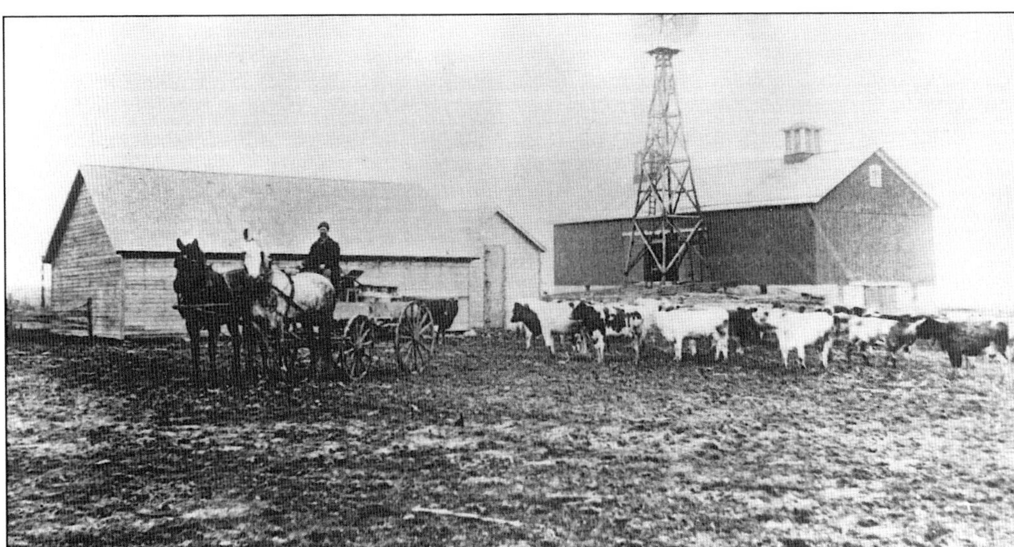

Bryant Durant purchased 195 of the original 1,000 acres from his brother James. The Durant Petersen House, which now serves as a living museum, was built by Bryant. It is likely that Bryant also built James's house.

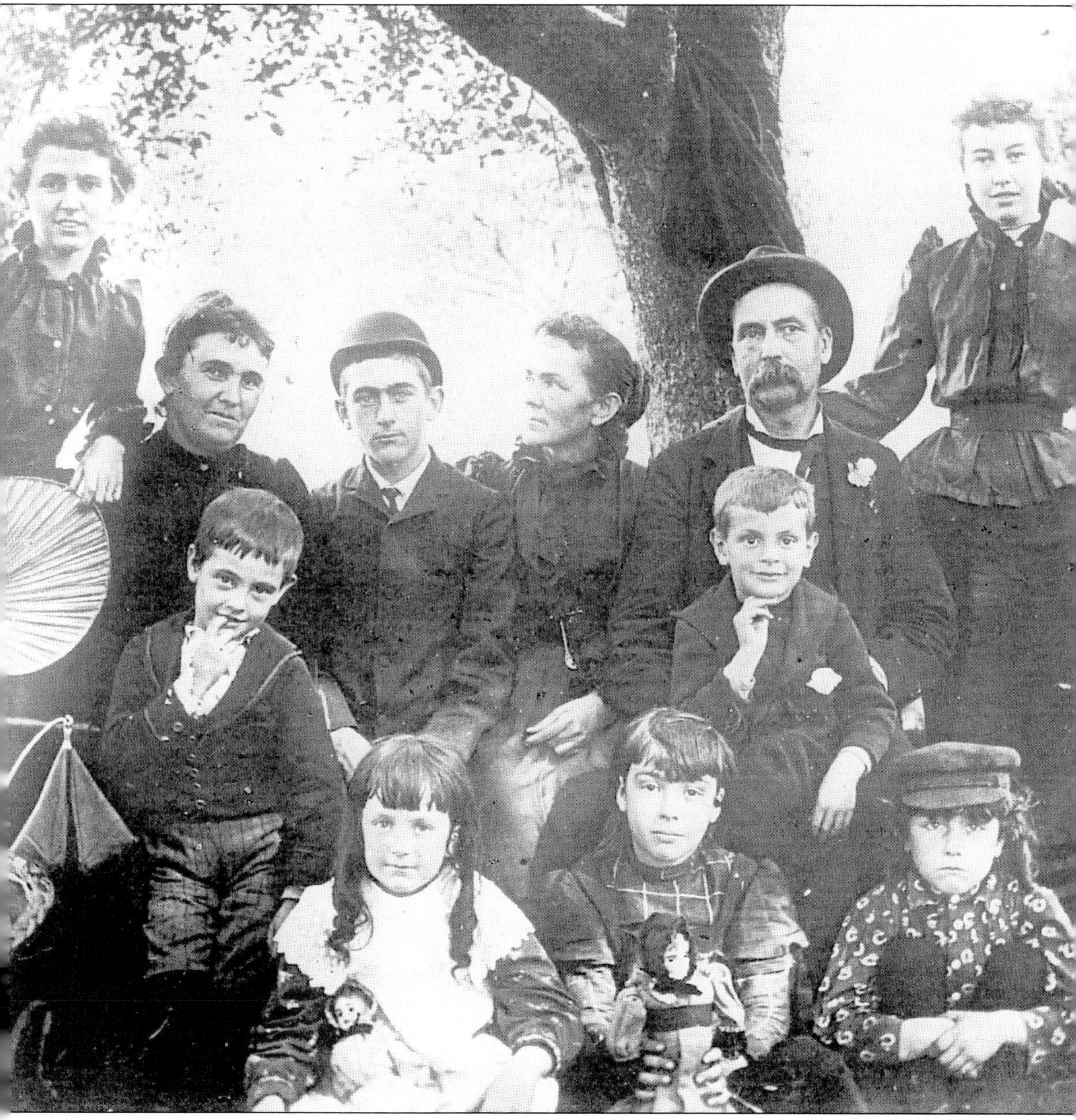

Charles Miller's parents came to St. Charles from Scotland in 1842, the same year Charles was born. James and Isabella bought several acres around Seventh and Oak where James set up his blacksmith shop. James taught Charles the blacksmith trade, and Charles worked at it until he was 24. It was then that Charles became interested in the paper-manufacturing business in St. Charles. He also held several civic positions such as circuit clerk, recorder for Kane County, and supervisor of St. Charles Township for many years. Pictured here are Charles, his wife, his son, and his son's family. They are, from left to right, as follows: (top row) Marion Miller Bagley, Mary Tuck Miller (Charles's wife), Charles Miller Jr., unidentified, Charles Miller, and Jessie Miller Johnson; (middle row) Fred Miller and Clarron Miller; (bottom row) unknown, Helen Miller Sampson, and Warren Miller.

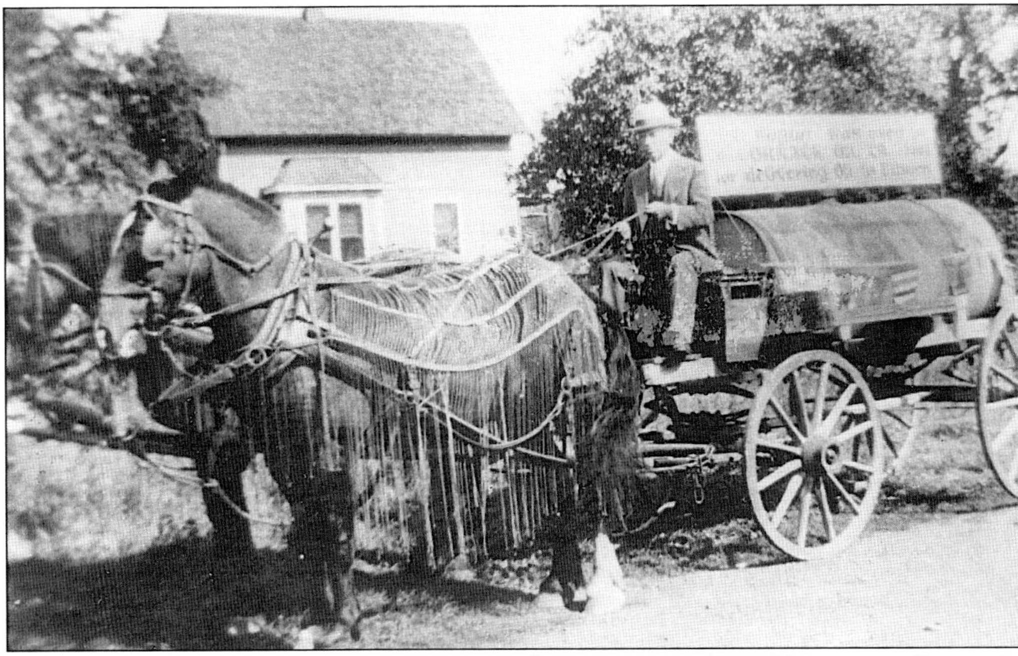

McCornack Oil delivered kerosene by horse and wagon to people and businesses all over the Fox Valley. These well-dressed horses were used to pull this kerosene truck to Elburn. The driver is Charles S. McCornack in 1904. The McCornacks were mostly farmers until Charles founded the oil company in 1904.

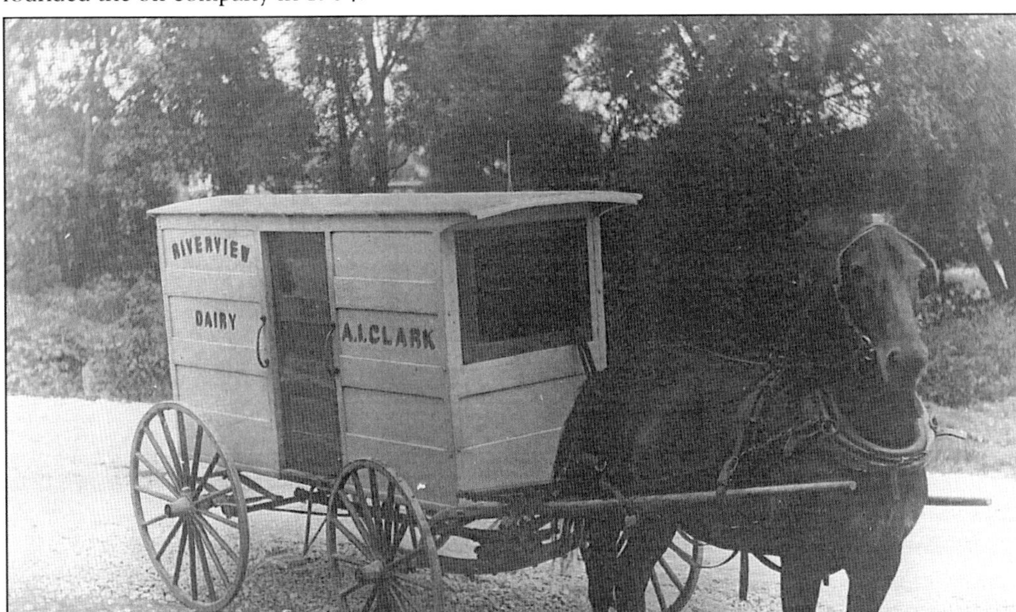


In 1945 Colonial sold the dairy portion of their business to Riverview Dairy. In a recorded interview with Beverly Davis Bell, she states that Malcolm Clark was son of the founder of Riverview Dairy Farm and that the Dairy was in operation as early as 1900. Anson Clark would deliver the milk with a horse and cart and also ladled the milk into his customers' containers just as Anderson did.

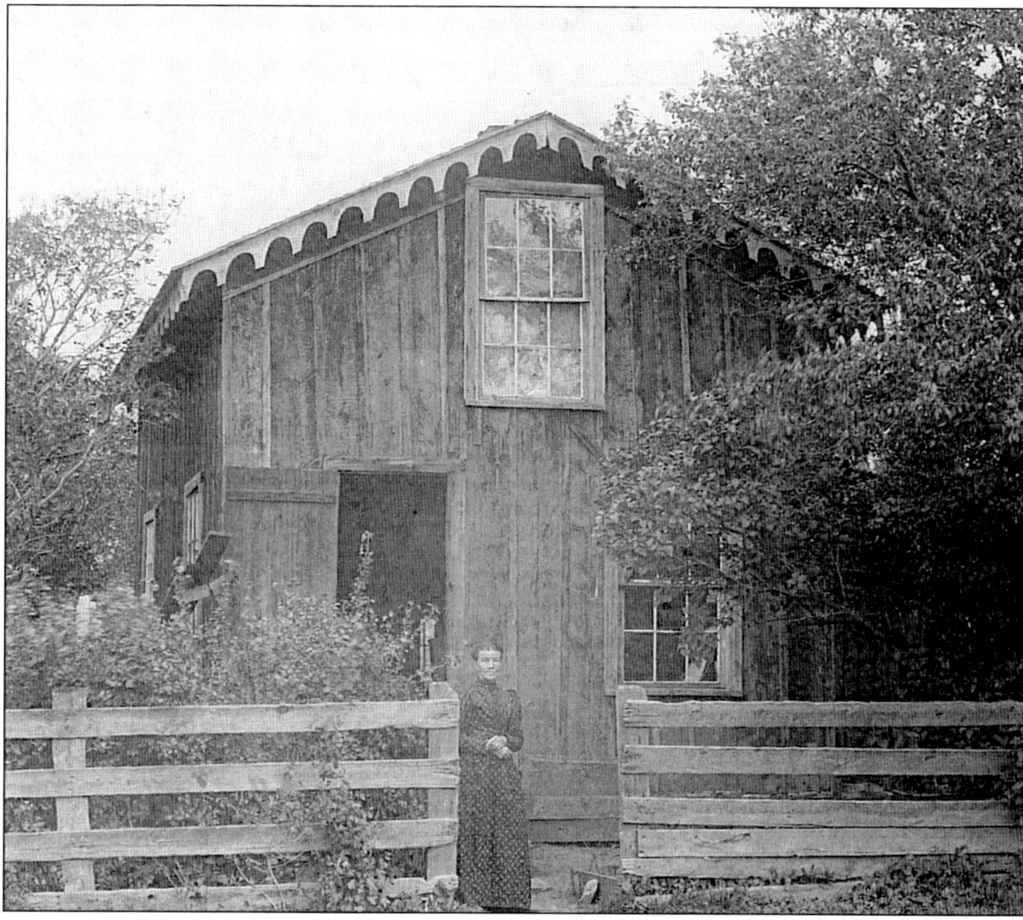

A colony of Swedish immigrants, who arrived in the Fox Valley in 1851, had heard of the job opportunities and excellent dairyland around St. Charles. A collection was started to build a Scandinavian Lutheran meetinghouse, and the house was constructed in 1852. The house above is said to have been that building. Local legend has it that the Swedish Church fell behind on the payments for this building in 1852. When the parishioners arrived to worship on Christmas day, they found it locked. One of the members broke the lock so they could worship. When they arrived the next Easter morning, their quaint church was gone. It had been whisked away in the night by the landlord to an unknown spot! Rather than rebuild right away, the money-poor Swedes from St. Charles journeyed to Geneva, about 2 miles south, to worship.

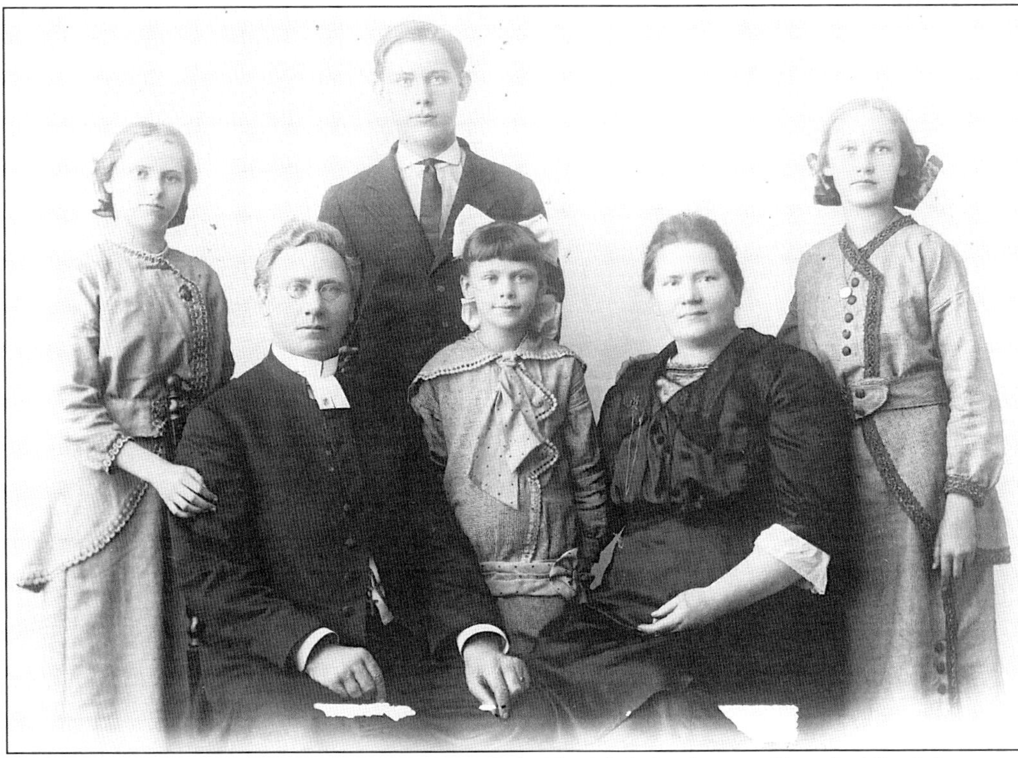

In 1905 Reverend Martinson was a pastor of the Swedish Lutheran Church. The Martinson family is pictured above. They are, from left to right, as follows: Martha, Reverend Martinson, Dong, Mrs. Martinson, and Margaret. Earl Martinson is standing in the rear.

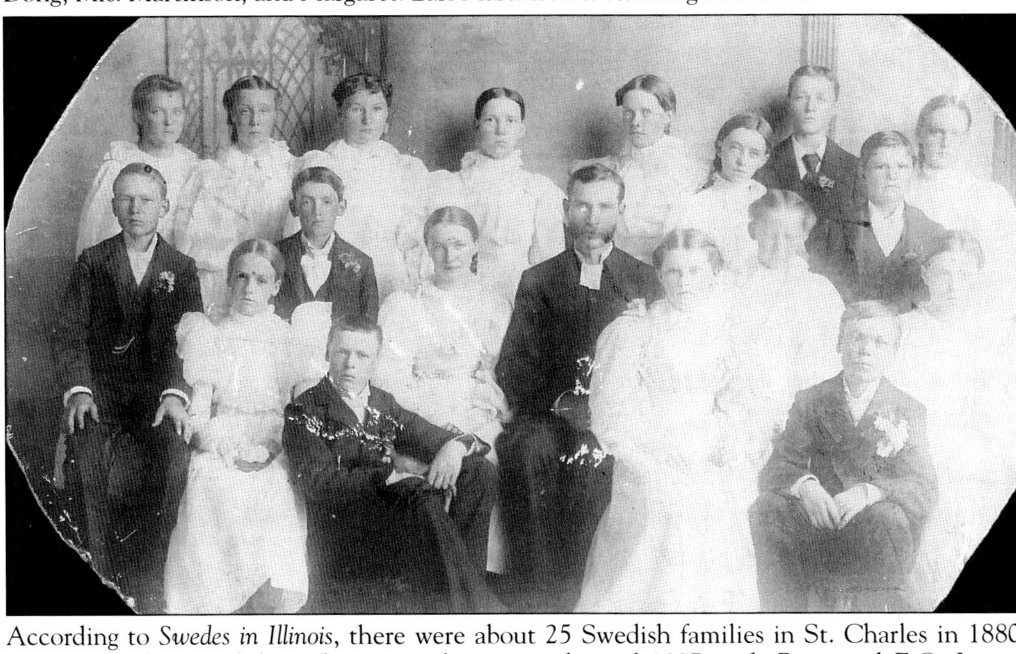

According to *Swedes in Illinois*, there were about 25 Swedish families in St. Charles in 1880. Pictured is the Swedish Lutheran confirmation class of 1897 with Reverend E.C. Jessup. Members are listed on the back of the original photograph.

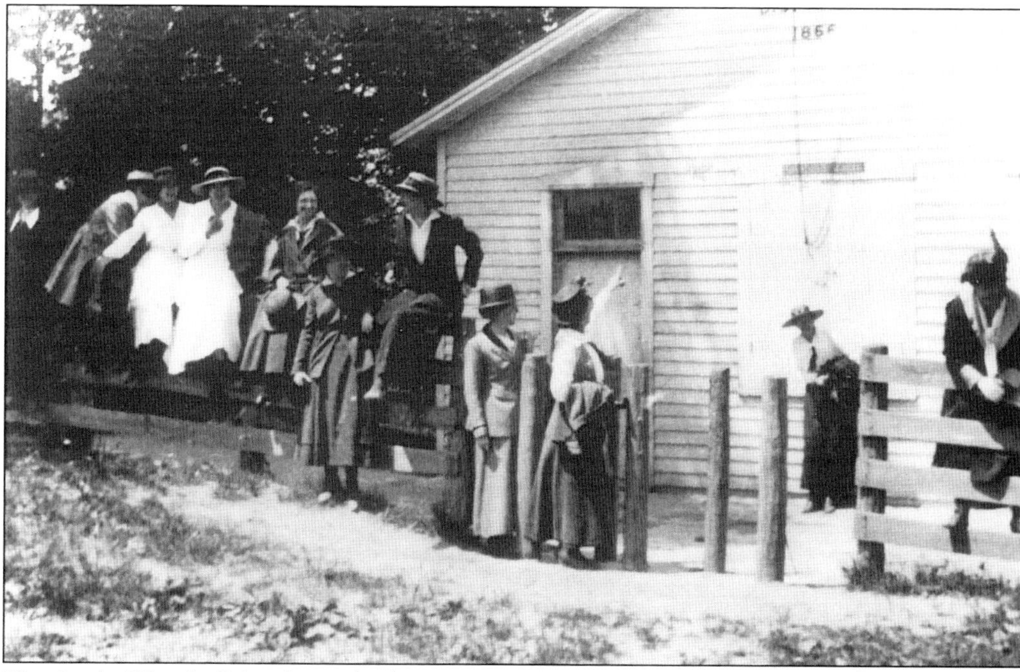

The Little Woods School was built in 1866. The Lutheran and Catholic Swedes provided language schools for their students from 1882 to 1888. Immigrant families saw to it that their children learned Bible history and grammar in Swedish in addition to learning the regular school subjects.

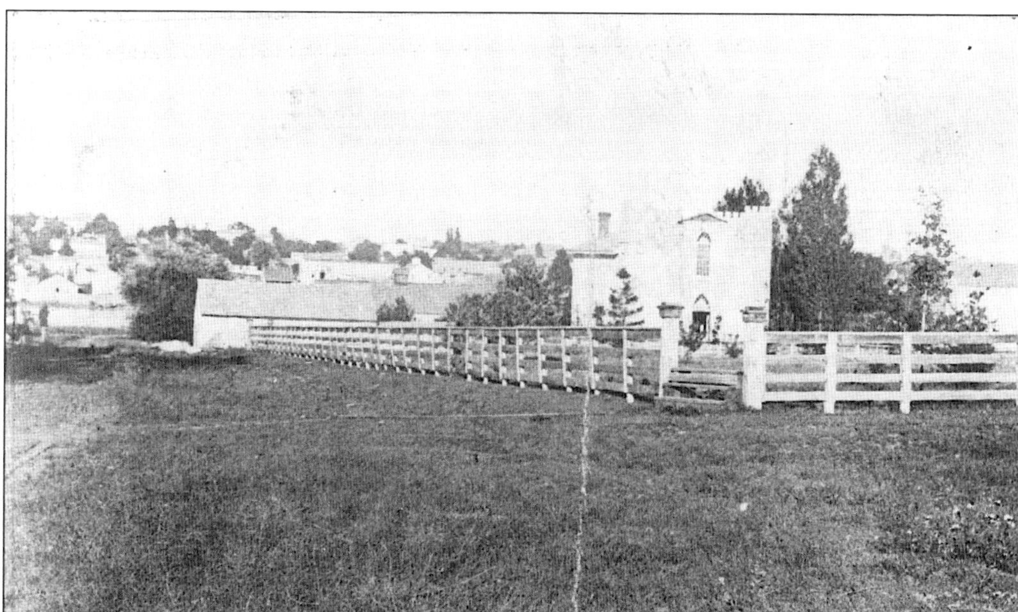

The slated fence encloses the old West Side Park. This view was taken from the northwest corner in 1872. Steps led into the park to allow people in but to keep cattle out. Farm animals ranged free and soon became a public nuisance. The Catholic church, before its steeple was added, is in the background.

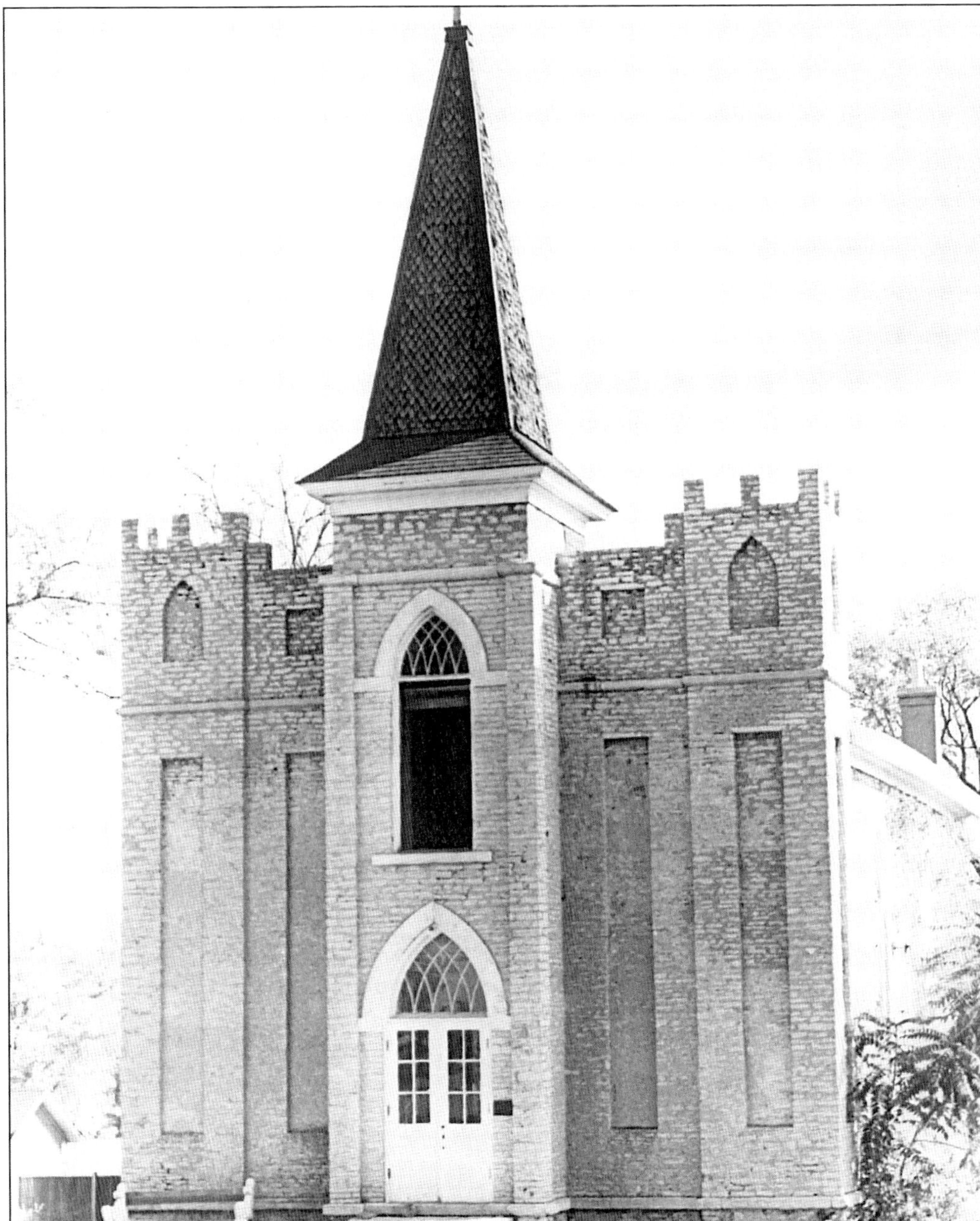

The largest group of Irish immigrated to the United States during the potato blight of the late 1840s. The early Irish settlers in St. Charles had been working on the Illinois Michigan Canal when a national depression first slowed then stopped construction in 1841.The majority of the Irish immigrants were Catholics, and religion played an important part in their lives. From 1830 to 1852, missionary priests traveled to St. Charles on horseback from Chicago or Joliet to hold Catholic services, which were held in private homes. The first Mass was celebrated in the home of Michael Flannery. The building of St. Patrick Catholic Church was begun in 1851, and it was completed and dedicated in 1852. The limestone for the church was quarried in St. Charles.

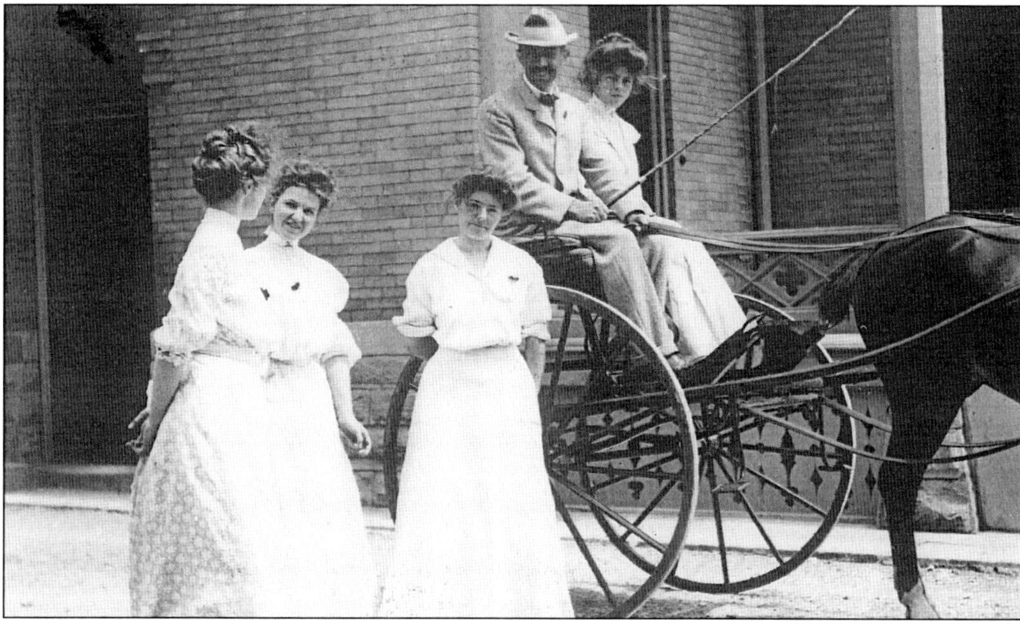

Solomon and Lydia Dunham came to Illinois in 1835 and settled northeast of St. Charles. Their farm came to be known as Oaklawn Farm. Their son Mark, born at Oaklawn, was credited with being the first breeder of Percheron (French) horses. Dunham consistently raised large numbers of domestic Percherons, the most prominent breed of heavy horses used in the 19th and early 20th centuries. Pictured above is Mary Louise Ward Dunham in the carriage about 1888.

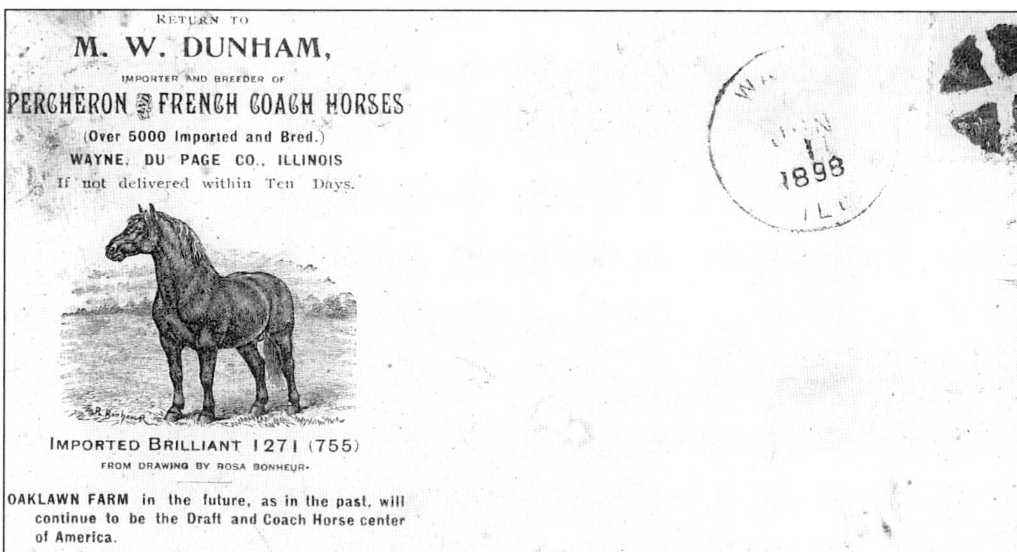


Brilliant 1271, Mark Dunham's most valuable sire, was imported as a four-year-old horse. Brilliant 1271 was described as "Weight 1,850; 16 hands high, long and very round body; extraordinary length of quarters, which are broad and level; very sloping shoulders of unusual depth; neck rather short; medium throttle; fine ear; wide between the eyes; slightly Roman nose; very broad breast; short legs and bone of uncommon width; good feet; immense stifle power." Dunham's envelopes advertised this most valuable asset.

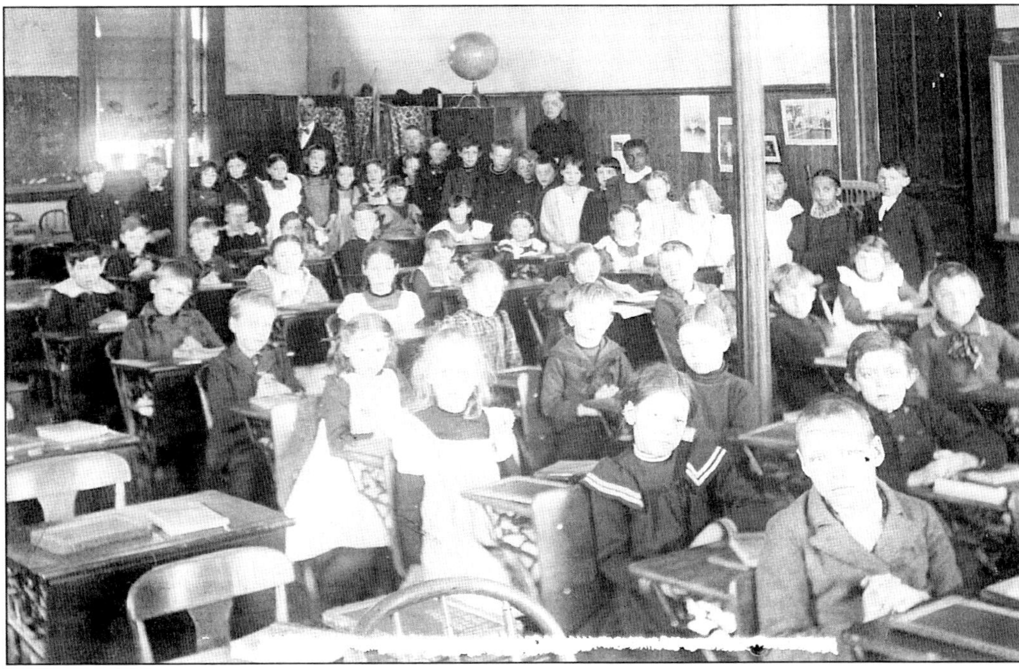

The first schools in the United States were private or parochial schools. Prudence Ward taught students out of her cabin from 1835 to the early 1840s. The public school on the east side was built in 1856 and was later replaced by Lincoln School. By 1885 the East Side School had 175 students and the West Side School had 156. Pictured are the first-grade students *c.* 1896.

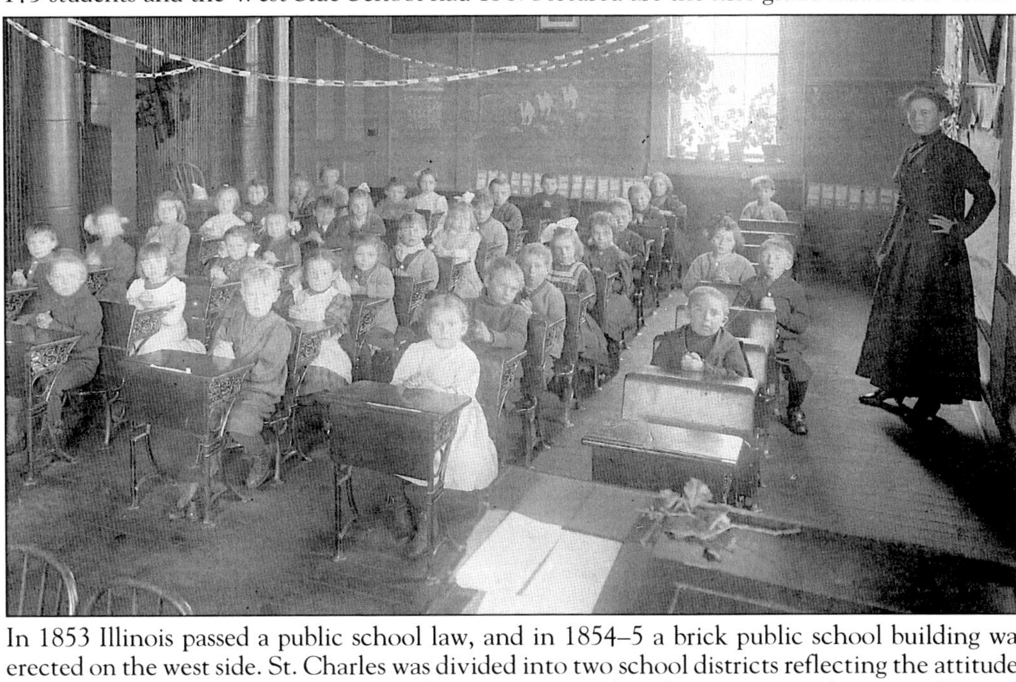

In 1853 Illinois passed a public school law, and in 1854–5 a brick public school building was erected on the west side. St. Charles was divided into two school districts reflecting the attitudes of the residents of the east and west sides. The West Side School was torn down in 1930, and the old bell, which summoned three generations of students, was moved to and mounted in Evan Shelby School.

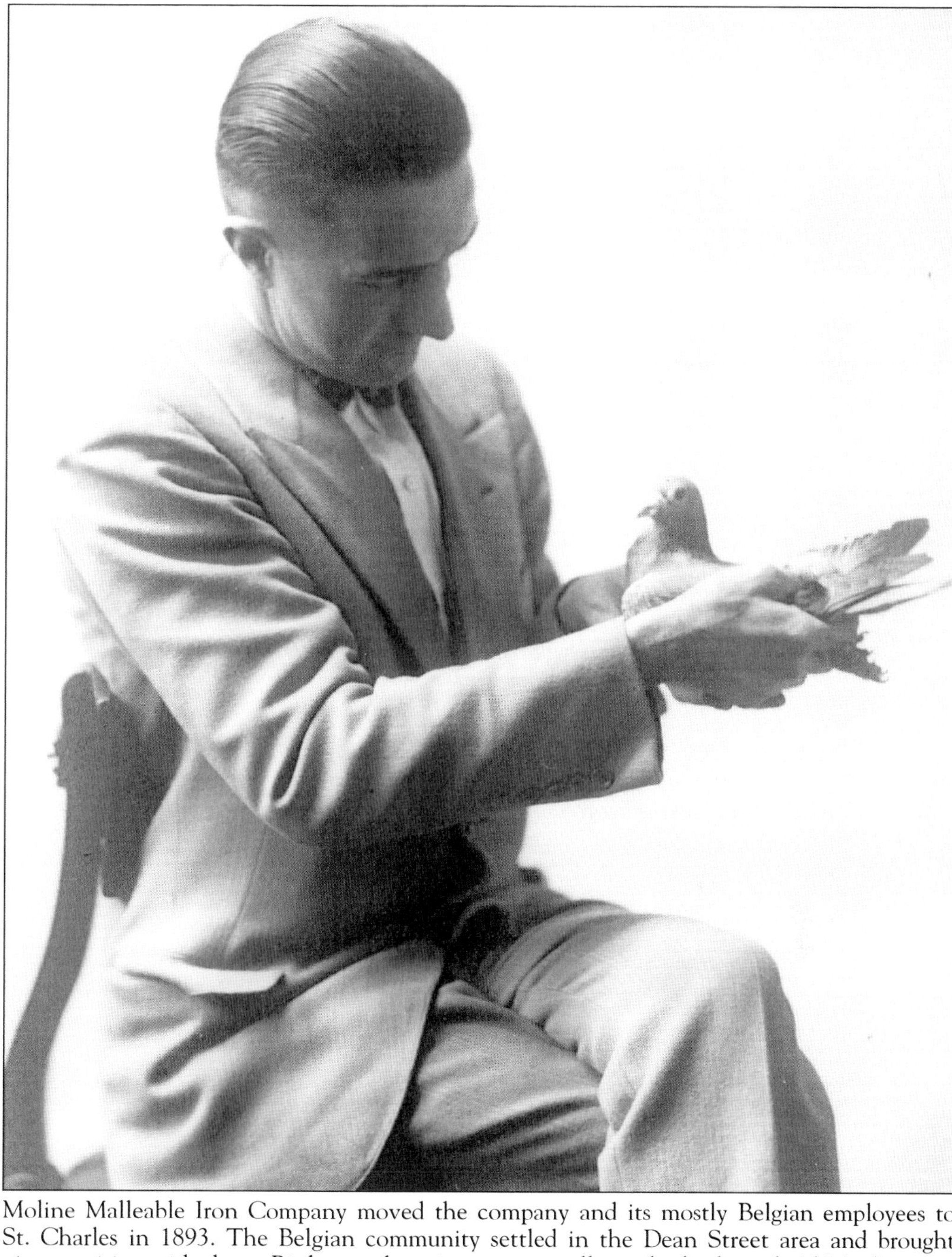

Moline Malleable Iron Company moved the company and its mostly Belgian employees to St. Charles in 1893. The Belgian community settled in the Dean Street area and brought pigeon raising with them. Birds were kept in coops, usually in the back yard. Al Mueleman is pictured holding a pigeon that won second place in 1924, 1925, and 1926 for the 500-mile race from Nebraska to St. Charles. This bird made it home in a day! Birds race distances from 100 to 1,000 miles. Pigeons cover the 100-mile course in about two hours. The 1,000-mile race lasts about 13 hours. Those who race the birds may have from 50 to 200 birds from which to train a racing team. Tiny cameras were strapped to pigeons during World War I to photograph over enemy territory, and the birds were awarded medals for their work.

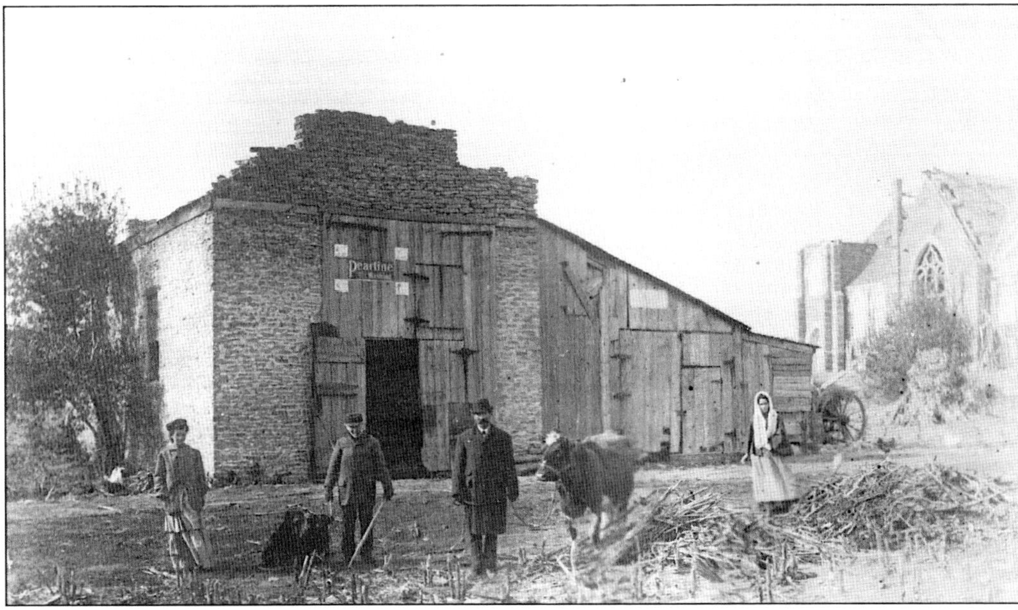

Michael Brennan (third from left) came to St. Charles in 1857. He worked at Butler Paper Mill as a machinist, and he owned the land from Seventh to Ninth Avenues where the engine house for the St. Charles branch of the Galena, Chicago, and Union Railroad stood. The engine went through the engine house to the turntable on the far side of the building.

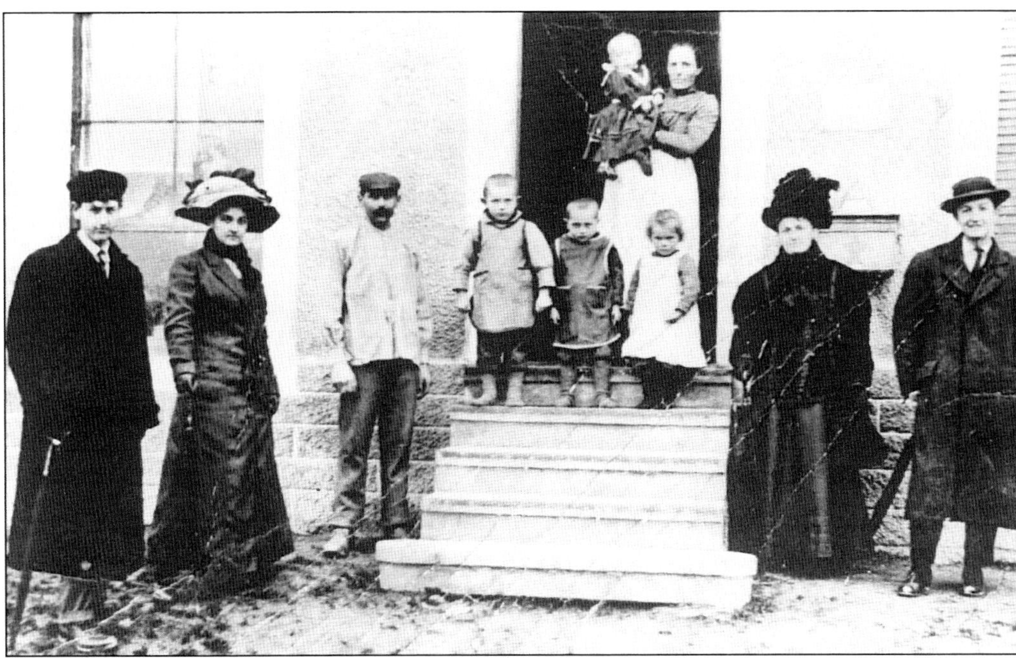
Pictured above is the Joseph Gartner family. The Gartners operated a restaurant and bakery, which was known area wide for their 5¢ ice cream and 25¢ Sunday chicken dinners. Joseph Gartner emigrated from Germany to St. Charles in 1890. In those days, you could get a free lunch at a tavern with a 5¢ beer.

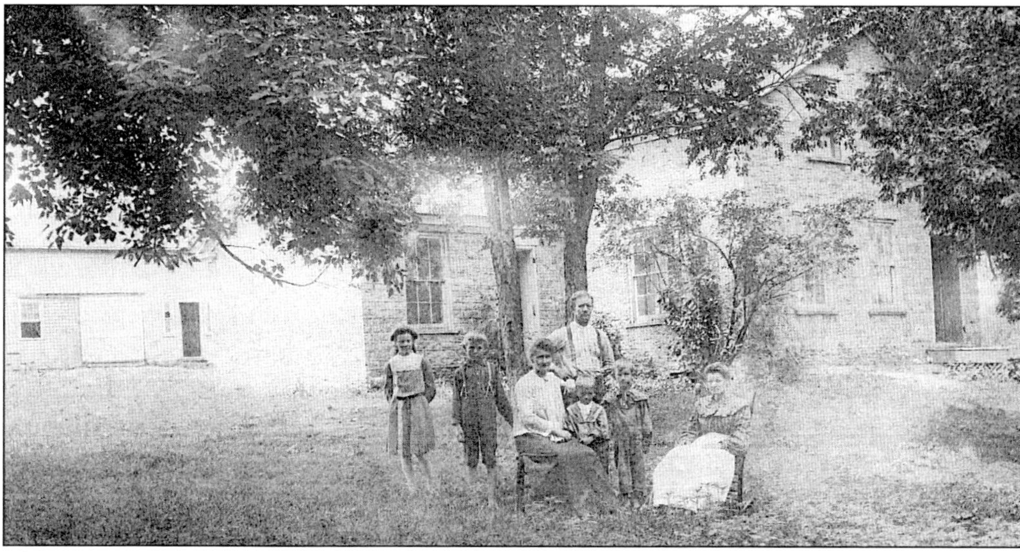

This 1908 picture of Mr. and Mrs. Manny Peterson was taken on the Silver Glen Farm that they rented to raise dairy cattle. Colonel Baker had been given the farm by John Gates because Baker admired it while they were riding past it in a horse and buggy one day.

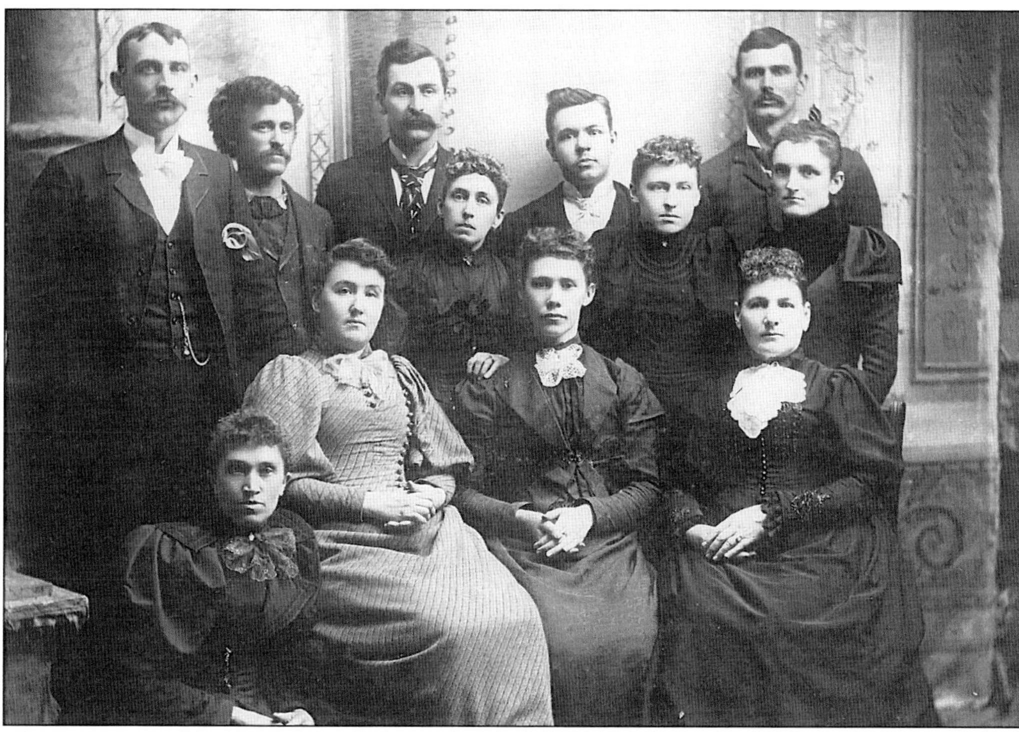

The Methodist Episcopal Society was one of the first founded in the village. They started building their sanctuary about 1843. This 1895 photograph is of a choir. Pictured, from left to right, are as follows: (bottom) Mrs. Thomas Marsden, Mrs. Oscar Howard, Mrs. George Turner, and Mrs. John Norton; (middle) Kate Brown, Mary Gorham, and Harriet Brownell; (top) Fred Grant, Oscar Howard, Cal Day, Harry Jordan, and U.S. Elliot.

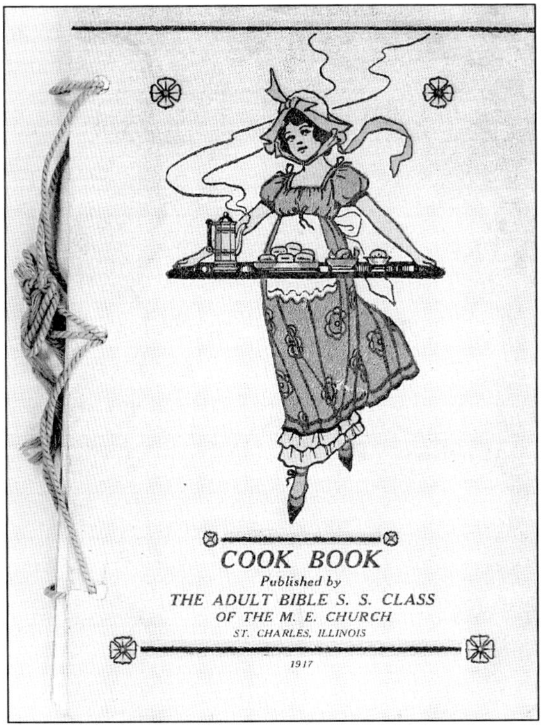


Cookbooks featuring local recipes were a popular method of fund-raising in the early 1900s just as they are today. This one was put together by the adult Bible Sunday school class of the Methodist Episcopal Church in 1917.

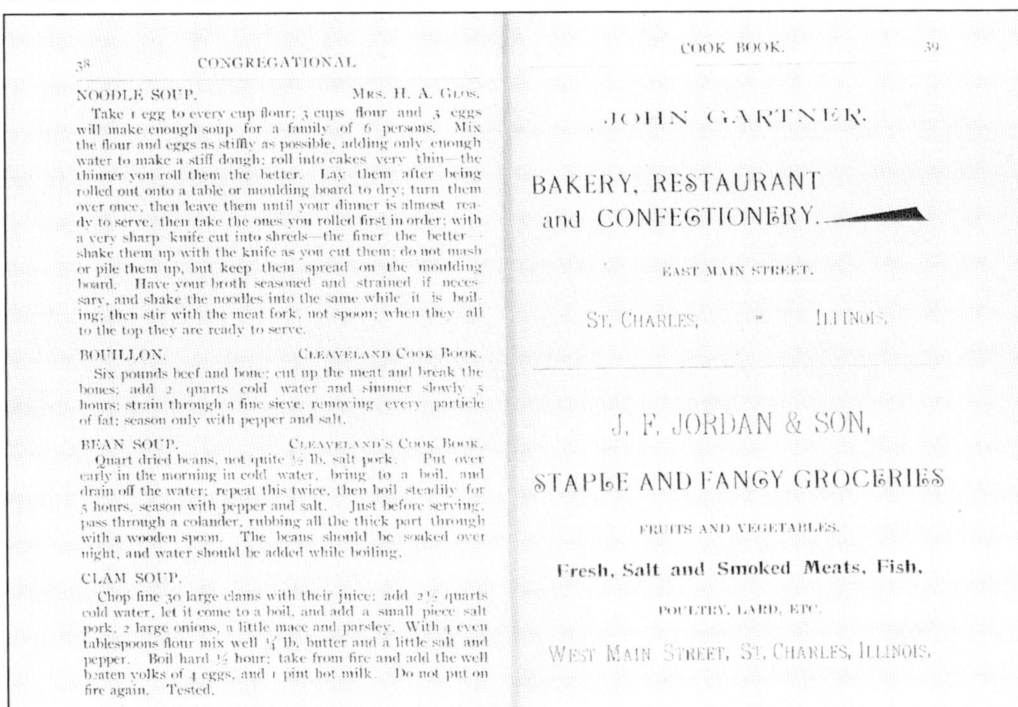

38 CONGREGATIONAL

NOODLE SOUP. MRS. H. A. GLOS.

Take 1 egg to every cup flour; 3 cups flour and 3 eggs will make enough soup for a family of 6 persons. Mix the flour and eggs as stiffly as possible, adding only enough water to make a stiff dough; roll into cakes very thin—the thinner you roll them the better. Lay them after being rolled out onto a table or moulding board to dry; turn them over once, then leave them until your dinner is almost ready to serve, then take the ones you rolled first in order; with a very sharp knife cut into shreds—the finer the better—shake them up with the knife as you cut them; do not mash or pile them up, but keep them spread on the moulding board. Have your broth seasoned and strained if necessary, and shake the noodles into the same while it is boiling; then stir with the meat fork, not spoon; when they all to the top they are ready to serve.

BOUILLON. CLEAVELAND COOK BOOK.

Six pounds beef and bone; cut up the meat and break the bones; add 2 quarts cold water and simmer slowly 5 hours; strain through a fine sieve, removing every particle of fat; season only with pepper and salt.

BEAN SOUP. CLEAVELAND'S COOK BOOK.

Quart dried beans, not quite ½ lb. salt pork. Put over early in the morning in cold water, bring to a boil, and drain off the water; repeat this twice, then boil steadily for 5 hours, season with pepper and salt. Just before serving, pass through a colander, rubbing all the thick part through with a wooden spoon. The beans should be soaked over night, and water should be added while boiling.

CLAM SOUP.

Chop fine 30 large clams with their juice; add 2½ quarts cold water, let it come to a boil, and add a small piece salt pork, 2 large onions, a little mace and parsley. With 4 even tablespoons flour mix well ¼ lb. butter and a little salt and pepper. Boil hard ½ hour; take from fire and add the well beaten yolks of 4 eggs, and 1 pint hot milk. Do not put on fire again. Tested.

COOK BOOK. 39

JOHN GARTNER.

BAKERY, RESTAURANT and CONFECTIONERY.

EAST MAIN STREET.

ST. CHARLES, - ILLINOIS.

J. F. JORDAN & SON,

STAPLE AND FANCY GROCERIES

FRUITS AND VEGETABLES.

Fresh, Salt and Smoked Meats, Fish,

POULTRY, LARD, ETC.

WEST MAIN STREET, ST. CHARLES, ILLINOIS.

Here is a page from the Congregational church cookbook. Not only are the recipes written very differently from ours today, but take a look at the list of ingredients. When have you last broken bones or made noodles for your soup?

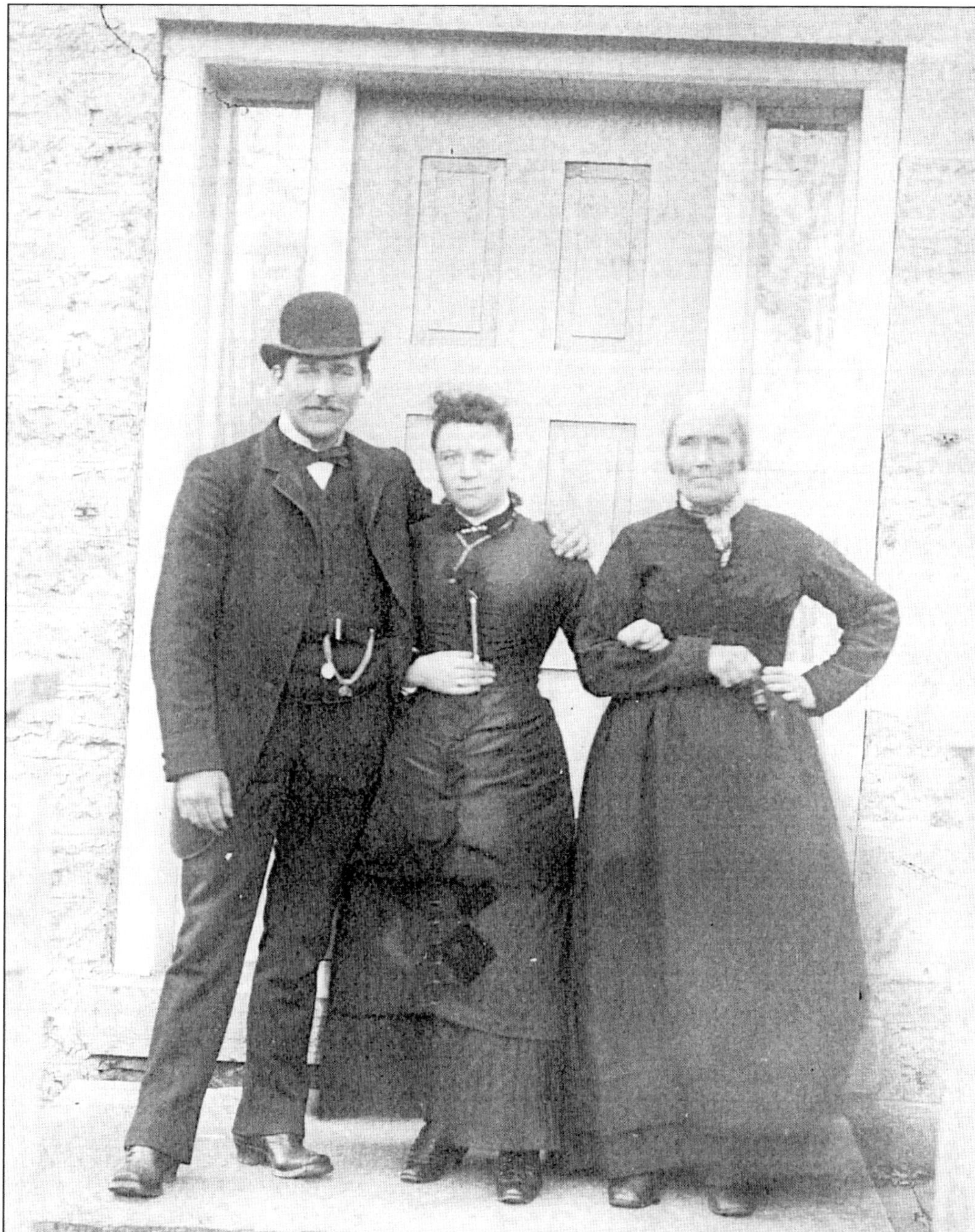

Marie Fulton is shown here in front of her house at 601 S. Sixth Avenue with two young relatives around 1885. The limestone used to build the house was most likely quarried in the Fox Valley. Marie was born in Ireland and immigrated to St. Charles in 1849. She lived here until her death in 1899, with the exception of four years she spent in Canada. The trio appears to be coming from or going to a wedding or a funeral by the appearance of their clothing. Mrs. Fulton's dress is now in the St. Charles Heritage Center archives. The niece may have been a teacher since she wears a pen hanging around her neck. The young man might even be wearing an Elgin watch on his fob.

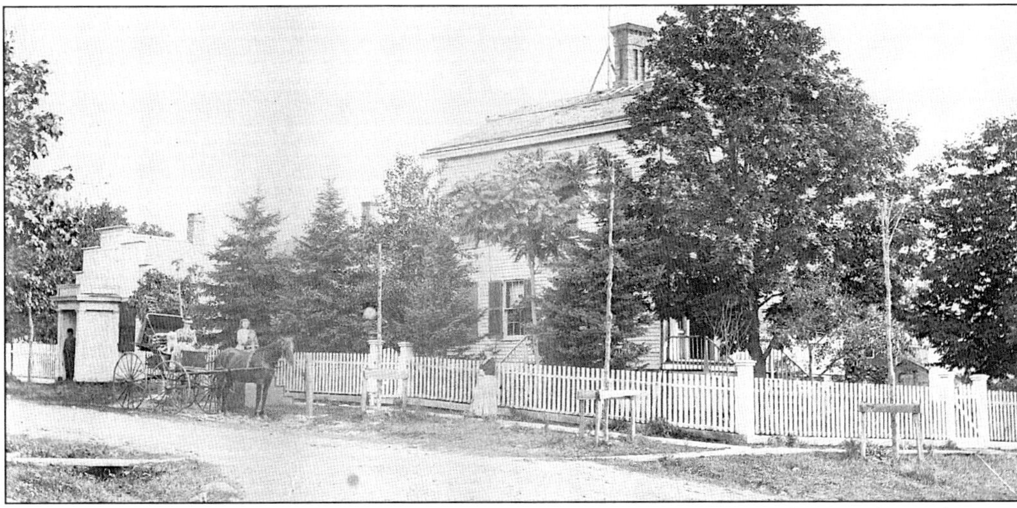

This photograph of the Stephens S. Jones residence, built in 1837, was taken in the mid-1800s. Gertrude Bundy Parker wrote that Grandma Bundy (Mary Jones Bundy) was in the buggy with "Fido," the poodle dog, and "Nellie," the horse. Harrison Smith is in the entrance to the old office. Harrison Smith was an African-American man who was given his free papers and brought north by Grandpa John (John Curtis Bundy).

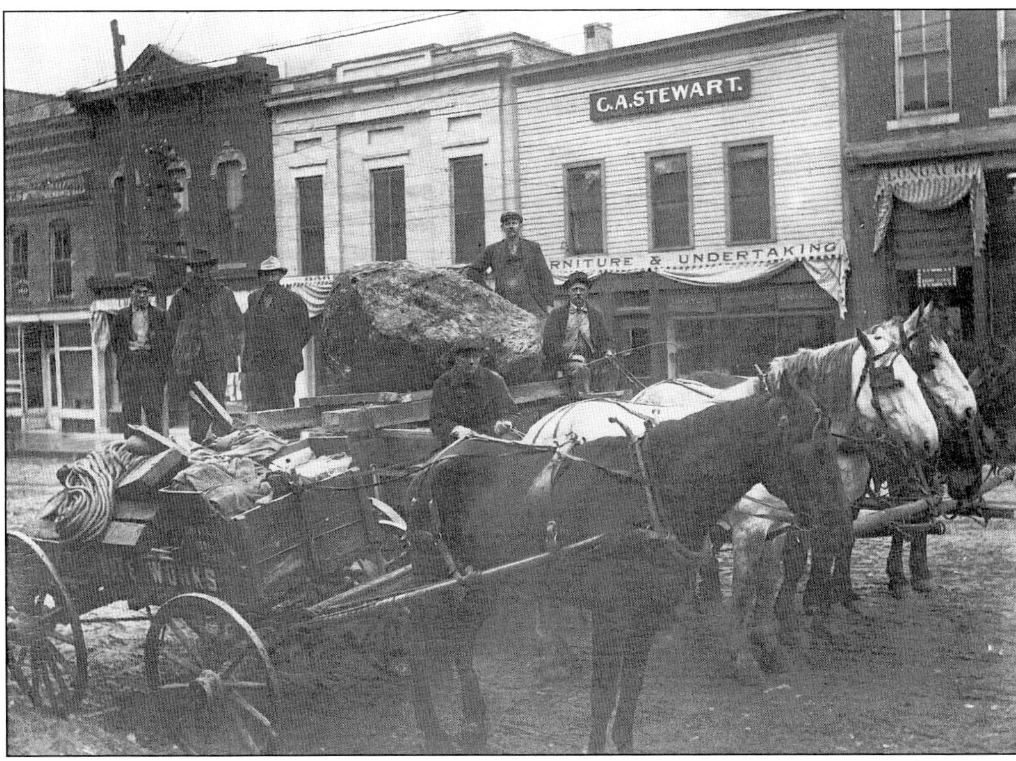


Maro the Magician (Edward T. Best) died in 1908. He wished to be buried in St. Charles and specified that this huge, 11-ton piece of granite be moved from Michigan to St. Charles and placed as a marker on his grave. These four horses earned their oats that day moving the boulder from the train to North Cemetery!

# Three

# MUSIC OF INDUSTRY
## *Milk, Pianos, and Chandeliers*

St. Charles picked up the pace after 1870 with a railroad, new industry, and more immigration. The village became a city in October 1874, and James K. Lewis was elected the first mayor. With the increased population, improvements were made which made to enhance urban life. Telephones were installed in the 1880s, and a library was built in 1889. Free mail delivery was available by 1904, and public utilities such as gas (1901), water (1906), and sewers (1912) were installed.

There were more means of transportation after the 1870s. Railroads and trolleys were additional ways of traveling, along with stagecoaches, boats, and horses, which had been in use for several years.

St. Charles also viewed itself as a healthy place to build new factories. It was a city of contented cows and people! Some of the new companies brought their workers with them. Others hired workers that lived in the area. Immigrants wrote home about the many opportunities in the Fox Valley, and the Belgians, in particular, sponsored the newcomers.

This was a city that took music into people's houses with the thousands of pianos that left St. Charles destined for countries near and far.

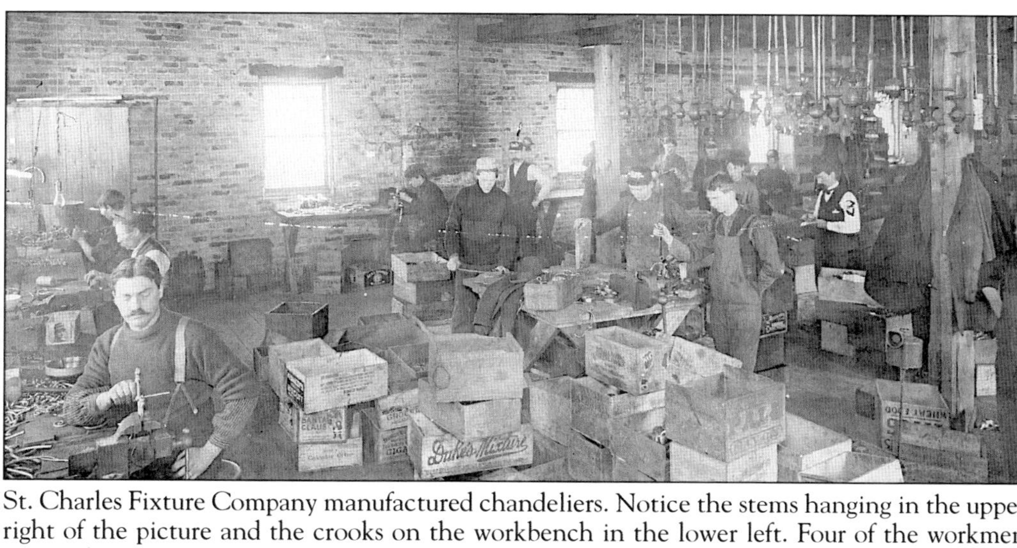

St. Charles Fixture Company manufactured chandeliers. Notice the stems hanging in the upper right of the picture and the crooks on the workbench in the lower left. Four of the workmen pictured are identified by number. One is Charles Nichol, two is Francis Parker, three is James Horne, and four is Joe McClanigan.

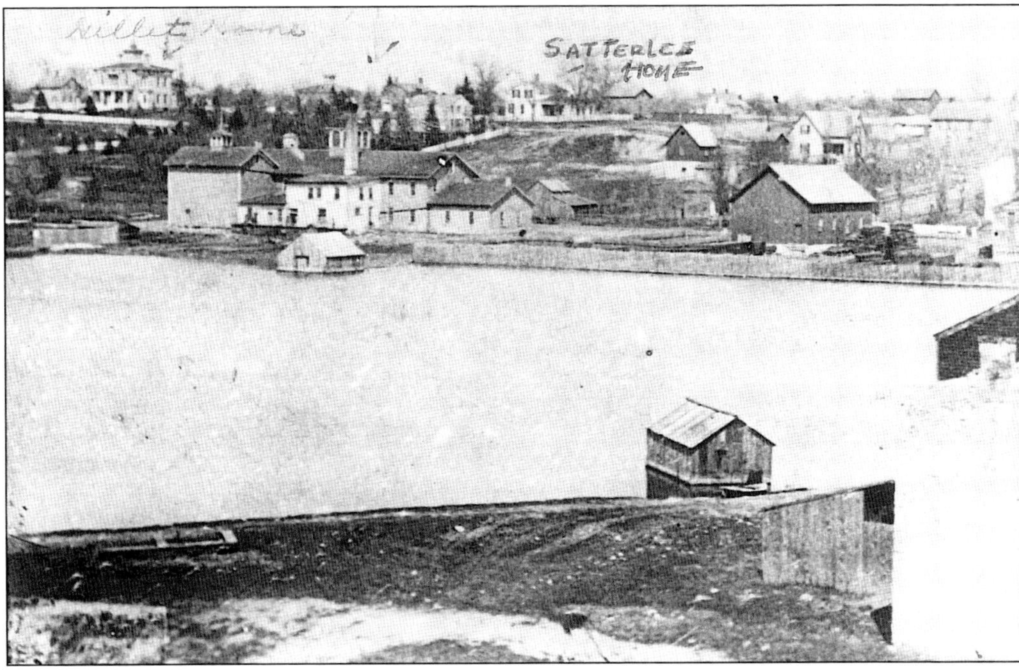


In the days before artificial refrigeration, milk was condensed and canned to be shipped to other locations. Pictured are the old milk sugar factory and the condensed milk factory looking from north of the present site of Hotel Baker.

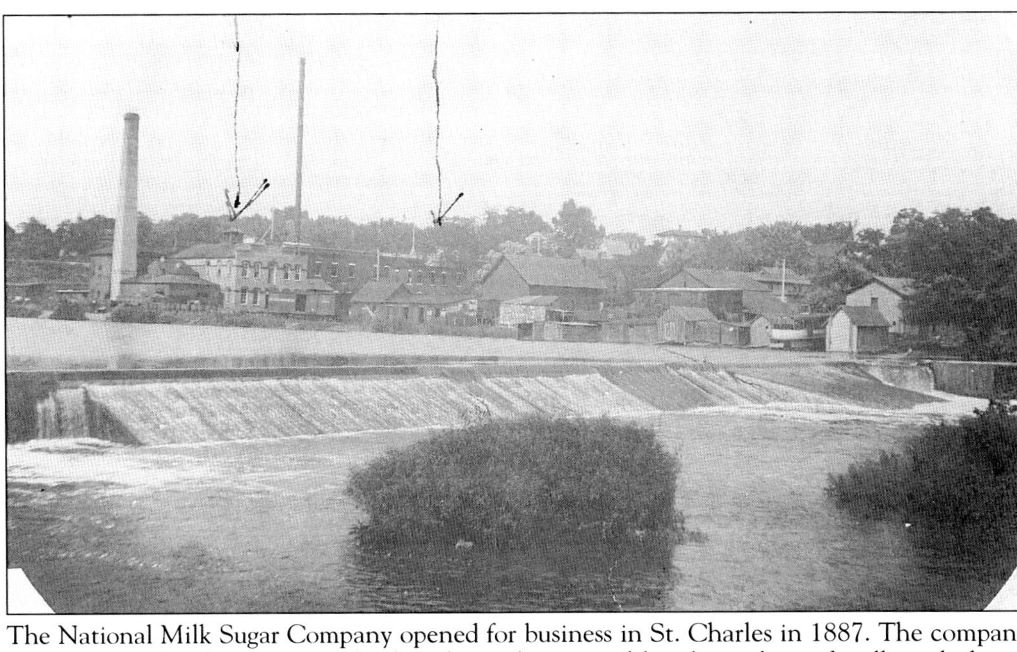

The National Milk Sugar Company opened for business in St. Charles in 1887. The company processed crude whey, previously thought to be a worthless byproduct of milk and cheese production. Sugar for medicinal purposes and infant food were made from the whey, and later, albumen and lactic acid were also extracted.

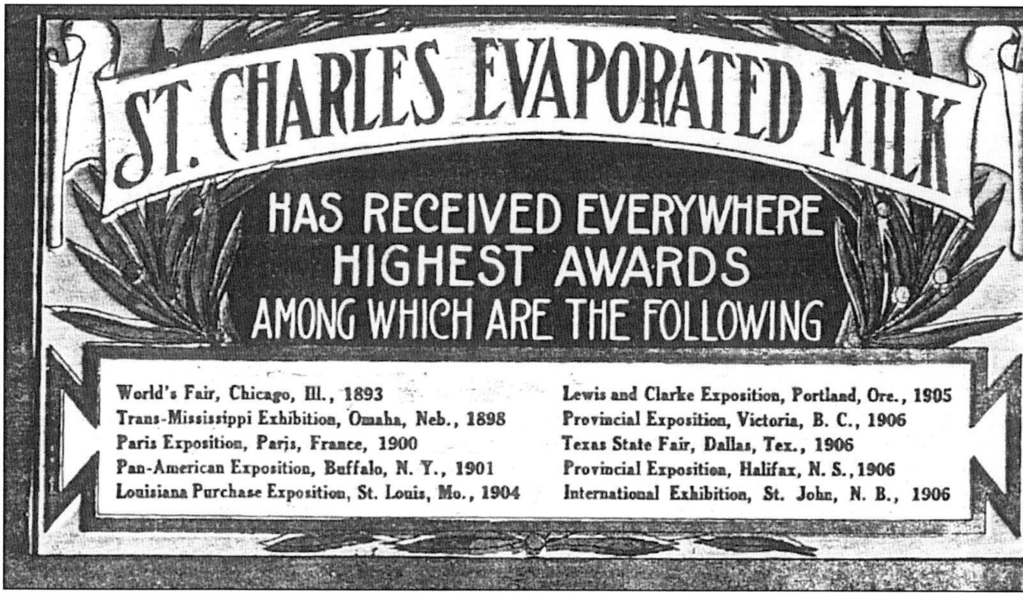


St. Charles Evaporated Milk was distributed in all markets of the world. The "Gold or Silver Cow" was the logo that thousands of people asked for when it was evaporated milk they wanted. The St. Charles Condensing Company was later sold to Borden's, but they still produced the St. Charles brand.

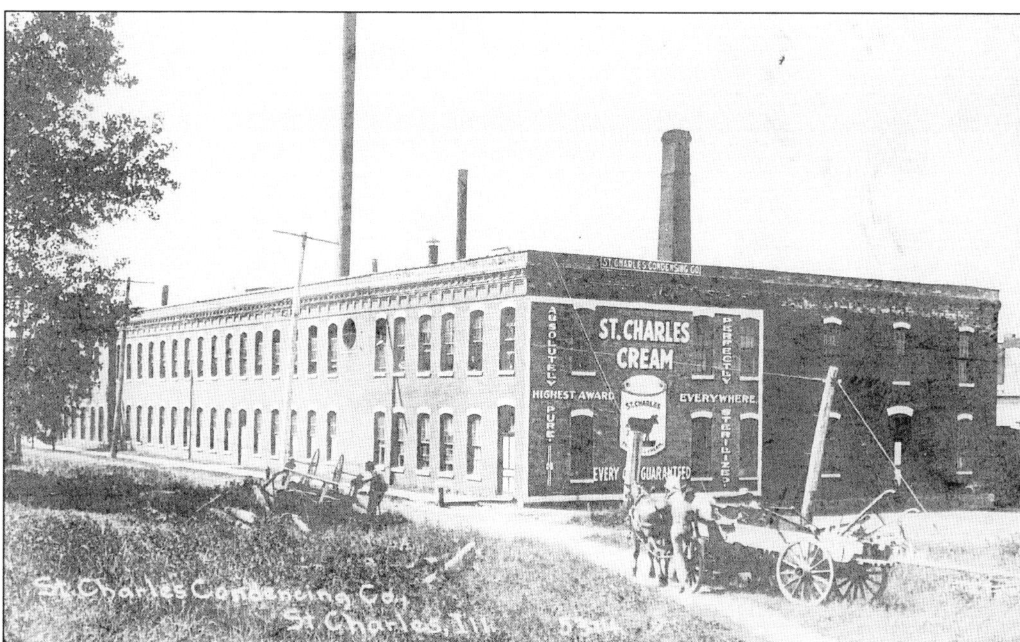


St. Charles Condensing Company employed 100 men. This plant was brought to St. Charles by Lorenzo Ward and was located in the long, red brick building that Ward had built in the 1870s on North First Avenue.

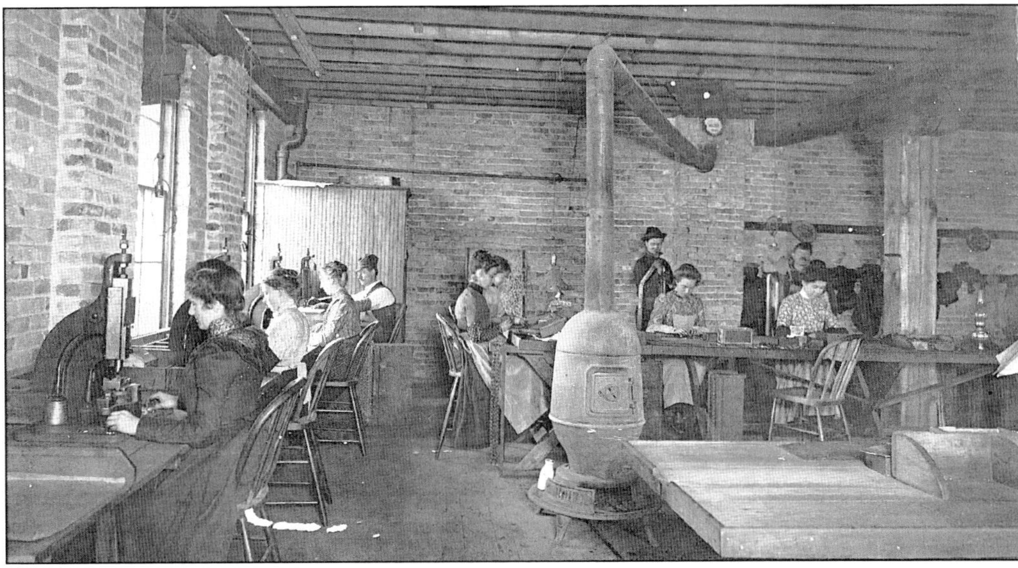

Crown Electrical Manufacturing Company located in St. Charles in 1892. Their first products were gas lighting fixtures, but with the affordability of electricity, the company changed from gas fixtures to the manufacture of a general line of electric lighting fixtures. They also manufactured chains for the hottest transportation device of the 1890s, the bicycle. This photograph shows one manufacturing area around 1910.

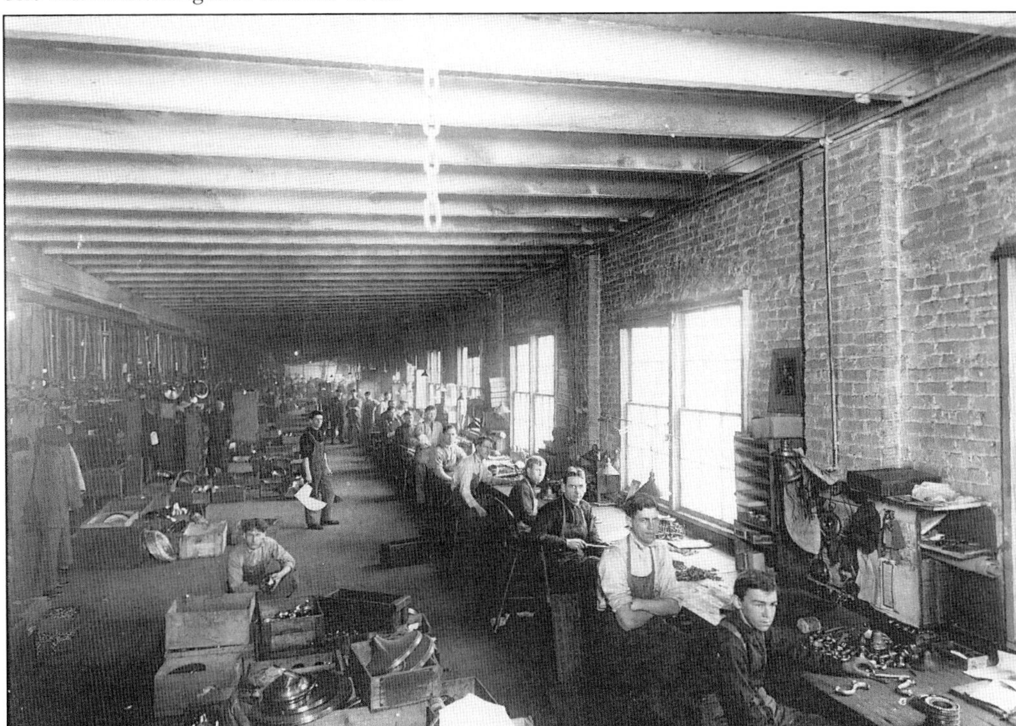

Crown Electric supplied commercial fixtures for hotels. Their largest order was for 5,500 lamps for the Hotel Stevens in Chicago. Crown Electric Company had over 700 chandelier designs and had a designer on staff to keep up with the home and hotel fashions of the day.

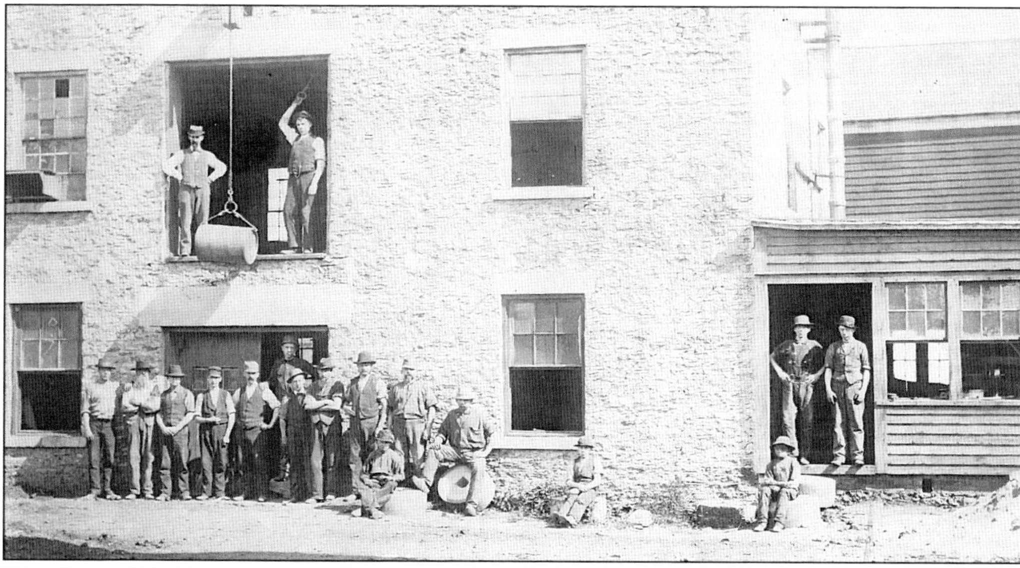

The Doige File Factory opened in 1877 and was located on a site behind the current Hotel Baker. About 25 skilled men worked in the factory. In the upper window are J.T. Gallegher and Hames T. Doherty. In the doorway, from left to right, are the following: Richard Garrity, Kollauf (unidentified surname), and G. Godfrey.

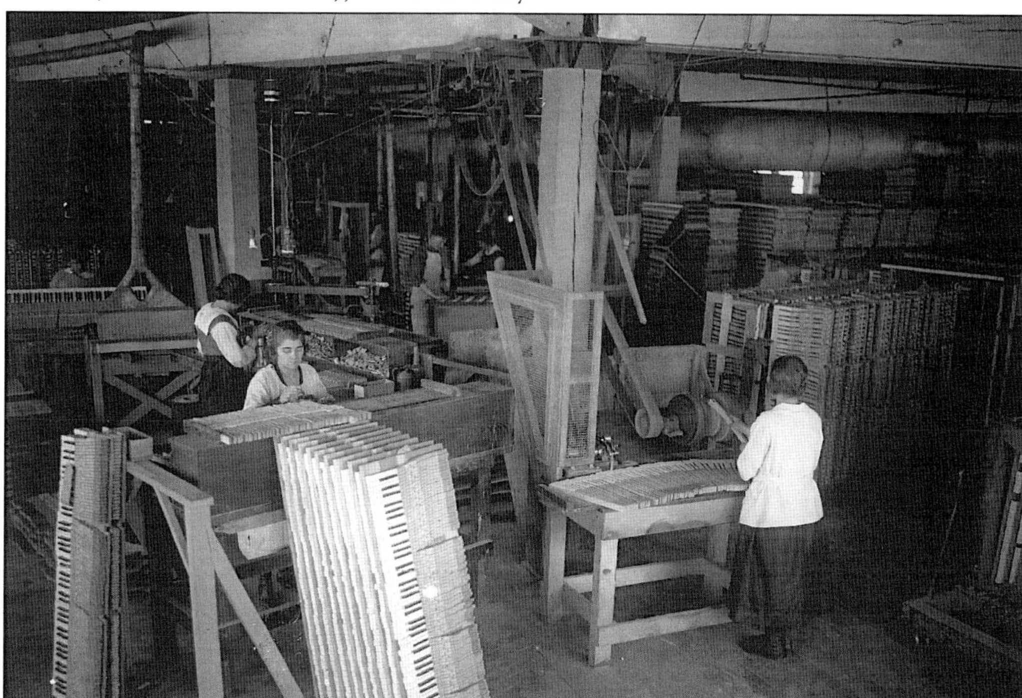

The Cable Piano Company was built along the Fox River in 1900 and operated until 1933. Despite being a very modern factory with good ventilation and free restrooms, Cable used a typical factory setup for the shafts on the ceiling and belts to direct the power down to the machines. This photograph shows the workers who are working on the keyboards, installing the black and white keys. Most of their employees were Lithuanians.

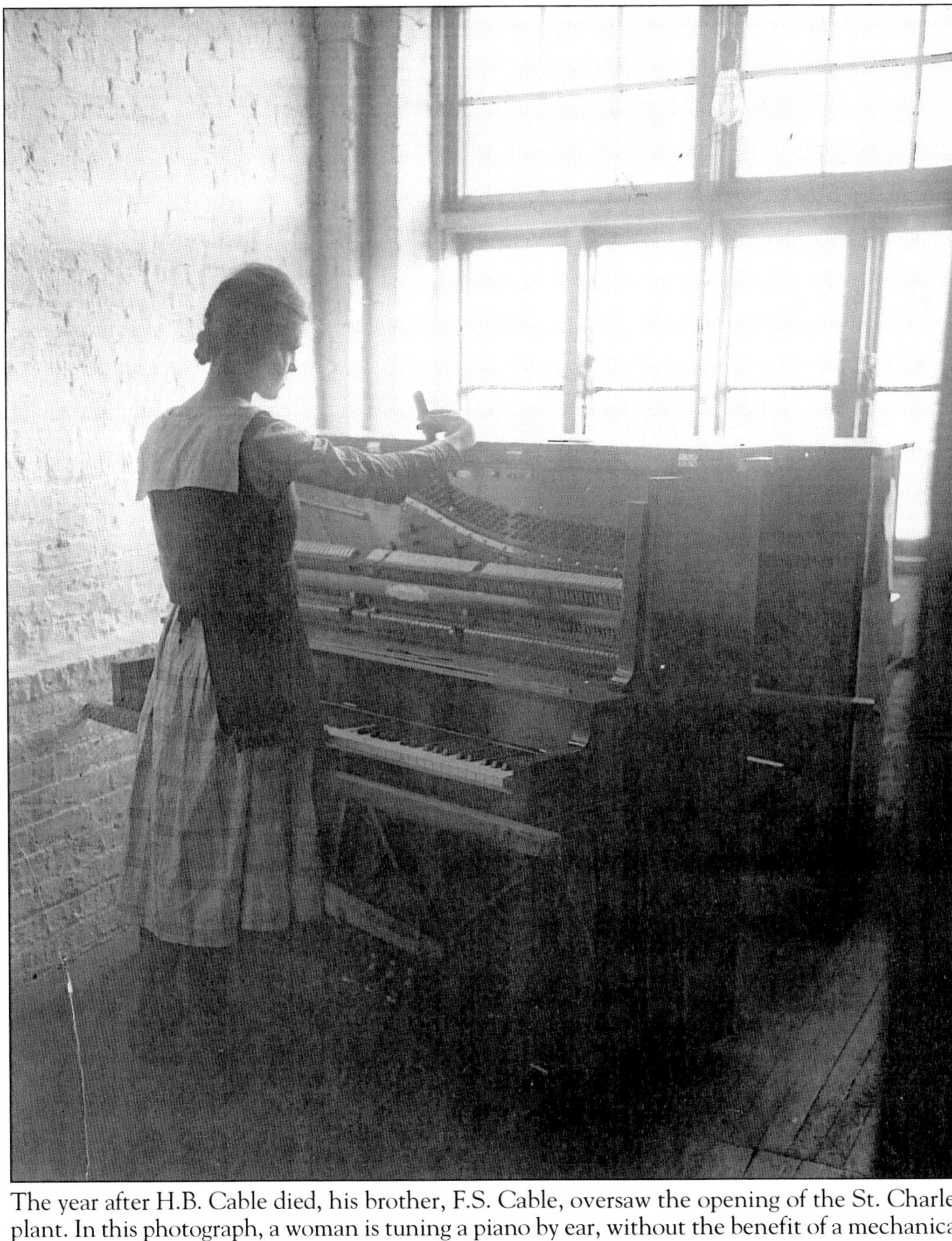

The year after H.B. Cable died, his brother, F.S. Cable, oversaw the opening of the St. Charles plant. In this photograph, a woman is tuning a piano by ear, without the benefit of a mechanical tuning device. She is shown using a lever to tighten the pin that holds the string. Cable Piano Company was different from other piano manufacturers in that they made all the components that went into their pianos on site. Cable polished and laid its own ivory and designed and built machinery needed to manufacture the pianos. Other piano manufacturers assembled parts from various manufacturers. Materials for Cable pianos came from all over the world. Ivory for the keys came from India and Africa, wool for the hammers came from Australia, and veneers came from Mexico, South America, and the gold coast of Africa.

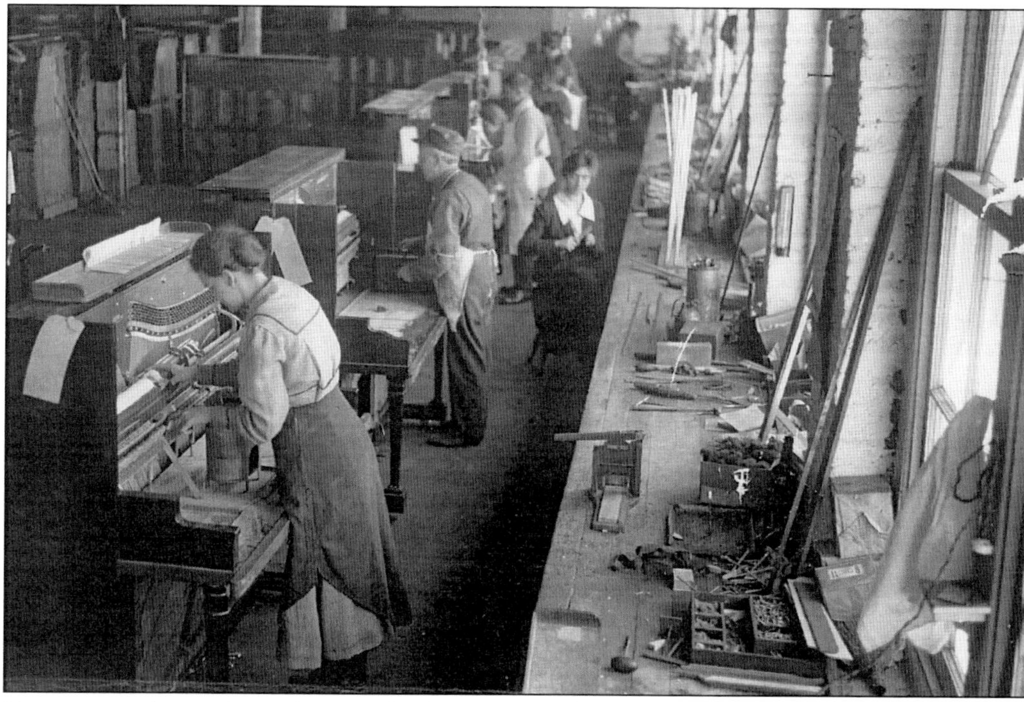

Here we see the workers adjusting the hammers on the piano action. Lighting was supplied by the long windows and the lights hanging from the ceiling every 15 feet. Supplies were stored in the darker section of the plant.

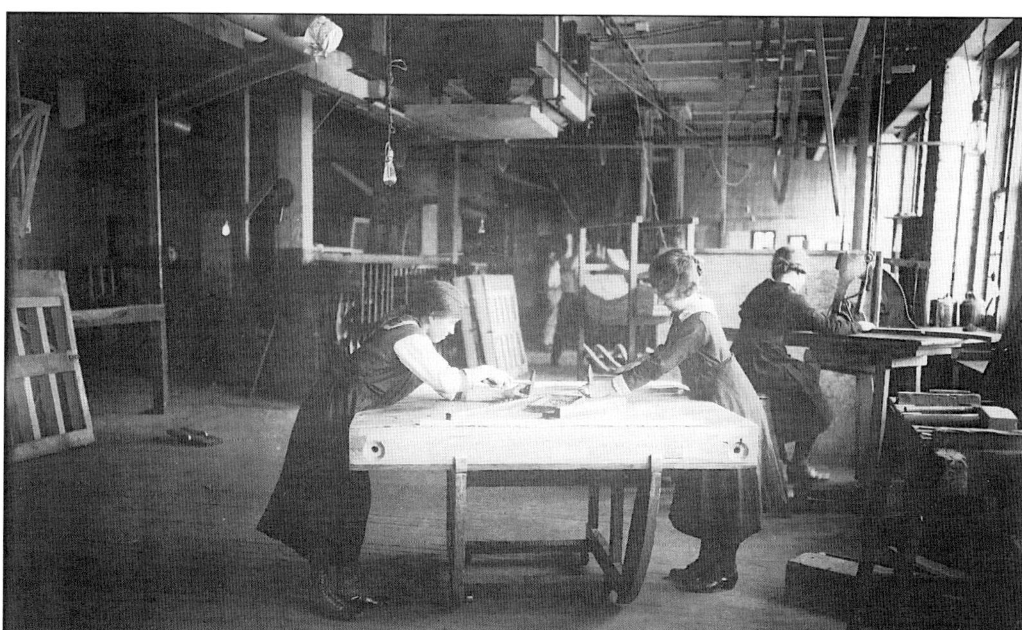

The women in this picture are adjusting the rib boards on sounding boards across which the strings are positioned. Women were a good, reliable source of labor at a bargain price, and more women were employed beginning in 1917, when the men in the labor force were called to war.

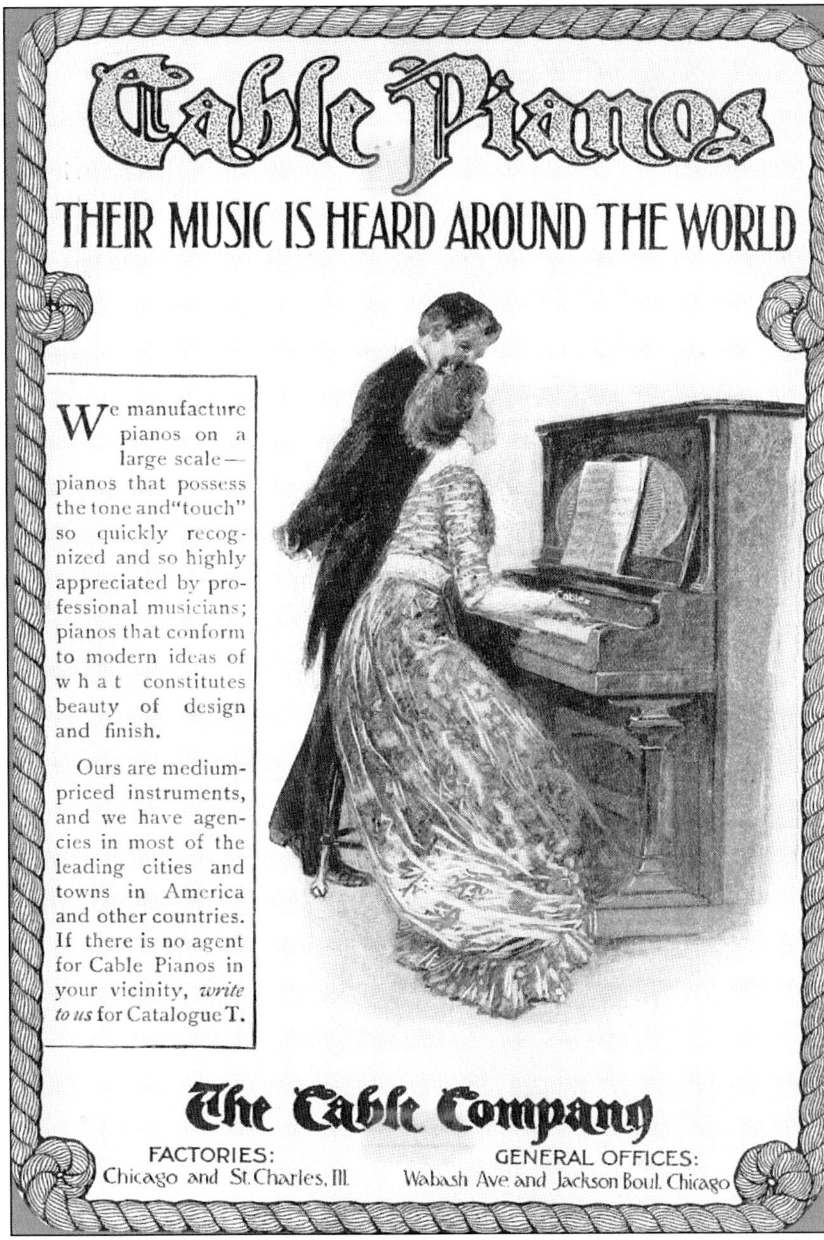


In 1913 Cable Piano Company was among the largest manufacturer of pianos, player pianos, and organs. Cable pianos were distributed all over the world. At first, the St. Charles plant's output was only two pianos a day. In 1905 that increased to 20, and at its peak, the St. Charles plant produced 35 pianos per day and employed up to 500 people. Cable pianos were medium-priced instruments and were found in middle-class homes and in schools. Before he started manufacturing pianos, H.B. Cable worked as a school superintendent and later worked for Barns & Company. He used the marketing methods he had learned as a book seller to market his pianos. Cable also printed sheet music and had demonstration studios so that a prospective buyer could test a piano before purchasing it. The Depression caused dozens of piano manufacturers to go out of business as sales plummeted.

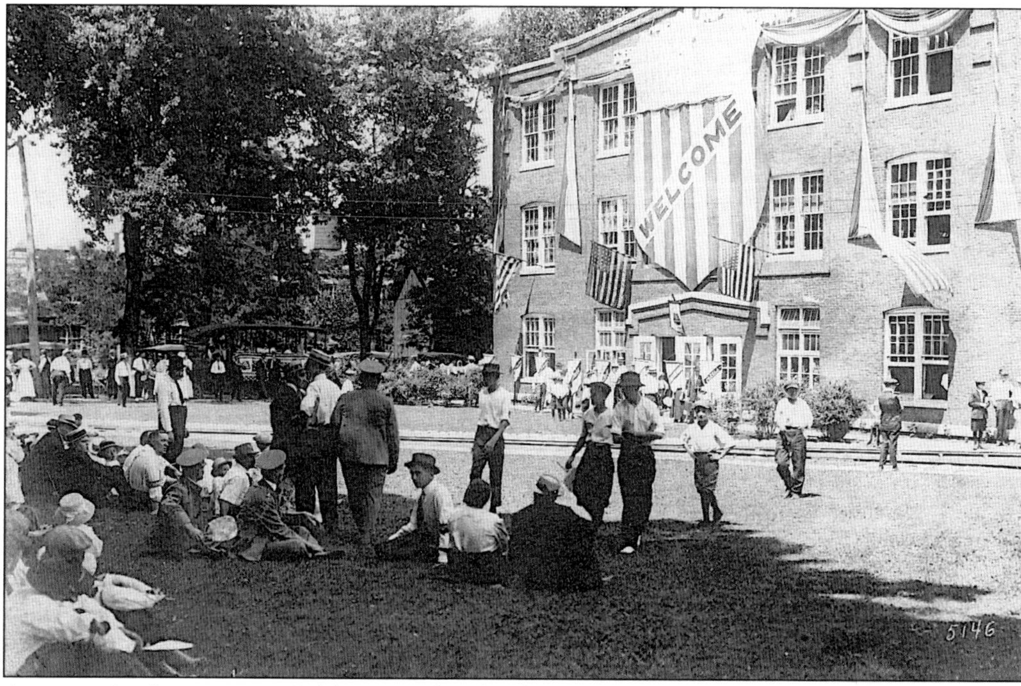


At its peak of prosperity, Cable seemed to be the perfect place for employment with healthy working conditions. The company's 11 acres along the Fox River were known for well-kept lawns and flower gardens. Baseball teams, brass bands, and an excellent male chorus represented the Cable Piano Company. The annual company picnic was held on the banks of the Fox and included employees from Chicago's Cable plant.

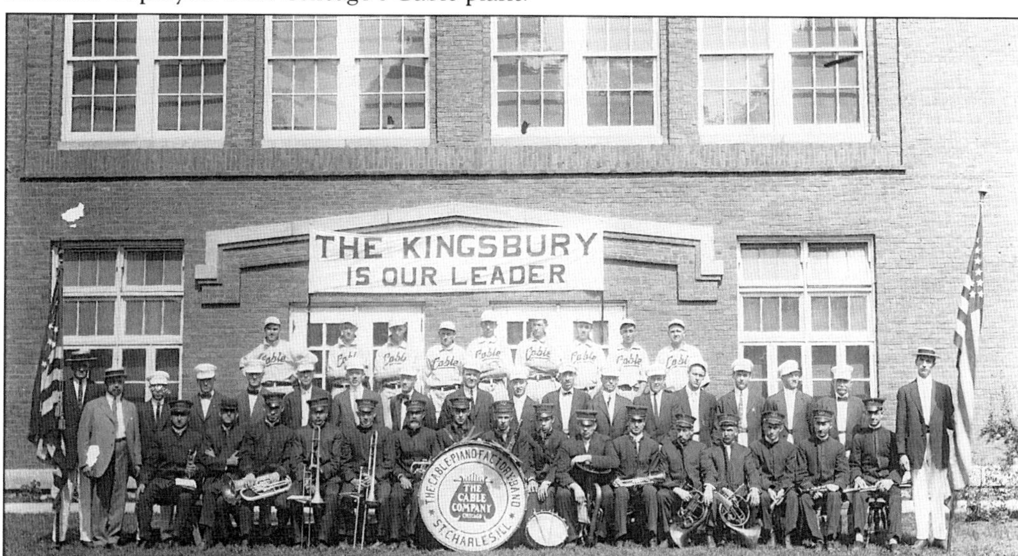


Factories of this era sponsored sports and musical teams. Cable was there helping make any patriotic parade a success. The only person identified in this photograph is Elmer Carlson, who is behind the drum with a clarinet. Pianos made in St. Charles included the Kingsbury (see the banner) and Wellington upright pianos, Convoer uprights and grands, and Eureka player pianos.

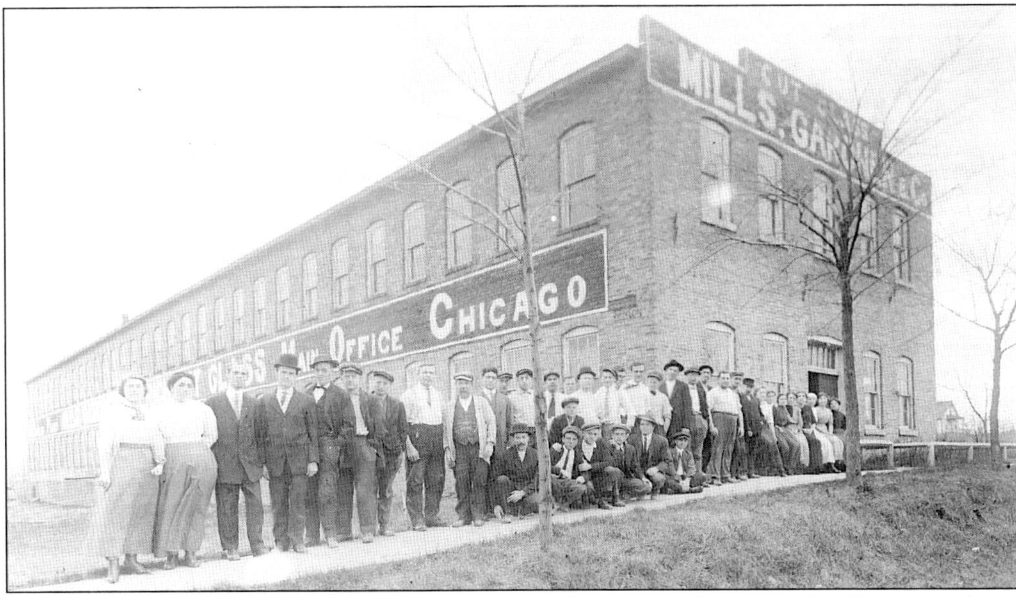


Another turn-of-the-century manufacturer in St. Charles was the Heinz Brothers, which was considered one of the largest cut glass manufacturing companies in the Midwest. At their peak in 1905, they employed 80 to 100 people. The factory was known internationally for its beautiful cut glass and expert craftsmanship. The German-born Heinz brothers had perfected a method of polishing with acids, which made their glassware more brilliant than their competitors'.

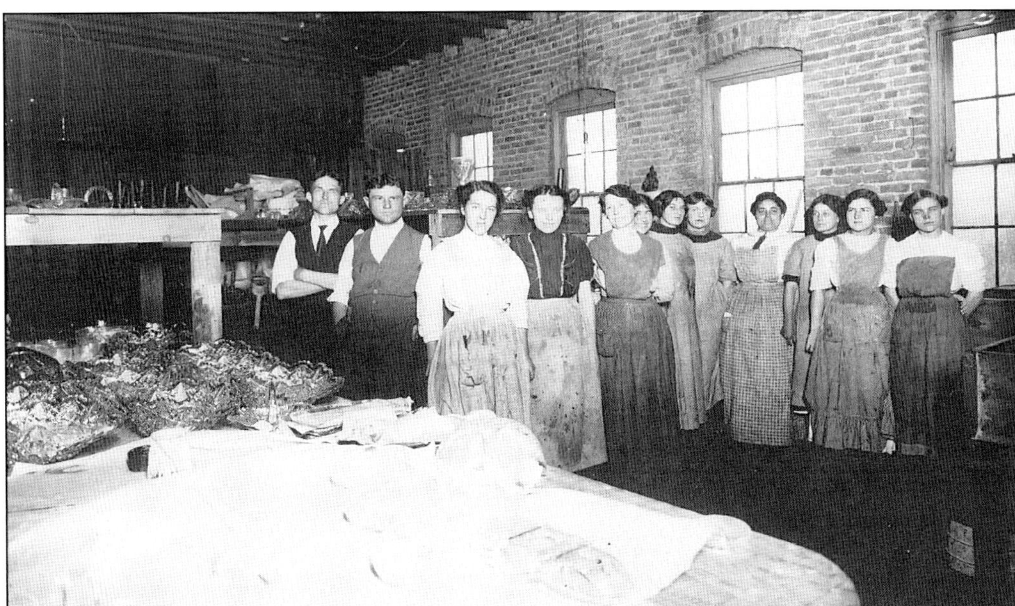

These are the workers from the inspection and wrapping department of the factory. Here you can see some of the glassware produced at Heinz Cut Glass. From left to right are as follows: Herman Eichman, Otto Heinz, Mabel Ladue, unidentified, Mrs. Quinlan, Clara Schmidt, Blanch Holden, Martha Eyner, Myrtle Anderson, Margaret Nelson, Grace Bosey, and Clara Dale.

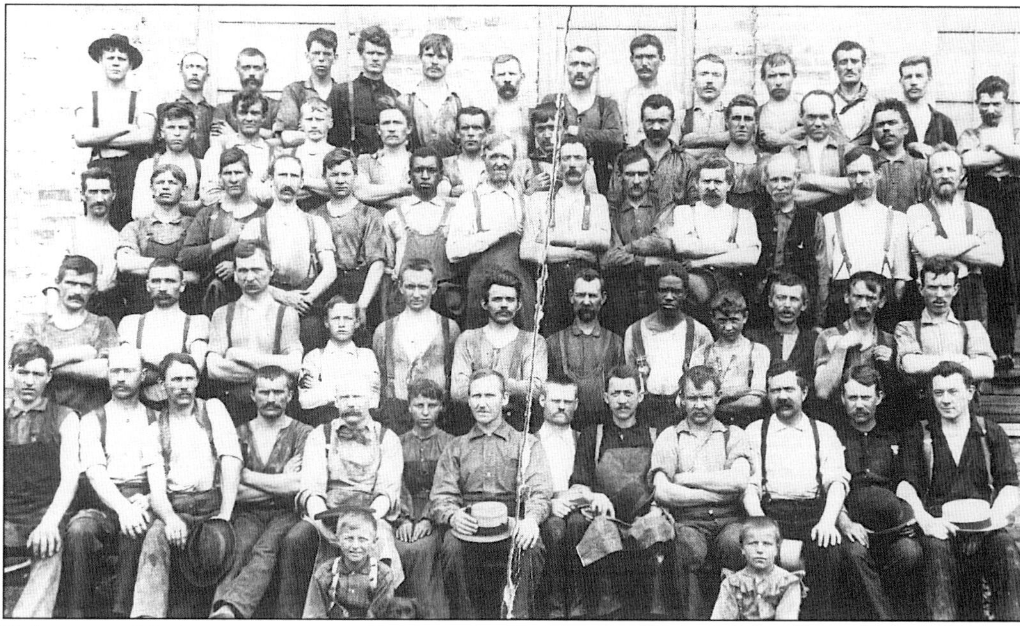

Belgium and Lithuanian immigrants were the backbone of the workers that Moline Malleable Iron Company moved to St. Charles from Moline in 1893, after the Moline factory was destroyed by fire.

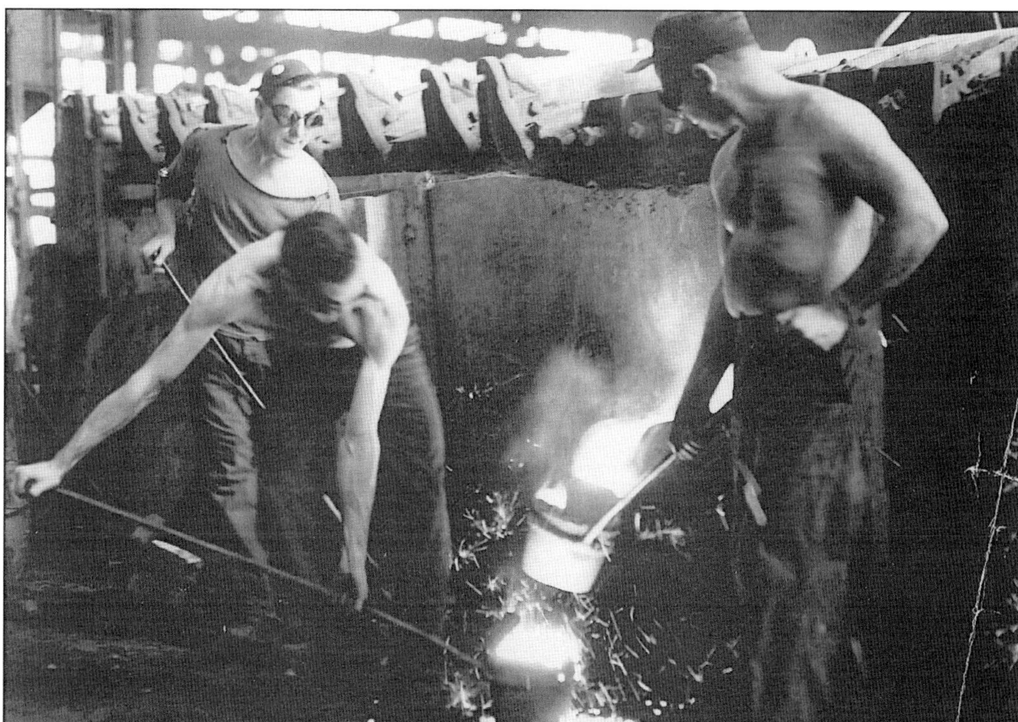

Ninety of the 300 men Moline brought with them were molders such as those seen above. Products included castings for agricultural implements, various castings for manufacturers of iron work, and power transmissions for elevating and conveying machines.

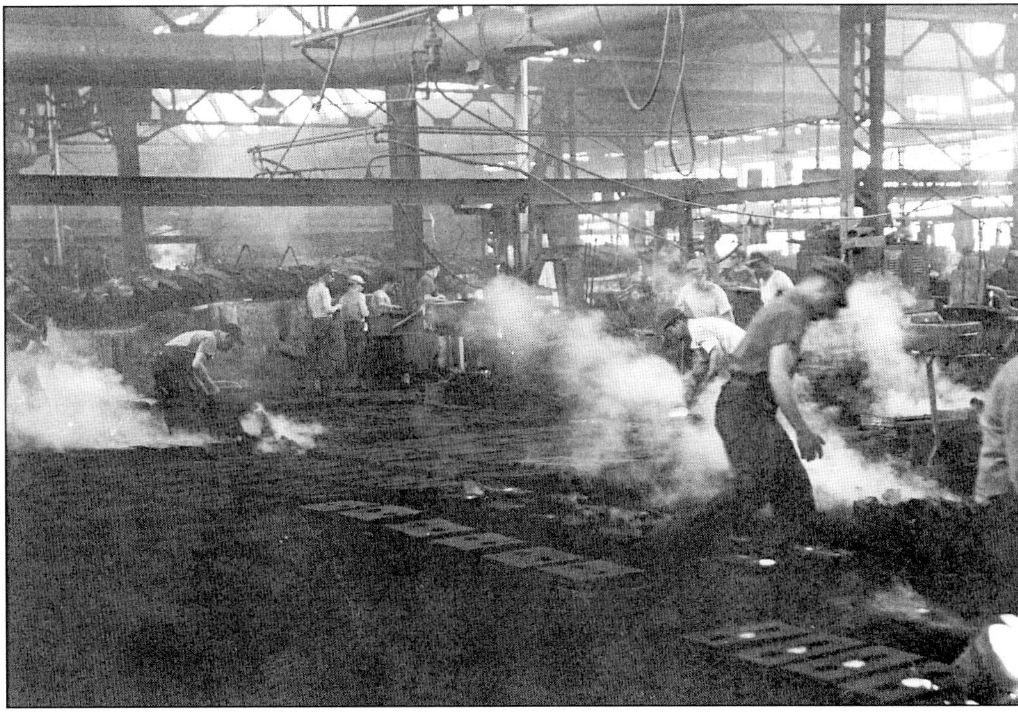

This influx of people increased the population of St. Charles several hundred fold at a time of renewed business activity in the city. T.E. Ryan of St. Charles and Gray & VanAllan of Chicago were the parties responsible for enticing Moline Malleable to relocate to St. Charles. The company later sponsored workers who emigrated from Belgium.

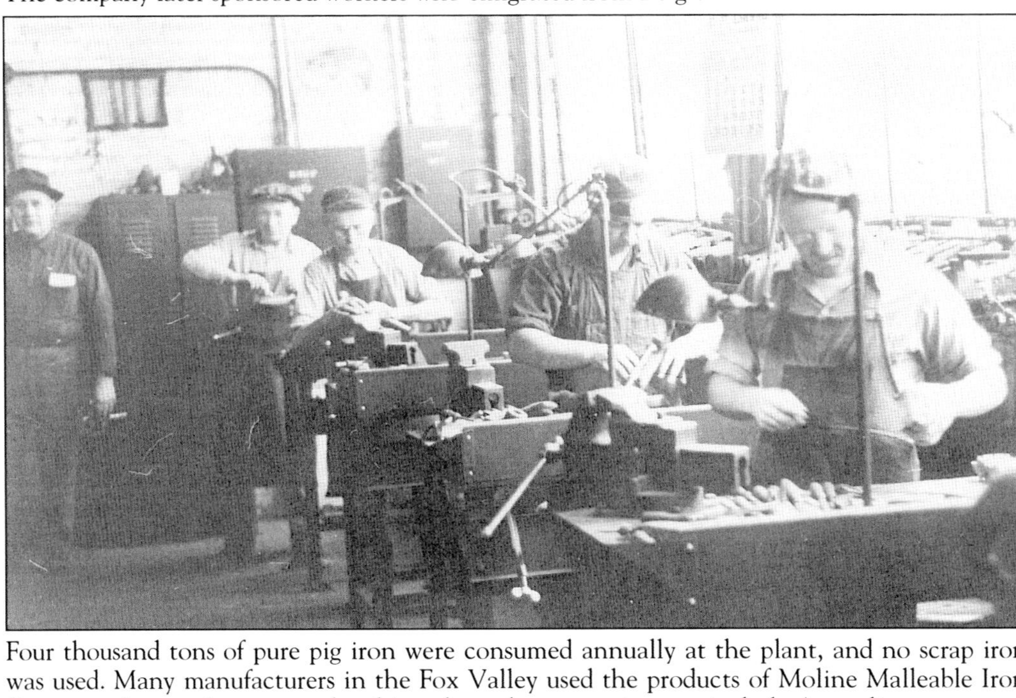

Four thousand tons of pure pig iron were consumed annually at the plant, and no scrap iron was used. Many manufacturers in the Fox Valley used the products of Moline Malleable Iron Company, but products were also shipped to other countries, particularly Australia.

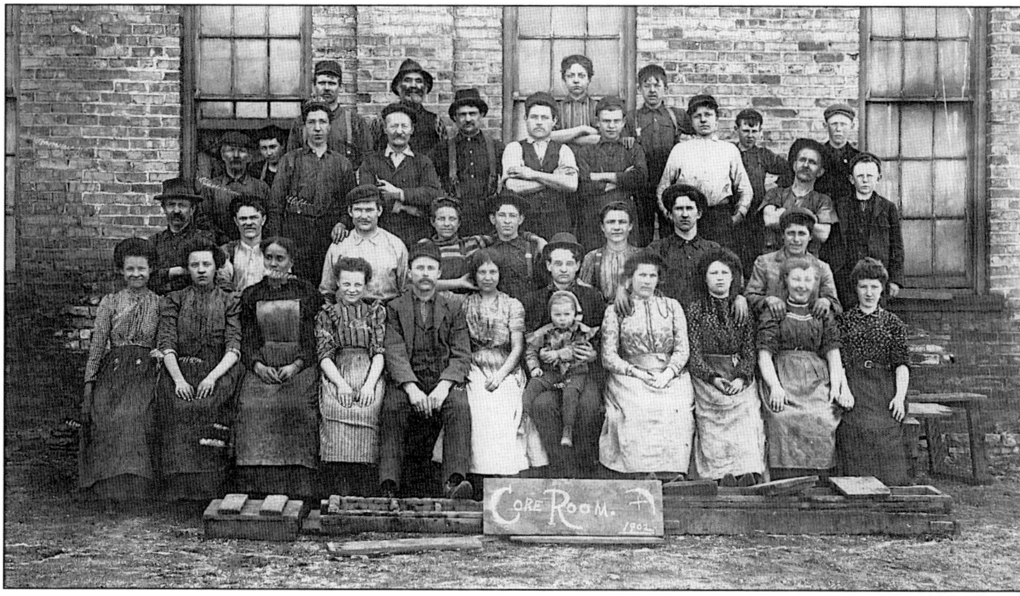


Chains, big and small, were a major early product. But in later years, the company focused more on bearings and towbars. Look at how the work force had changed by 1902. Who is missing, and who has entered the work force?

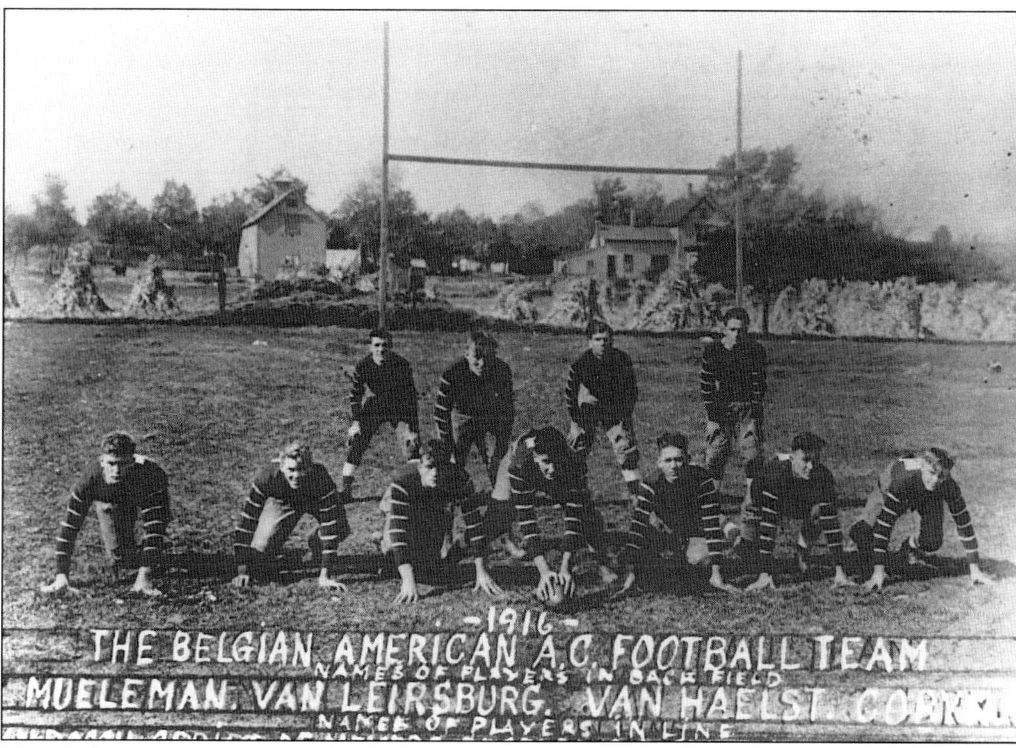


Here is the Belgian-American football team in 1916. The company sponsored athletic programs with not only football teams but also basketball and baseball teams. Possibly, they were competitors to the city's other sports teams such as that of the Cable Company. Many of the Belgian customs, such as rolle-bolle, are still in evidence in St. Charles.

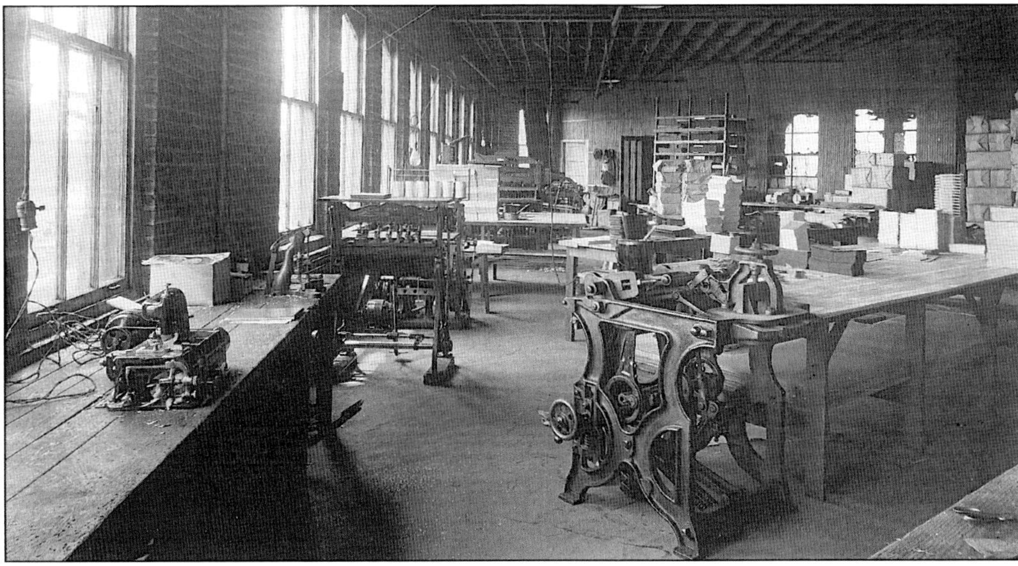

Holmstrom Bookbinding relocated to St. Charles in 1925 and took over the Heinz Cut Glass Factory building. The shop was equipped to produce high-quality bookbinding as well as novelties. They printed wedding and graduation books as well as cookbooks and music books for Cable Piano Company.

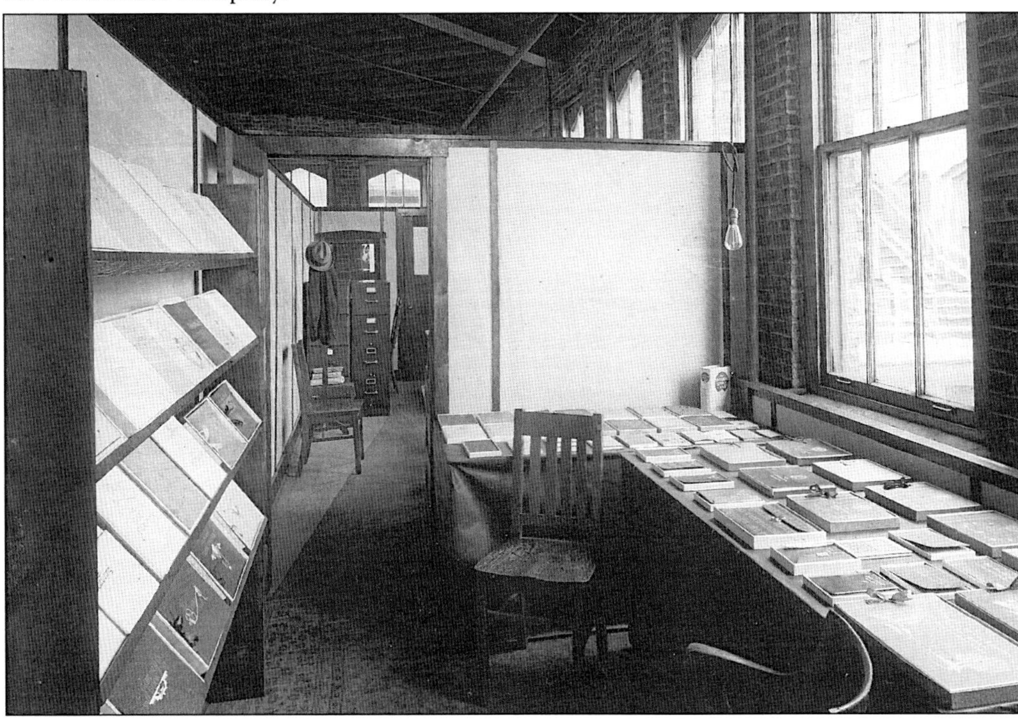

Earling "Ike" Holstrom remembers that his father's company also put the programs together for the opening of the Arcada Theatre on September 6, 1926. In an interview for the *St. Charles Chronicle*, Holstrom reminisced, "We had to keep running back and forth between the theater and the shop to make more and more programs. We even put our visiting Chicago relatives to work. The people just kept flocking to the opening."

# *Four*

# Freedom Calls

## *Biscuits, Gettysburg, and a Horse*

Feelings for abolition ran high in St. Charles and all of northern Illinois. Kittredge Wheeler related the following story to the *Saturday Evening Post*. "When *Uncle Tom's Cabin* was published, father read it to the children. The publication of this heart-stirring story found a circle of open-mouthed children gathered around the fireplace while my father read aloud. The pauses were frequent, for he was compelled to make constant use of the waistband of his hickory shirt in dashing the tears from his overflowing eyes . . . These evenings we laughed and cried with Uncle Tom, little Eva and the other personages of the great story were surpassed only by the nights when we heard stranger stories from the lips of slaves."

Kittredge had heard the eye-witness accounts of the "peculiar institution" of slavery from escaping blacks, so it is not unusual to find such a commitment to defend the union and perhaps end the evil of slavery all in one unifying action. The Underground Railroad was not a subway system but a series of safe houses about a day's distance apart from south to north. Hundreds of paths and thousands of safe houses or stations existed throughout the northern states. Escaped slave Harriet Tubman made 19 trips to lead 300 slaves out of bondage.

In the mid-1800s, when St. Charles was a community of less than 500 families, over 450 men and boys volunteered with the 8th and 7th Illinois Cavalry and the 52nd, 127th, and 141st Infantry. The sons of St. Charles and Kane County were passionate abolitionists and unionists. They were in the thickest of fighting from start to finish.

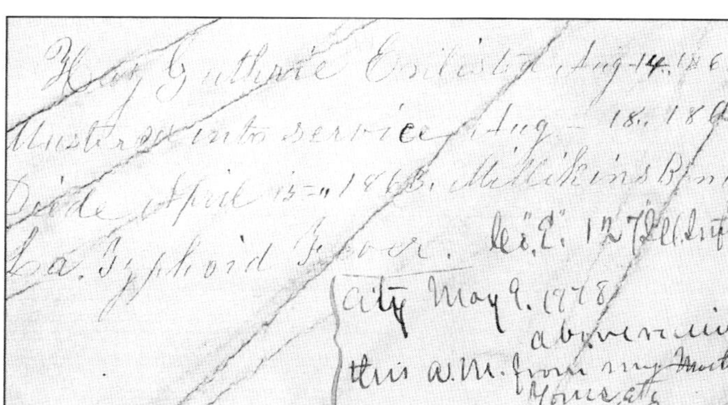

Lucy Whipple Campbell kept a notebook in her nurse's uniform as she was working with the sick and wounded during the Civil War. She would record the names of those who would soon die, so they would not be listed as the unknown dead. In this way, she brought comfort to the dying men and offered those back home a final resolution to the fate of loved ones.

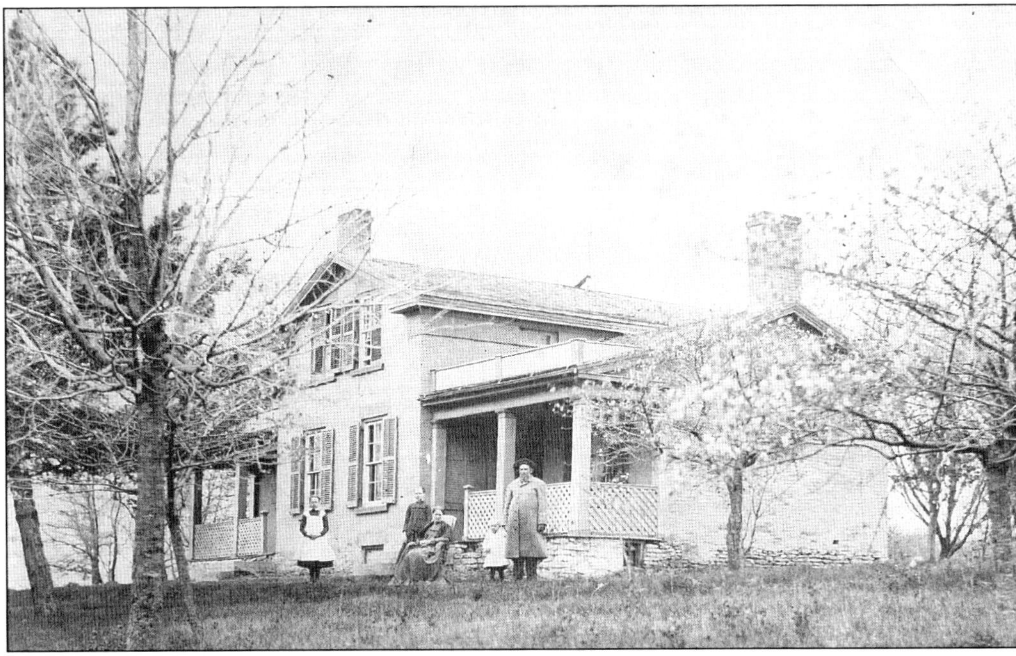

James T. Wheeler emigrated from Canada, where he had been a school teacher. Brainard T. Wheeler and his family are shown above in front of the home James built in 1851. This house was reported to be one of the "stations" of the Underground Railroad when Kittredge Wheeler was a boy.

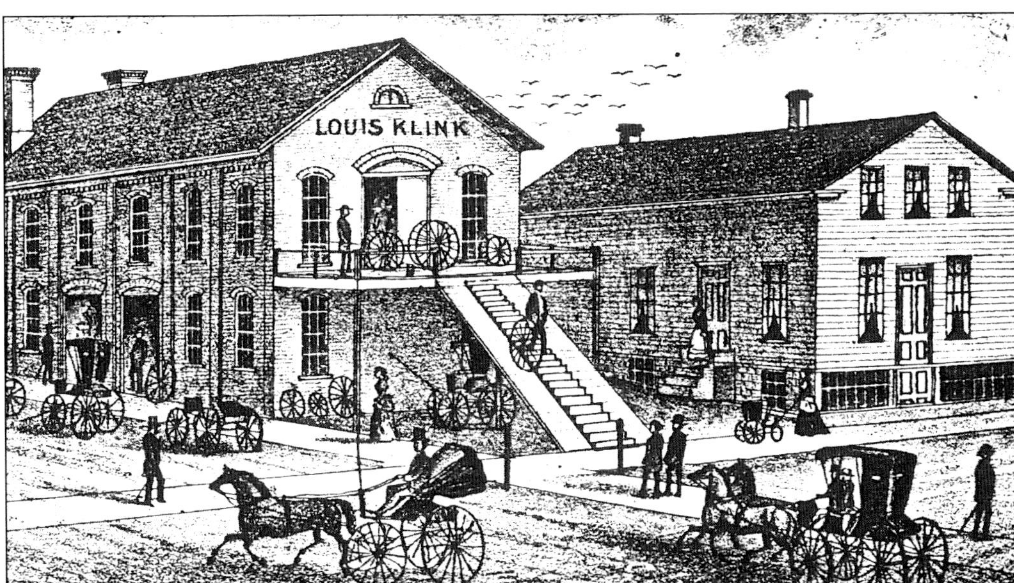


Another station was in the basement of Klink's Wagon and Carriage Shop. Louis Klink would receive word to pick up a load of straw with a spring wagon at a certain place. A slave or two would be part of the load. He stowed the slaves in his basement, and as soon as he felt it was safe, he took them to the next stop.

Joanna Garner was a former slave who stayed in St. Charles in the 1860s. This was, potentially, a dangerous decision. Instead of continuing on to Canada, she settled here and worked for a family on the west side of the river. This family gave her a block on Sixth Street and a small house in return for her services. Her descendants still live on that land. This photograph is of one of Joanna Garner's descendants.

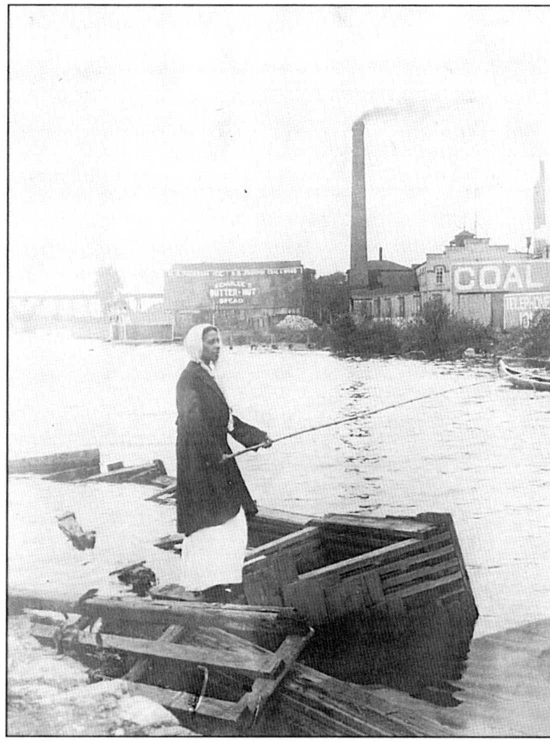


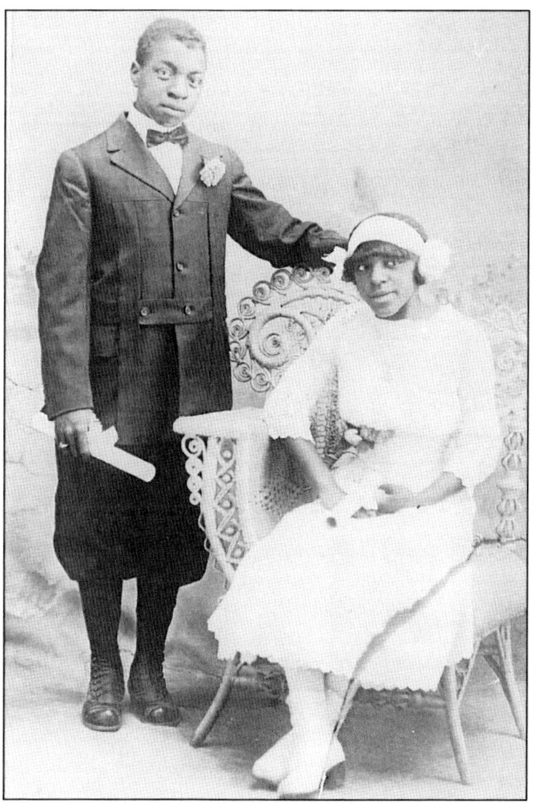

William Luckett and his sister Harriet Luckett Harris were great-grandchildren of Joanna Garner. William's artistic talent was evident at an early age, and after training at the Art Institute of Chicago, he worked as a commercial artist in Chicago. Harriet fostered over 40 children while she lived in "Belgian town" on Dean Street.

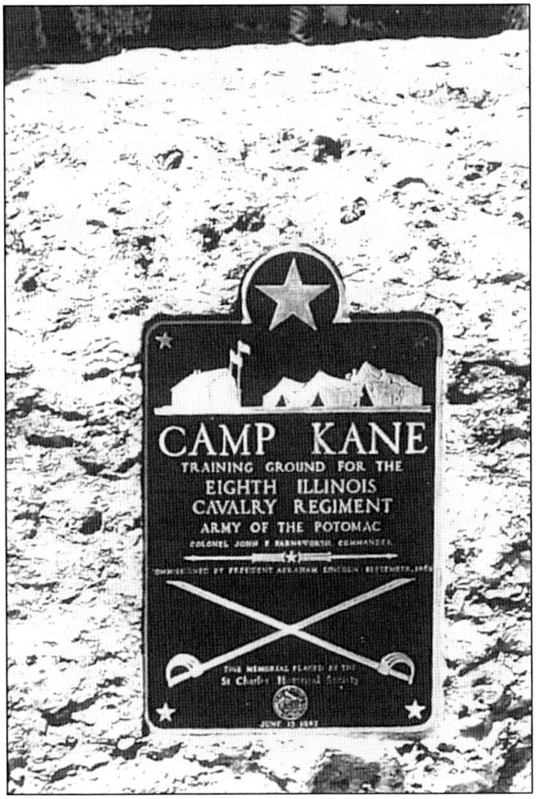


Not only did St. Charles rally to the flag, but it also served as the site of a major Illinois Civil War training camp. From 1861 to 1864, Langum Park was the site of Camp Kane, a 20-acre training facility for the 8th Illinois Volunteer Cavalry and later the 17th Illinois Cavalry. Of the more than 2,000 men who were trained at Camp Kane, 194 were killed in action or died from disease or accident, 185 were wounded, and five died in Confederate prisons.

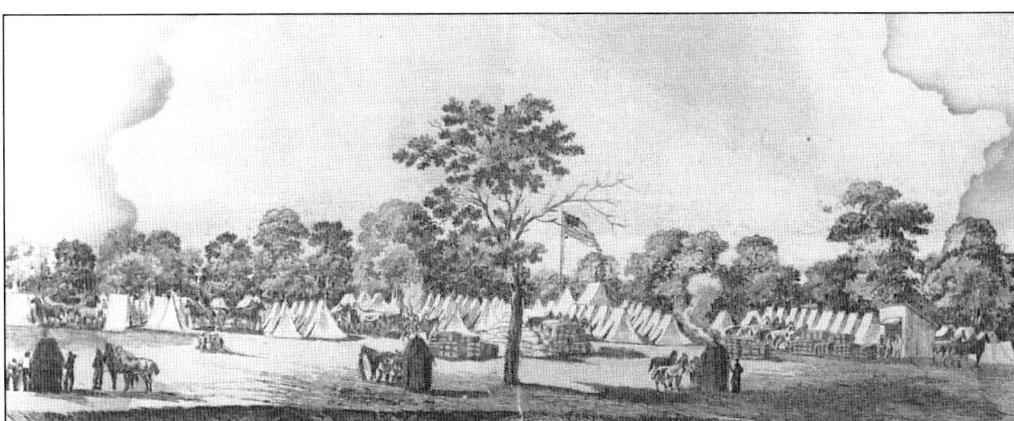

Camp surgeon Dr. Abner Hard wrote that young volunteers came to the camp so quickly, many had to be temporarily sheltered in private homes until tents and other garrison supplies could arrive. There was a general holiday mood, and area residents went to watch the drilling and training maneuvers, especially at the beginning of the war when spirits were high in anticipation of an early end to the rebellion.

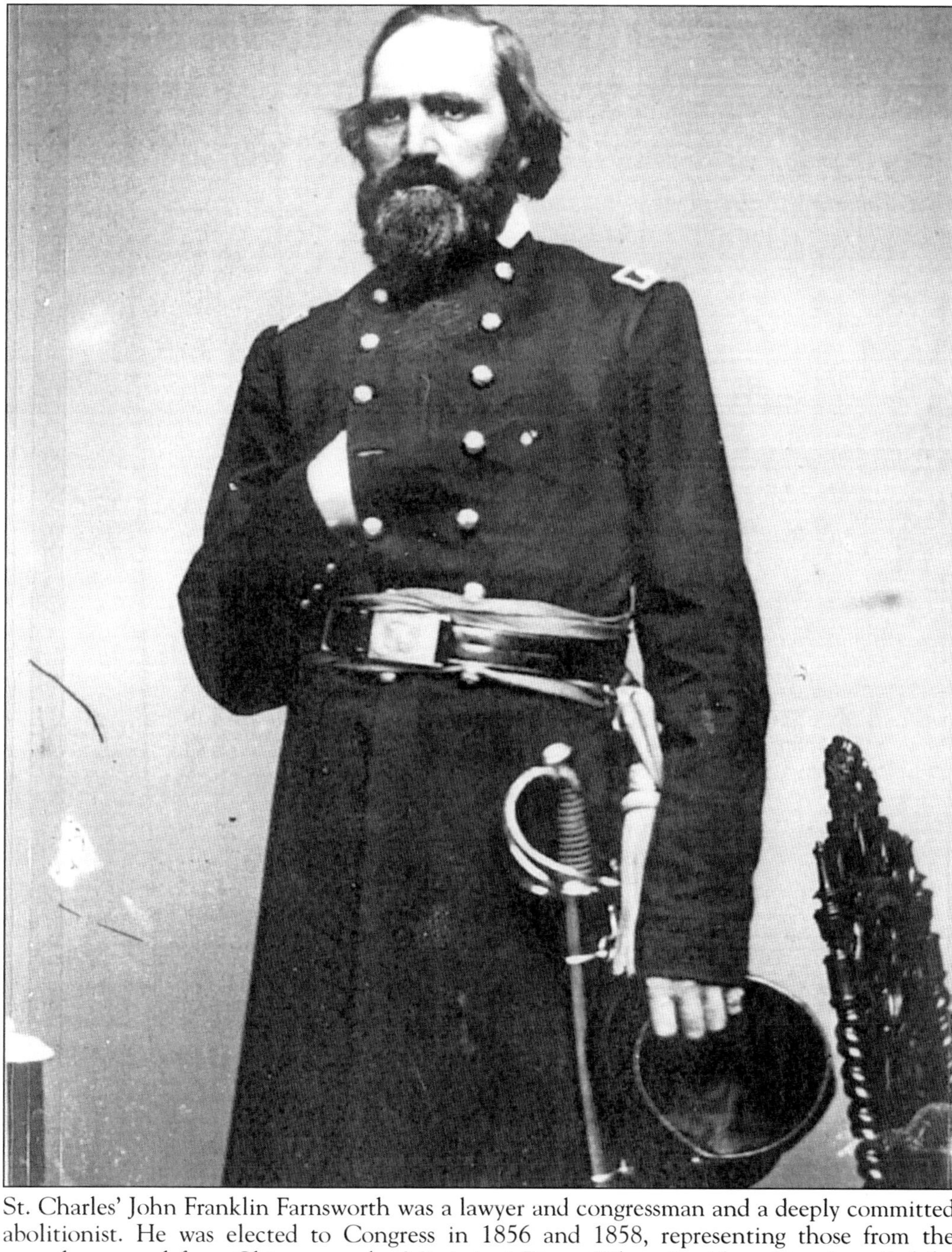

St. Charles' John Franklin Farnsworth was a lawyer and congressman and a deeply committed abolitionist. He was elected to Congress in 1856 and 1858, representing those from the area that spread from Chicago to the Mississippi River. When President Lincoln called for 500,000 volunteers, Farnsworth asked for and received permission to raise a cavalry troop in Illinois. Colonel Farnsworth's call was for 1,200 men. By September 1, 1861, most of the men had arrived and the Eighth Cavalry Regiment was being formed at the campsite, then designated Camp Kane. President Lincoln called the Eighth Illinois "Farnsworth's Big Abolition Regiment." Farnsworth was again elected to Congress in 1862 and resigned his commission as brigadier-general in March 1863, to take his seat in Congress.

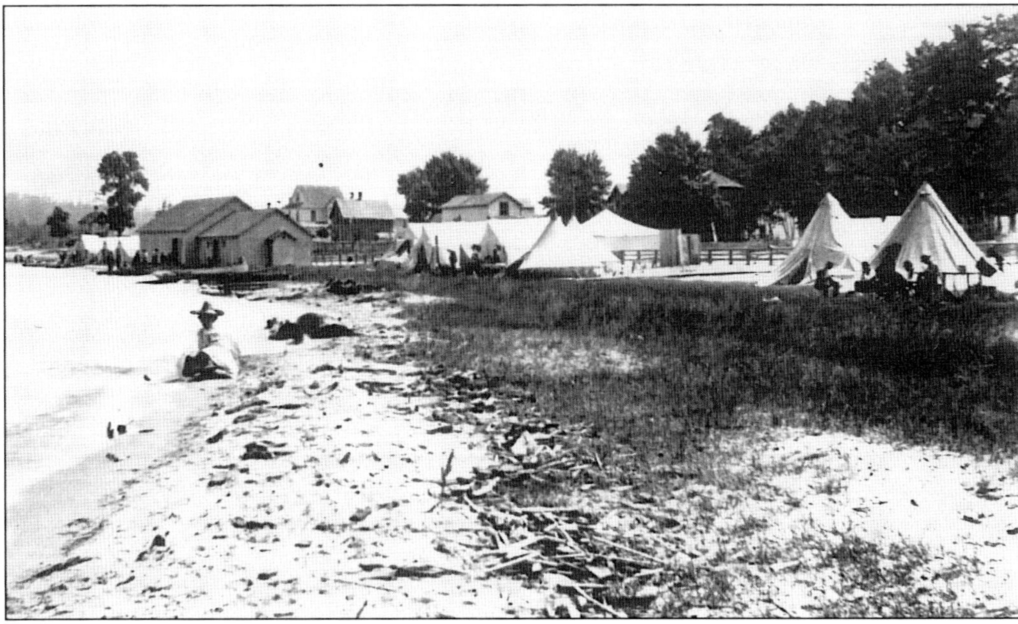

On September 18, the men of Kane County were formally mustered into the United States Military Service. At the conclusion of a little more than a month of training, horses and men were sent to Washington for their first posting. The ladies of St. Charles gave them large boxes of bandages and old linens to take along into battle. Both Northern and Southern women helped in this way. The effort was known as the sanitary commission, the predecessor to the Red Cross for soldiers.

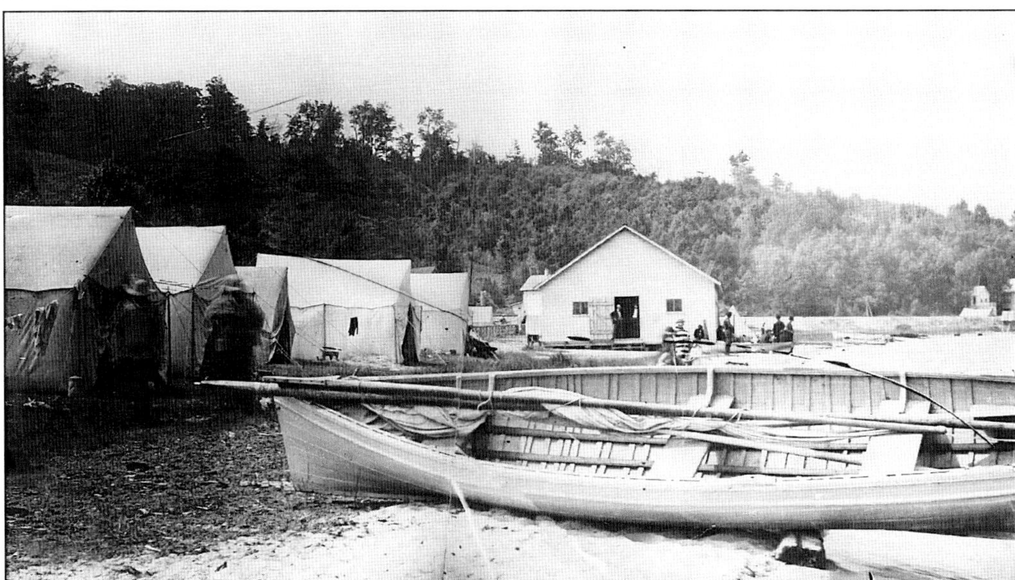

In 1863 General John F. Farnsworth, serving on the military affairs committee of Congress, was asked to raise yet another unit, the 17th Illinois Cavalry Regiment. Major John L. Beveridge of the Eighth Illinois Cavalry was promoted to colonel and given command of the new regiment. In the fall of 1863, recruiting and training was held at Camp Kane, and the troops were mustered into service in January and February of 1864. Camp Kane was then deactivated.

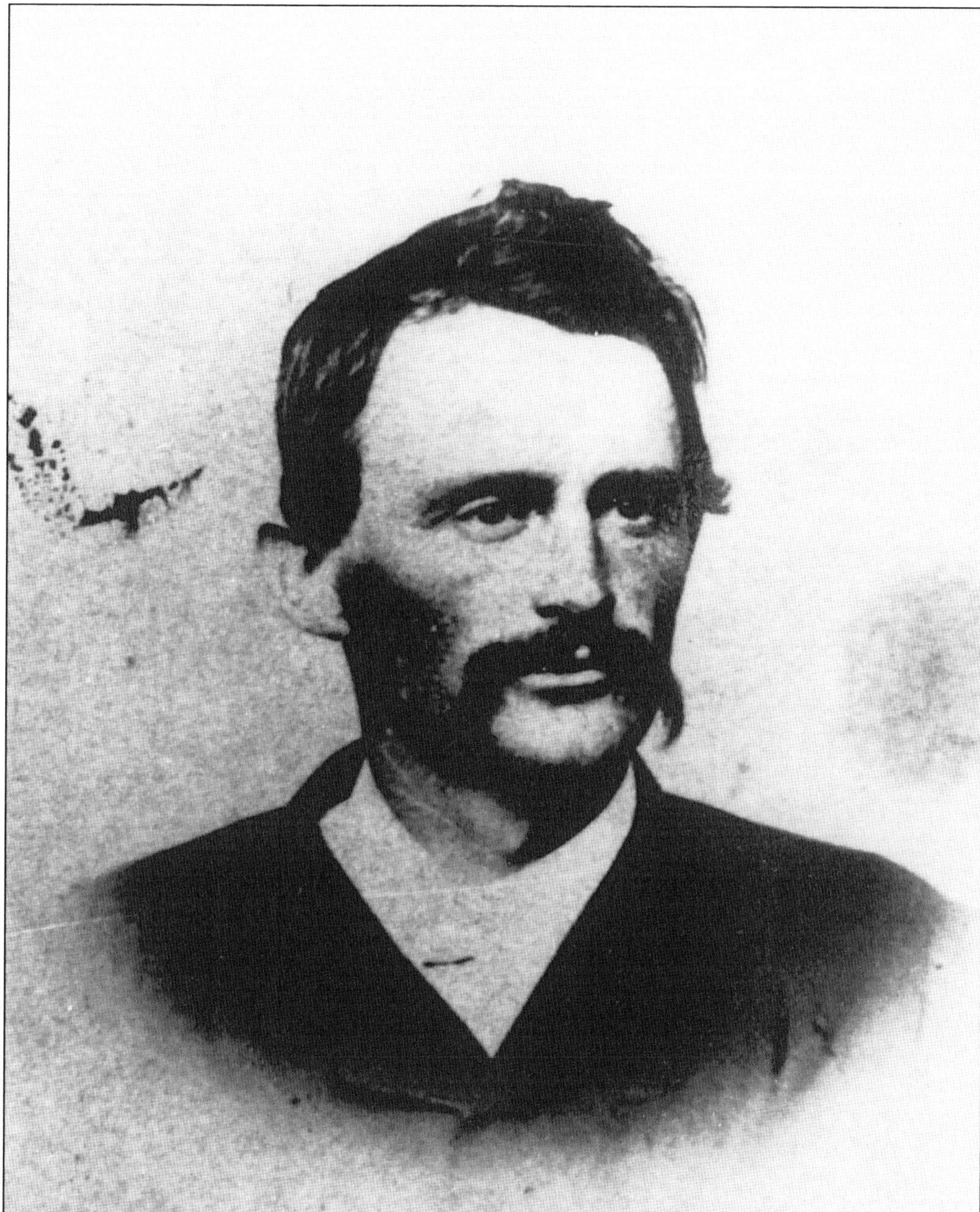

Elon Farnsworth, nephew of General John F. Farnsworth, joined the newly established Eighth Illinois Cavalry as a first lieutenant. He had previously served in the quartermaster department of the army in the Utah expedition and later hunted buffalo and carried mail to the newly discovered mines at Pike's Peak. On the eve of the battle of Gettysburg, he was promoted from captain to brigadier general. On July 3, 1863, General Kilpatrick ordered Farnsworth and his brigade to charge Longstreet's Confederate position in a hopeless charge, which he and his men did not once but three times. When Farnsworth fell, he was still shouting to his men to fight. The local chapter of the Women's Relief Corps and the local post of the Grand Army of the Republic were named for Elon J. Farnsworth after his heroic death.

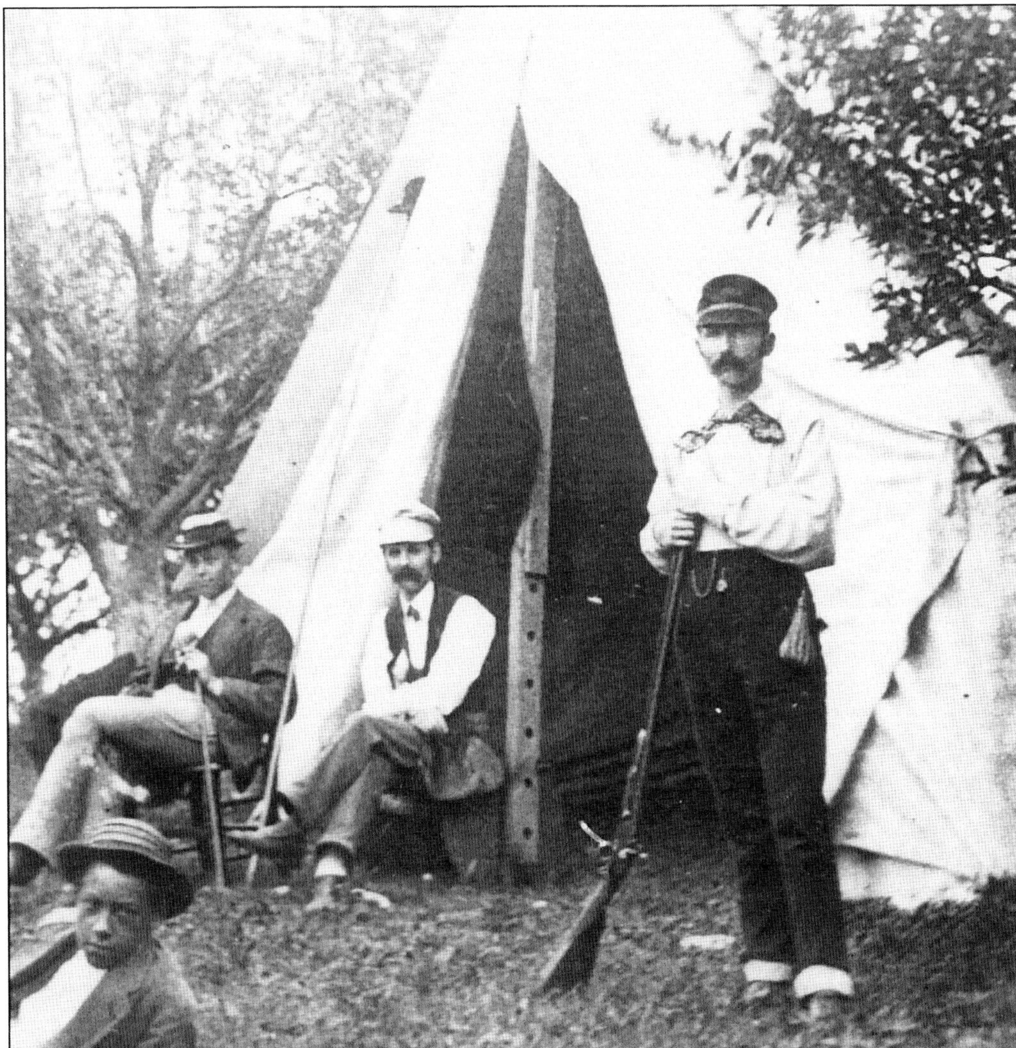

According to Lt. Col. Abner Hard, "Of the 200 regiments of brave and loyal troops that Illinois sent out to battle in the war of the great rebellion, none had a more brilliant career or shed a brighter light upon the State of the Nation than the Eighth Illinois Cavalry. No regiment was made up of a better class of men, mentally, morally, or physically than the Eighth." Elon Farnsworth was but one of seven in the Eighth Illinois who rose to brigadier general. The others were L. Beveridge (later governor of Illinois), William Gamble, D.R. Clendennin, George A. Forsyth, Daniel Dustin, and Dennis Hyner (who became advertising manager of *The Chicago Tribune*). This regiment took part in 26 actions that included Manassas and Gettysburg. By the end of 1863, losses to the Eighth Cavalry totaled 23 killed, 116 wounded, and 37 missing.

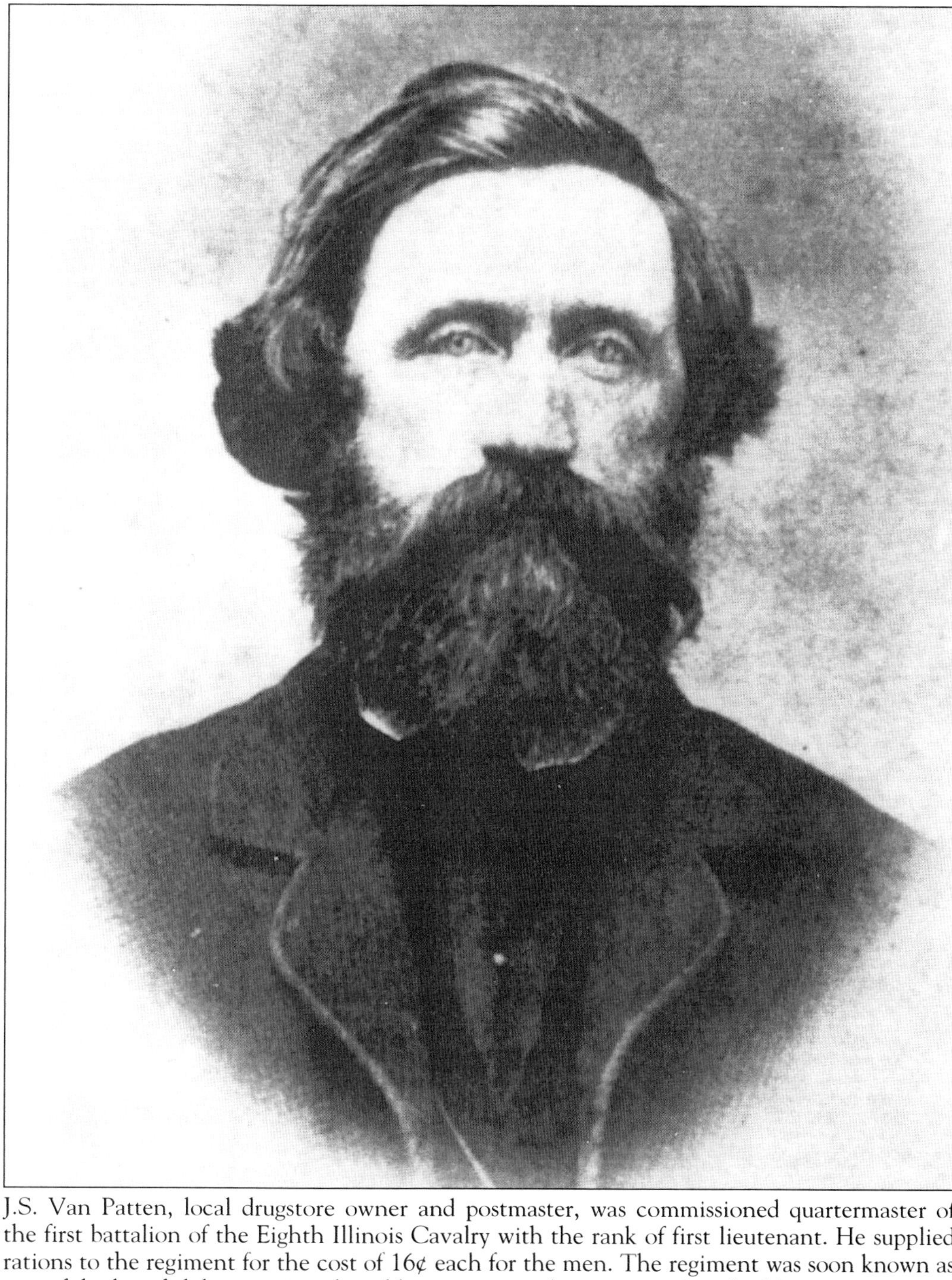

J.S. Van Patten, local drugstore owner and postmaster, was commissioned quartermaster of the first battalion of the Eighth Illinois Cavalry with the rank of first lieutenant. He supplied rations to the regiment for the cost of 16¢ each for the men. The regiment was soon known as one of the best fed, best equipped, and least expensively maintained in the Union army. It was also more quickly prepared than most of the others. Early in October, the horses were shipped to Washington, and the men left on October 14. In 1862 he was promoted to regimental quartermaster and served in that capacity until November 1862, when he resigned. He was then commissioned first lieutenant of Company M and was detailed April 1863, as acting commissary of subsistence of the cavalry division, Army of the Potomac.

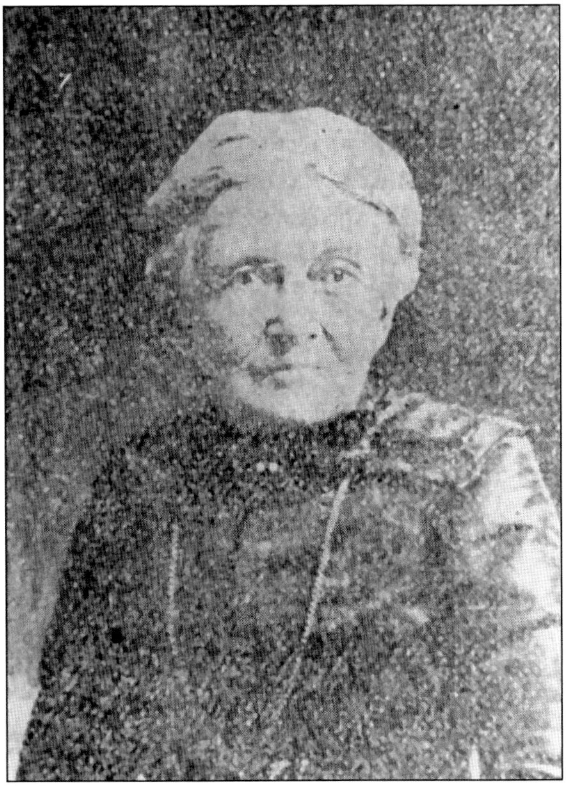

Lucy Whipple Campbell (and later Kaiser) led a tragic life prior to the Civil War, having lost her husband, business, and home in a cyclone. When the call for volunteers came, she enlisted as a regimental nurse. She went through the Siege of Vicksburg and the Battle of Shiloh. At Shiloh, her tent was struck with a cannon ball, destroying her trunk with all her belongings.

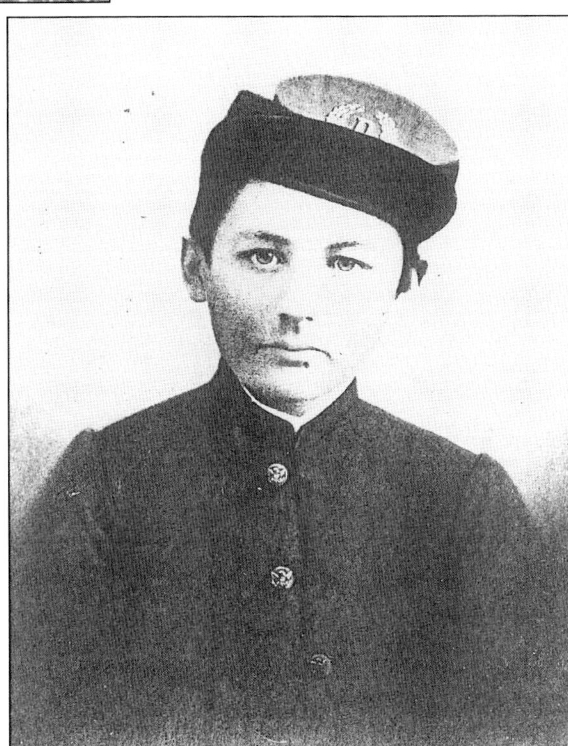

The *St. Charles Chronicle* reported in 1924 that there were 2,865,028 soldiers in the Union Army in the Civil War, and of these, 231,051 were under 16; 104,798 under 15; 1,525 under 14; and 225 under 12. C. Perry Byram enlisted at nine and a few months. He was the drummer boy in Company D of the Illinois 24th.

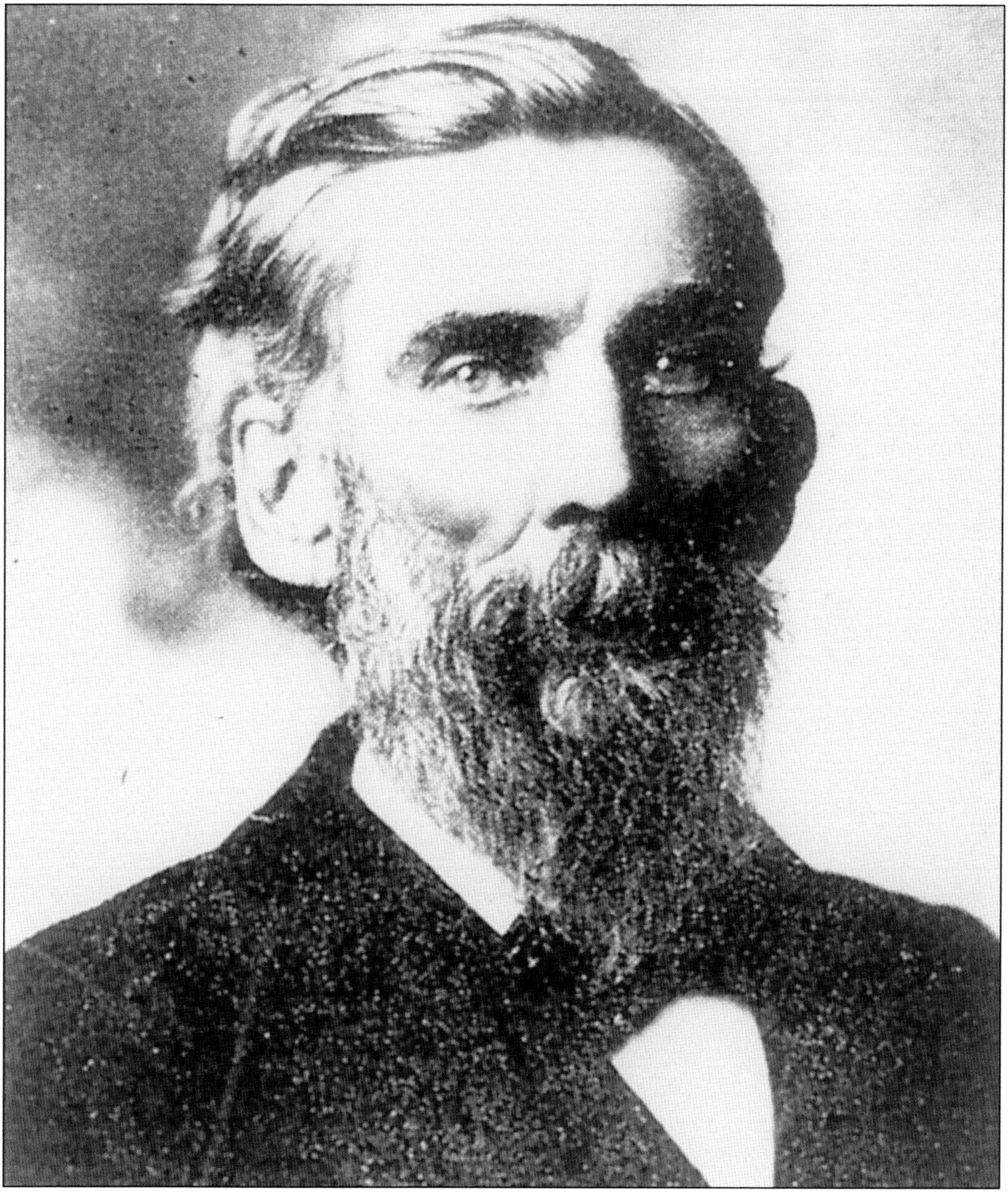

John F. Elliott, born in 1834, immigrated to St. Charles in 1855. He enlisted in Company K of the 36th Illinois and served one month as a private before becoming a first lieutenant. Elliott was captured at the battle of Stone River near Atlanta along with 80 others. They organized a plan for escape, but the day it was to take place, the guard they had turned was replaced. Not long afterwards, they were notified that they were to be transferred to Richmond. At this time, Elliott and a Lieutenant Burrett were charged with passing counterfeit money. When Burrett's name was called he responded, but Elliott did not. His fellow prisoners assured their captors that he had escaped, which he did shortly afterwards. With $9 in Confederate money, seven small biscuits, a compass, and a map, he travelled through Confederate country until he reached safety within the Union lines at Corinth, Mississippi. After a furlough home, he rejoined the 36th at Murfreesboro.

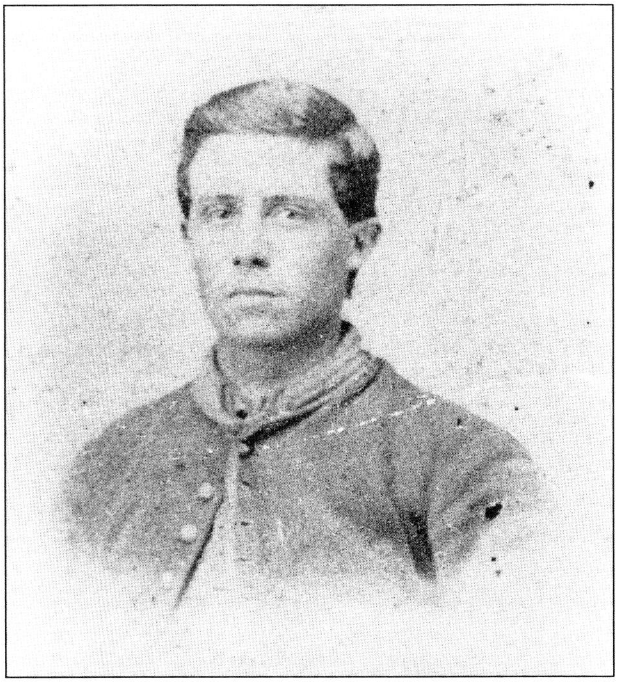

Morgan Hughes was a bugler in Company E, Eighth Illinois Cavalry, who trained at Camp Kane. Agatha Myers, his granddaughter, attended the dedication of Camp Kane and took the bugle along. "My grandfather used that bugle to play taps at President Abraham Lincoln's funeral in Washington, D.C.," she said.

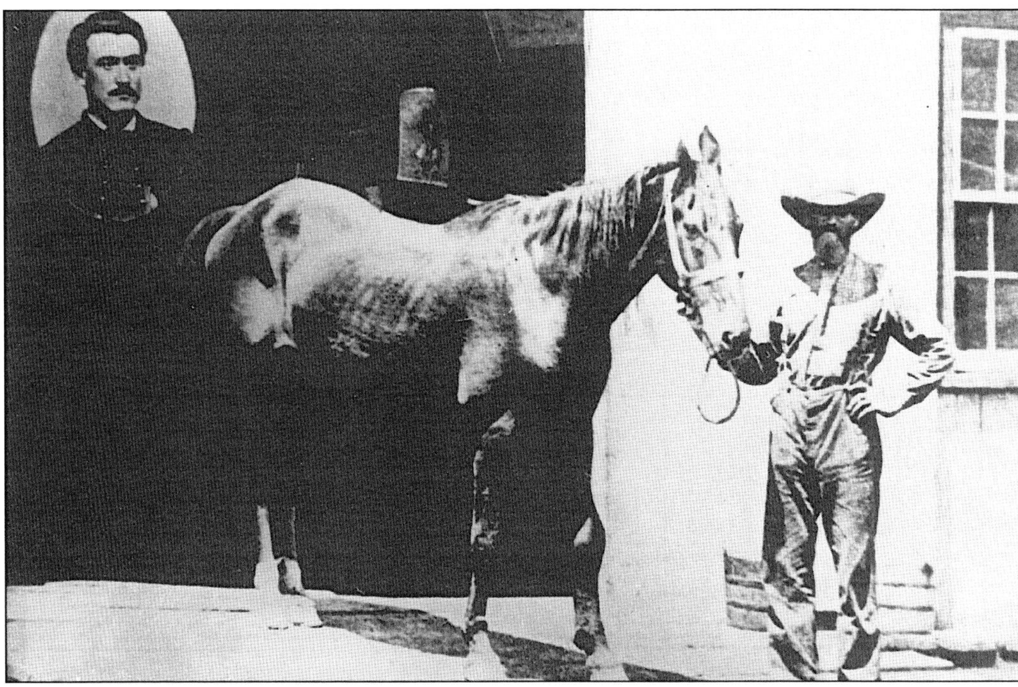

St. Charles not only had famous soldiers in the Civil War, but also had a brave and courageous horse that deserved a medal. Charley the horse was sold to the government for a cavalry horse in 1861 and was ridden in service for four years. He was wounded twice, once in the head in Naperville, Virginia, and once in the fore leg at the Battle of Beverly Ford. S.D. Wesson was his last passenger and is pictured with him. In 1883 Wesson offered to show the ball that wounded Charley's leg.

William C. Hazelton joined the fighting Eighth Illinois Cavalry as a second lieutenant but was promoted to captain near the end of the war. Captain Hazelton was a farmer, teacher, civil leader, and a family man. Contrary to popular belief, Northern men made better soldiers than Southerners because they followed orders better and were less inclined to try to do their own thing in battle.

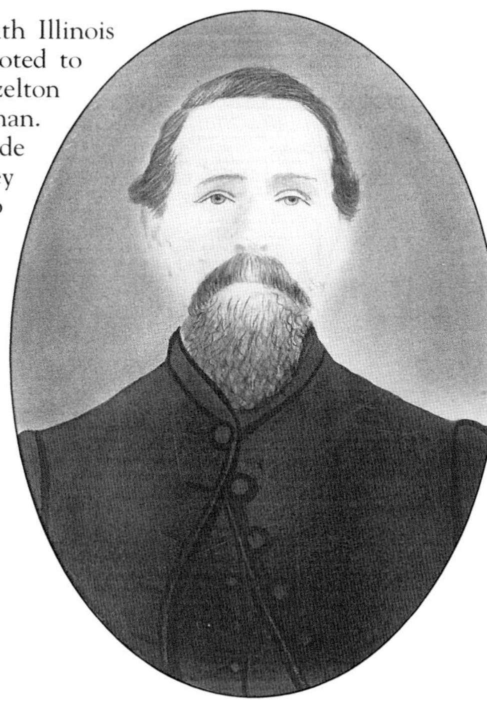

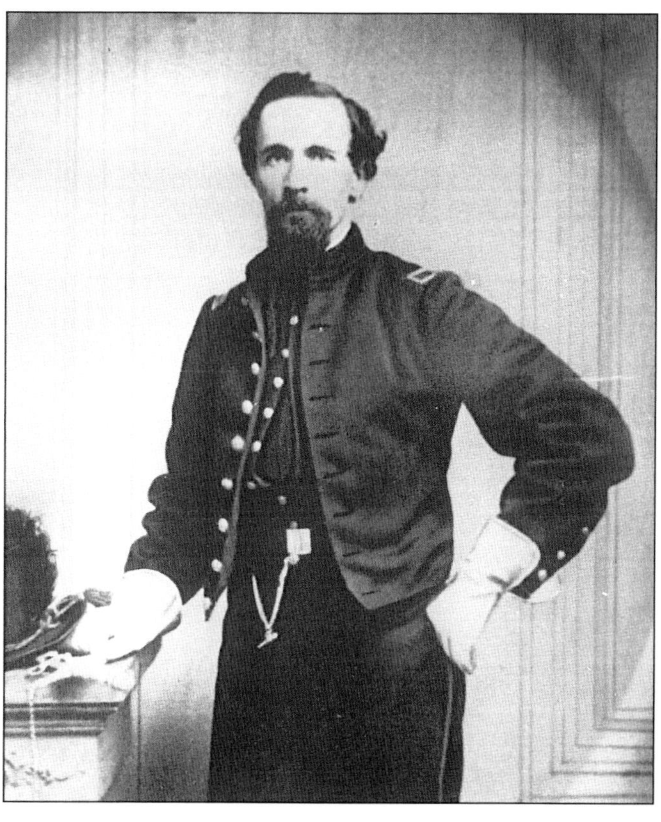

Felix McFarland was born in Ireland and immigrated to Illinois in 1850. McFarland worked as a farmer and as a laborer. He enlisted as a private in Company E of the 127th Illinois Infantry Regiment on August 14, 1862, and mustered out on June 5, 1865. McFarland returned to farm near St. Charles after the war.

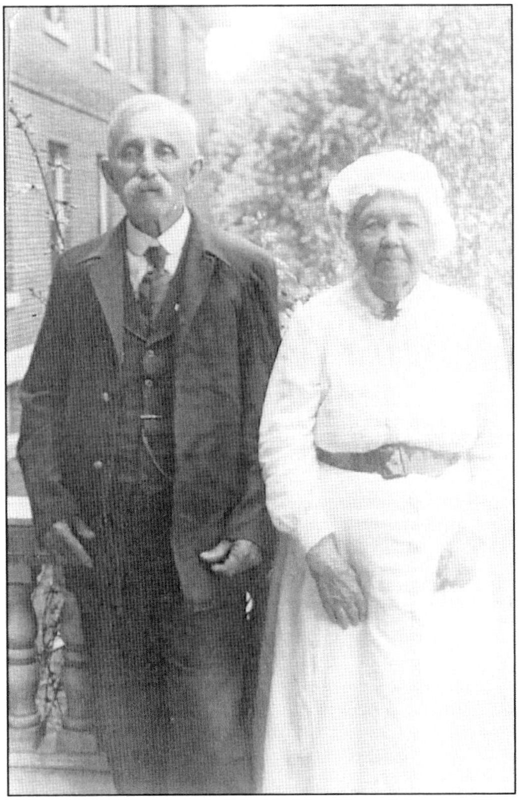

Gabriel A. Warner moved to St. Charles in 1882. He had served in the Third New York during the Civil War and was an active member of the St. Charles GAR chapter. Warner is shown here with his wife Sophie sometime before 1919.

The drum these veterans are taking on the trolley is in the St. Charles Heritage Center collection. These men were probably travelling to attend a reunion or participate in a parade in the 1890s. In many fighting units, young boys manned the fifes and drums, freeing the older men to fight.

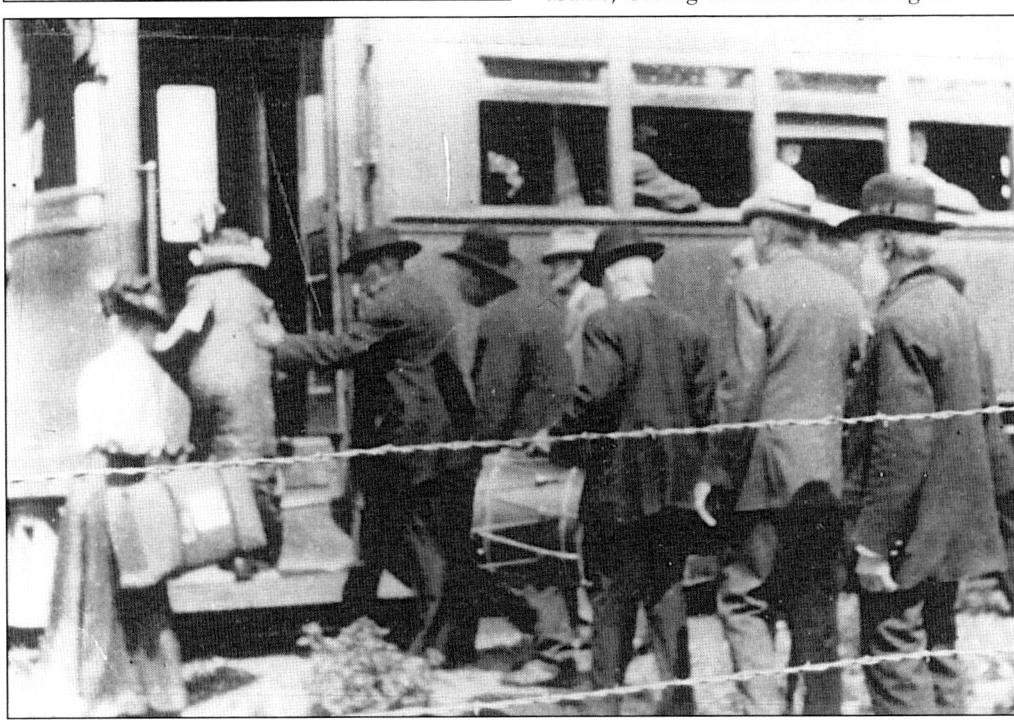

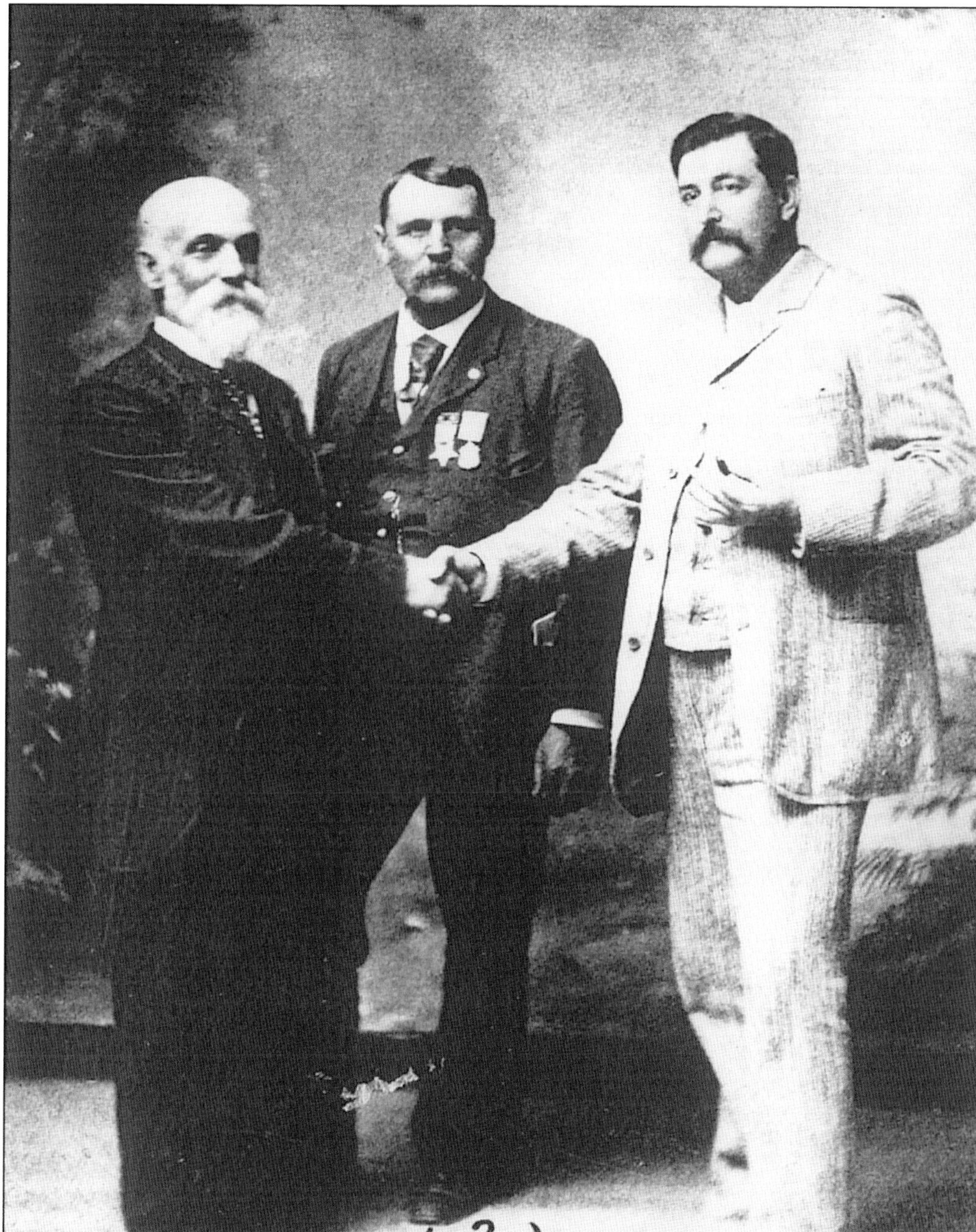

Second Lieutenant Marcellus E. Jones (left) of Company E, Eighth Illinois Cavalry, is credited with firing the first shot at Gettysburg at 7:30 a.m. on July 1, 1863. As a cavalry officer, he carried a revolver and a saber. Private Thomas B. Kelley (middle), also of the Eight Illinois, was on duty when he noticed the rebel flag and advancing Confederate column and sounded the alarm. Seeing the confederates approach, Jones borrowed a carbine from Sergeant Levi Shafer of Naperville and fired the shot. To the right is Colonel W. Marion McCarty of the First Texas Legion, who led the advancing Confederate column. This photograph is possible because Lt. Jones missed when he fired at McCarty.

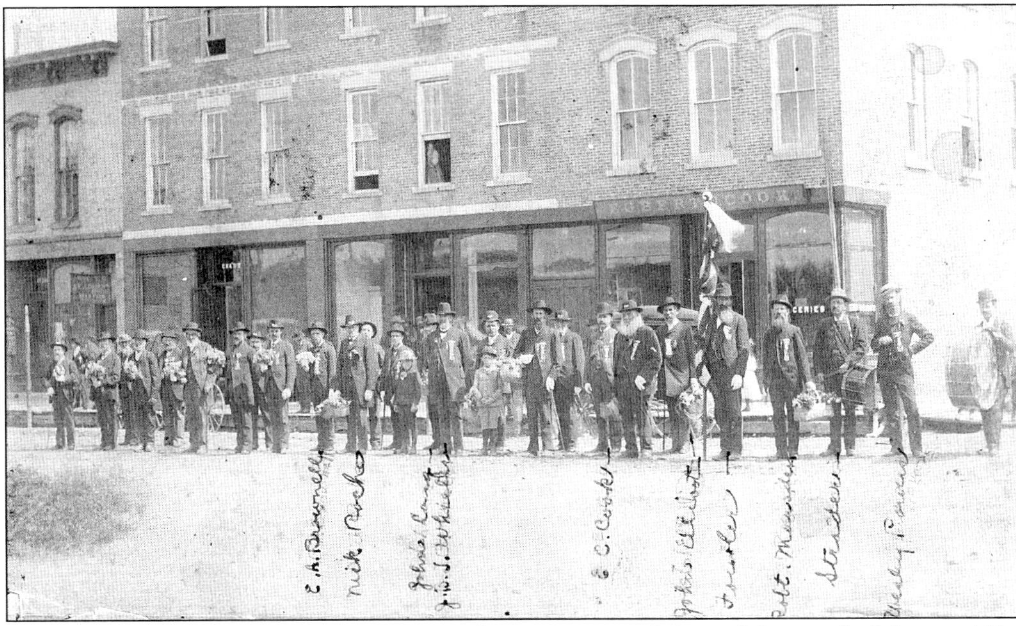

These veterans are lined up at the corner of West Main and Second Streets for Memorial Day in the 1890s, either before or after a parade. Some are identified on the photograph. By the mid-1900s, only a handful of Civil War veterans survived. Most had been young children at war.

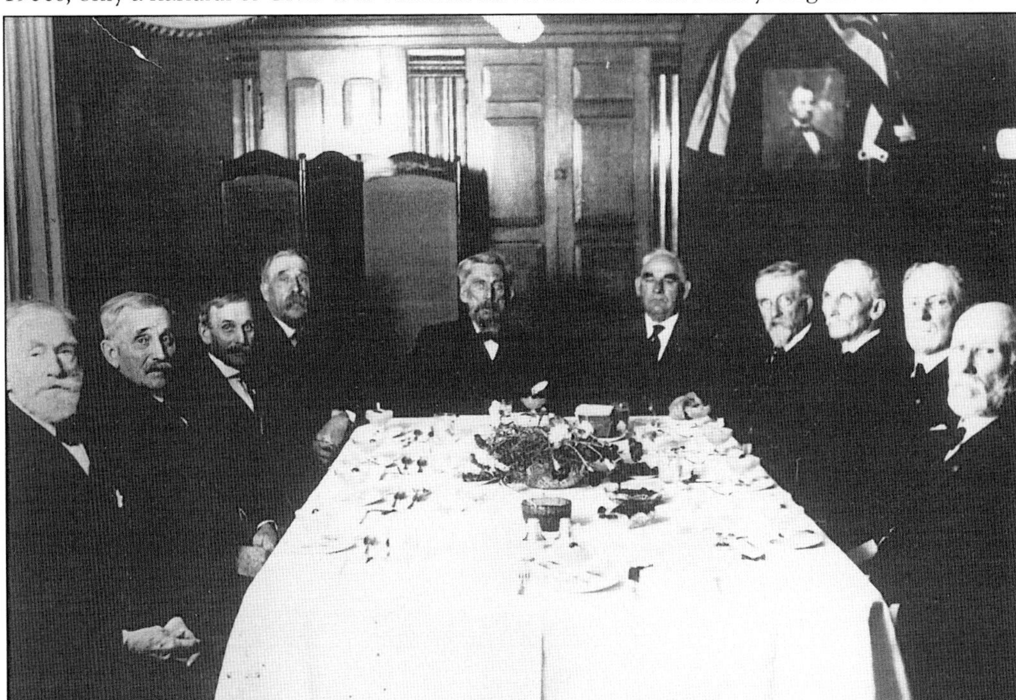

This 1914 photograph shows the attendees at a reunion of the Elon J. Farnsworth Grand Army of the Republic Post 45 veterans. From left to right are as follows: Mr. Bowman, G.A. Warner, Mr. Conners, E.P. Phillips, F.J. Elliot, J.B.T. Wheeler, unidentified, L.A. Brownell, T.E. Ryan, and Robert Marsden.

# *Five*

# DANGER LURKS AHEAD
## *Fires, Floods, and Wrecks*

St. Charles suffered through its share of disasters over the years, both natural and unnatural. Cholera invaded the river towns from 1849 through 1854, and the newly arrived Swedes were especially hard hit in 1852. Often there was either too little or too much water. Fires and floods were common in the early days. Before the days of civic fire departments, people "subscribed" to a firefighting service, very much like making insurance payments.

It took several beginnings to get a railroad to St. Charles, and the failure of the 1853 venture was a stunning blow to the growth of the town. Ira Minard and hundreds of other men staked their fortunes on the St. Charles & Galena Air Line Road. The rail bed was graded from Chicago to St. Charles, the culverts were built, and piers and abutments for a bridge across the Fox River were built. Nine miles of track from Chicago was completed when E.C. Litchfield, who had taken controlling interest in the stock, sold his interest to a competing line that bypassed St. Charles. The road ended at the Des Plaines River, leaving the useless piers standing unused in the Fox River as a reminder of this disaster. It wasn't until the 1870s that trains were seen in St. Charles again.

Other tragedies touched the lives of those in St. Charles too. Raids and riots and even the sinking of the *Titanic* affected those who lived in St. Charles.

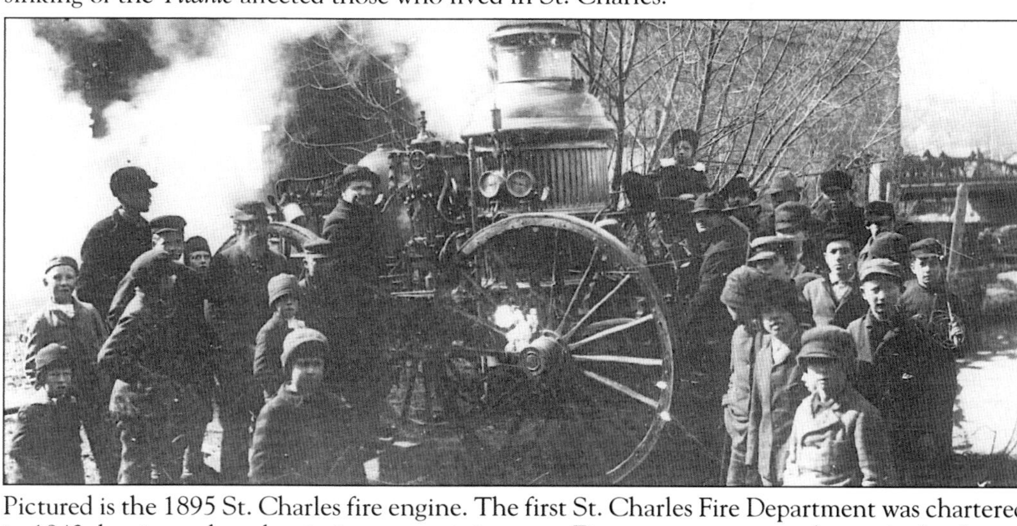

Pictured is the 1895 St. Charles fire engine. The first St. Charles Fire Department was chartered in 1842, but it was by subscription not a civic group. Fires were a constant danger in the days of wooden buildings and kerosene lighting. The fire of 1866 was called the great fire. It destroyed the west side paper mill, which had been burned once before in 1856.

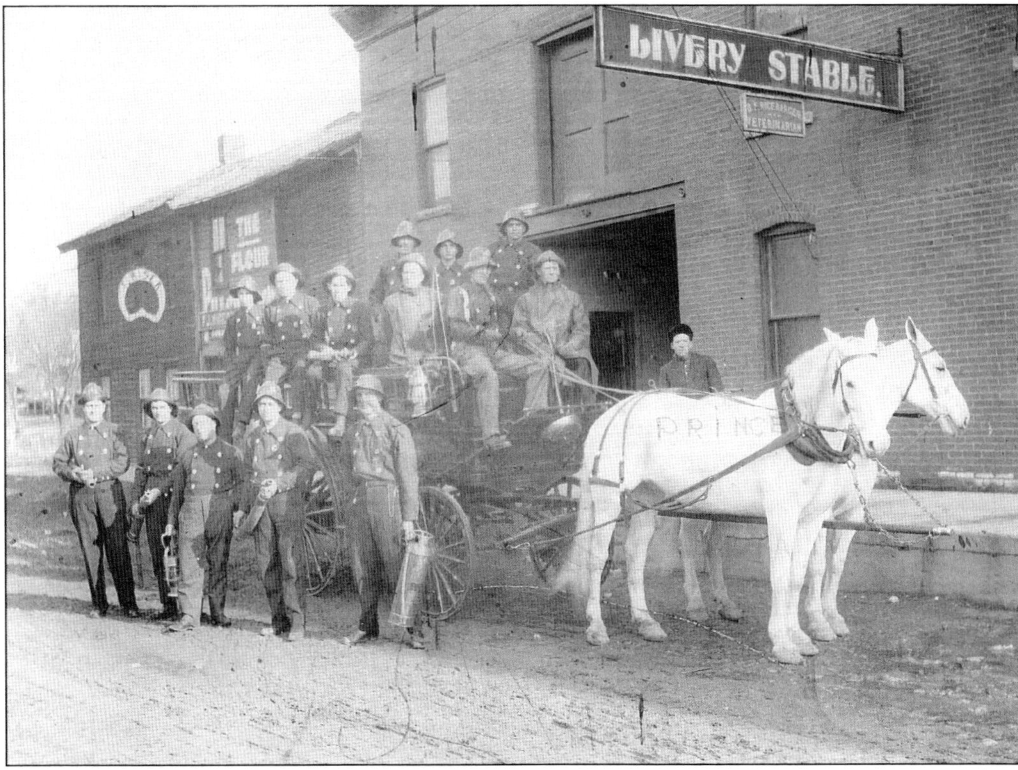


This photograph is of the volunteer fire department in the 1880s. Uniformed men are in front of the Livery Stable that also housed the veterinarian named Ricebarger. The men are wearing six-button tunics. The beloved lead horse was named Prince.

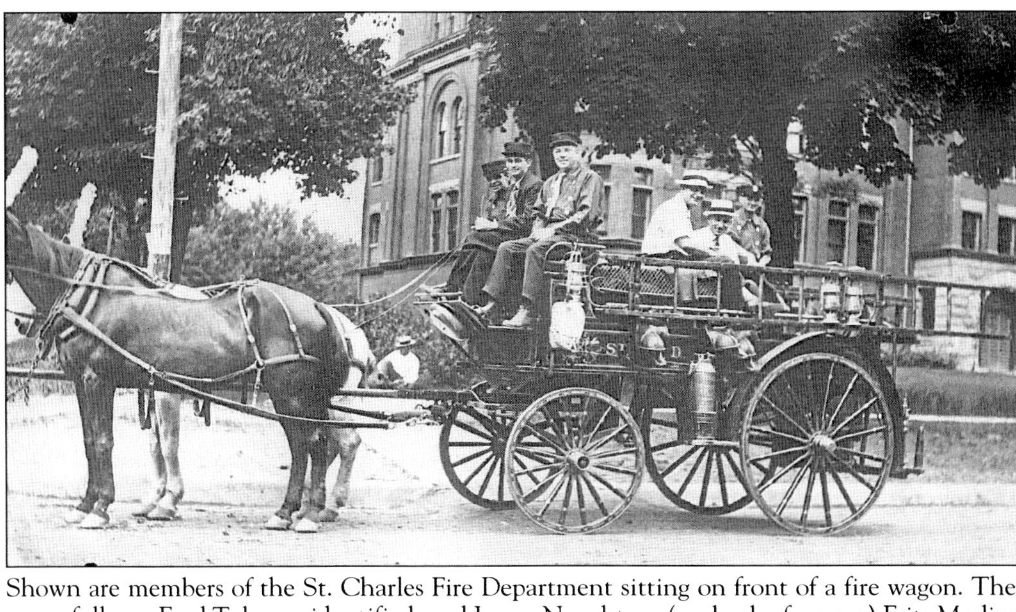

Shown are members of the St. Charles Fire Department sitting on front of a fire wagon. They are as follows: Fred Tyler, unidentified, and James Naughton; (on back of wagon) Fritz Modine, Roscoe Wagner, and Tom Haines. These horses are outfitted with colorful plumes, and the firemen's helmets are shown hanging on the side of the wagon.

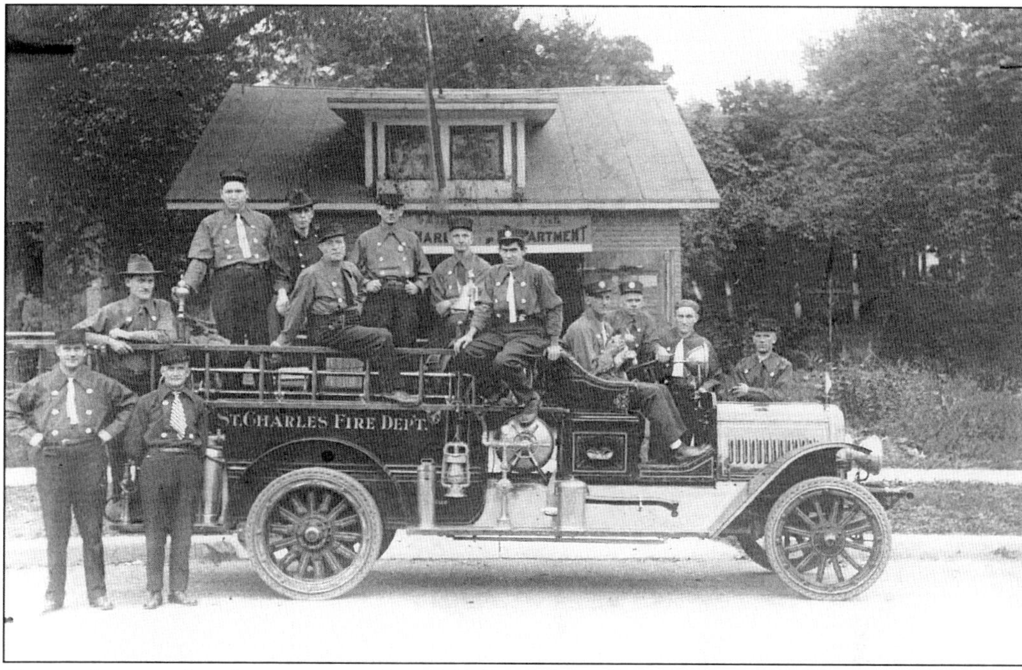


Here is the civic fire department with a 1913 DeKalb truck. The city waterworks were completed in 1910, which made water more easily available than pumping it from the river. This used vehicle was purchased by the city in 1915. It was the first motorized vehicle for the department.

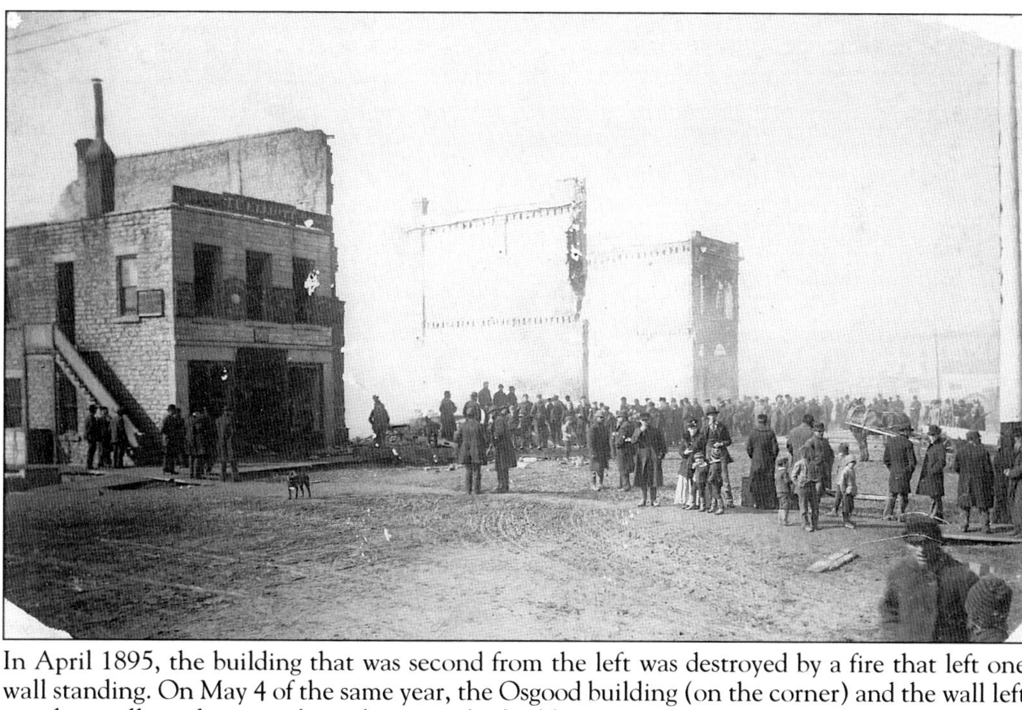

In April 1895, the building that was second from the left was destroyed by a fire that left one wall standing. On May 4 of the same year, the Osgood building (on the corner) and the wall left standing collapsed in a cyclone that tore the building to pieces in an instant. Buried beneath the ruins were the bodies of seven people, three of whom were found alive in the rubble.

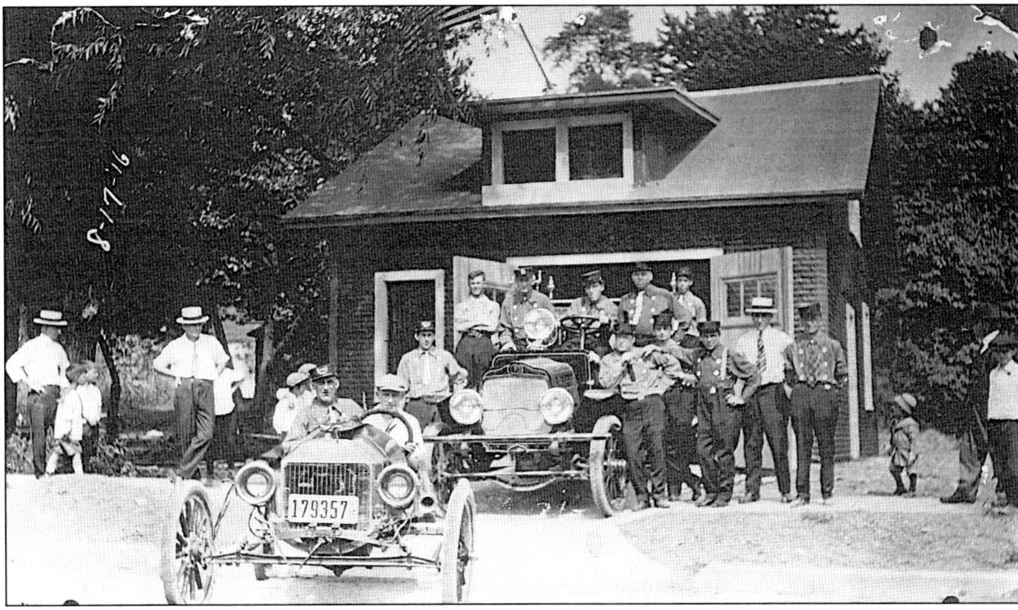

This zippy speedster was used by the chief as the lead vehicle for the St. Charles Fire Department in 1916. The firetruck carried an 80-gallon water tank, sufficient to put out small fires, and all the necessary equipment to hook up to the recently installed city hydrants. It also carried small ladders, hoses, tools, and firemen's protective clothing.

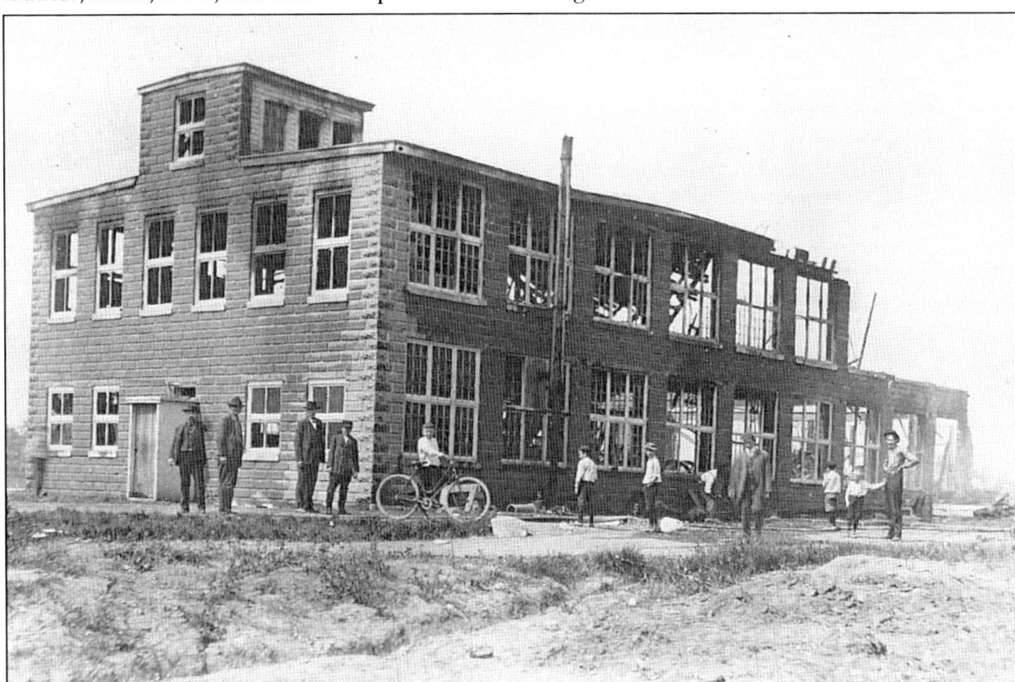
Adults and children gather among the remains of the St. Charles Net and Hammock Factory that burned in the early 1900s. After the fire, the building was rebuilt at the same location on North Sixth Street but was made larger. Couch Hammocks, basketball goals, and woven minnow seines were manufactured here.

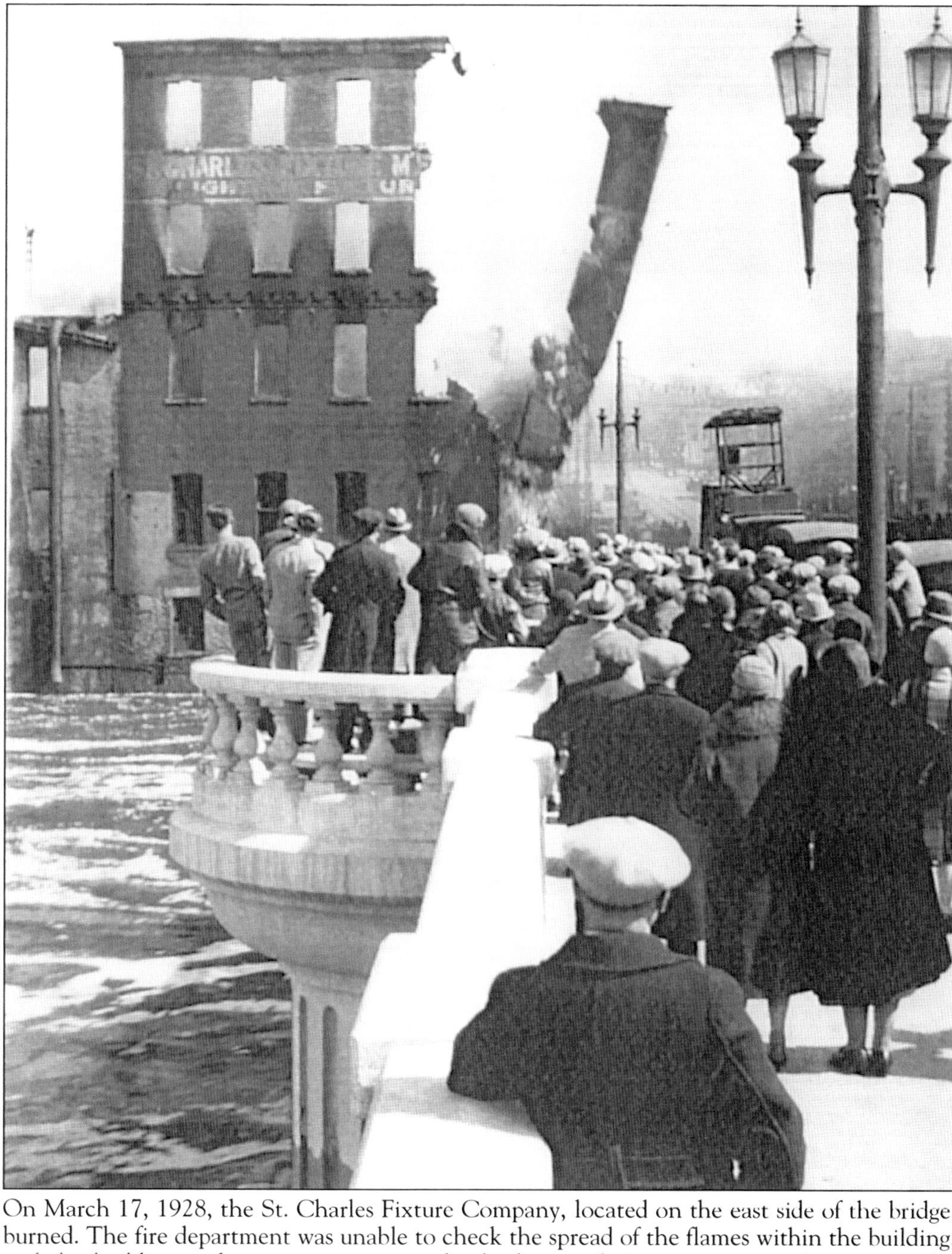

On March 17, 1928, the St. Charles Fixture Company, located on the east side of the bridge, burned. The fire department was unable to check the spread of the flames within the building, and the building and contents were completely destroyed. Spontaneous combustion on the second floor was blamed for the start of the fire. The firemen's effort was spent in keeping the fire from spreading to the surrounding buildings. This unique picture shows the fire just as the front wall was collapsing. St. Charles Fixture Company was one of the two chandelier manufacturers in St. Charles. Previous businesses in this location included the East Side Flouring Mill, the Fredenhagen Mill, and Steward and Pease (later named Stewart Brothers Mill).

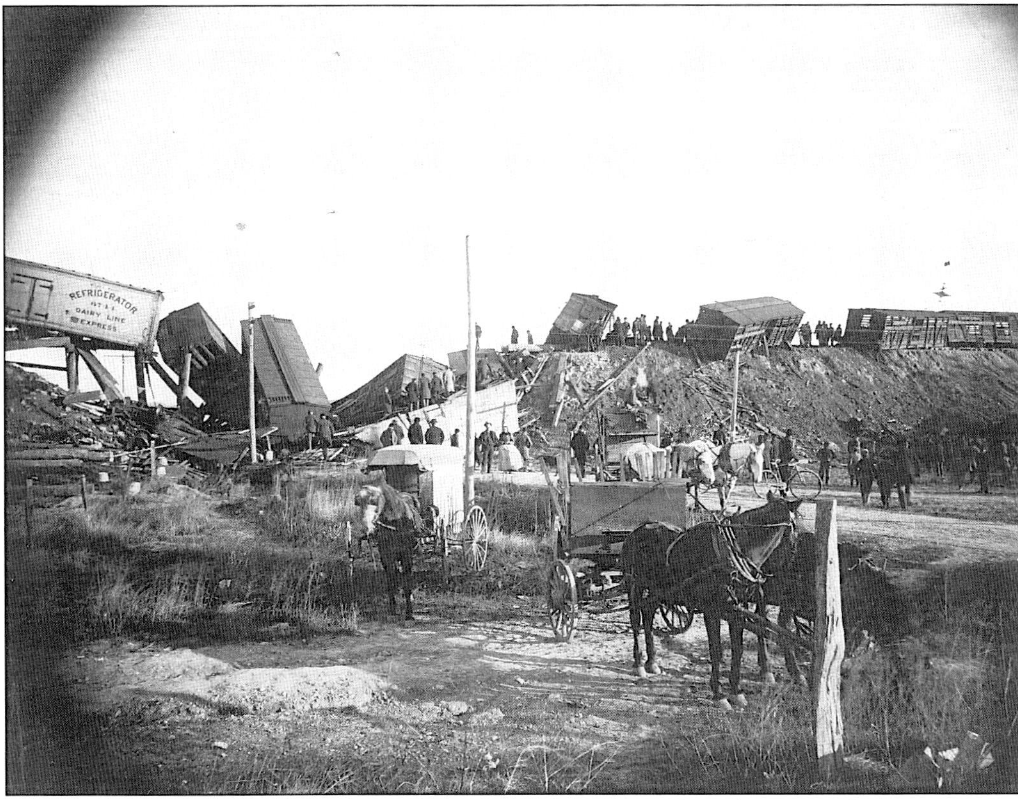


Fires were not the only disasters to plague the city. In 1905 the Chicago and Great Western freight train crashed on the Fifth Street overpass. This pass was over what is now Route 31. Spectators arrived on foot, by bicycle, and by horse, with or without wagons to view the remains. The wagon in the foreground belonged to J.E. Gordan & Son.

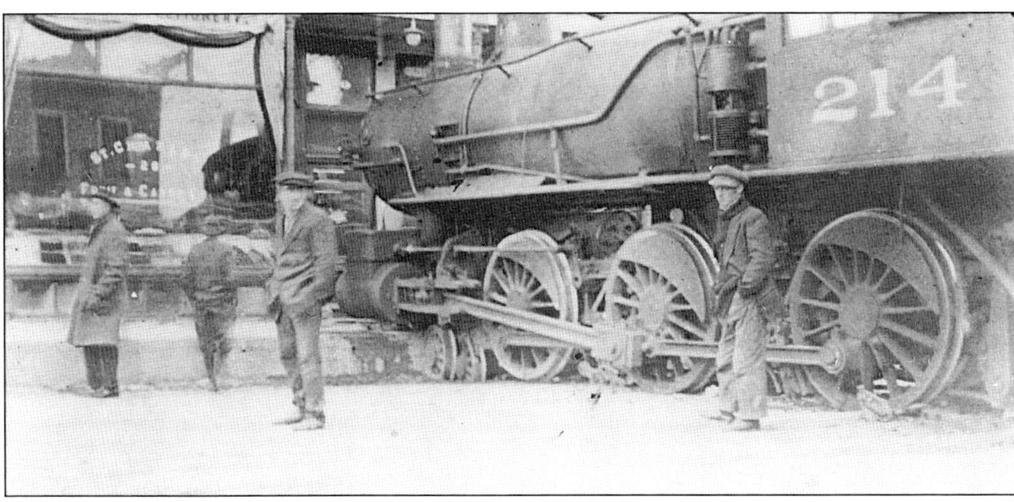


One of the more bizarre accidents was the crash of the Great Western engine number 214, which jumped the track on the spur line that ran along the river and crashed into a store front on Main Street in 1908. No one was injured, but the St. Charles Fruit and Confectionery Shop was slightly damaged.

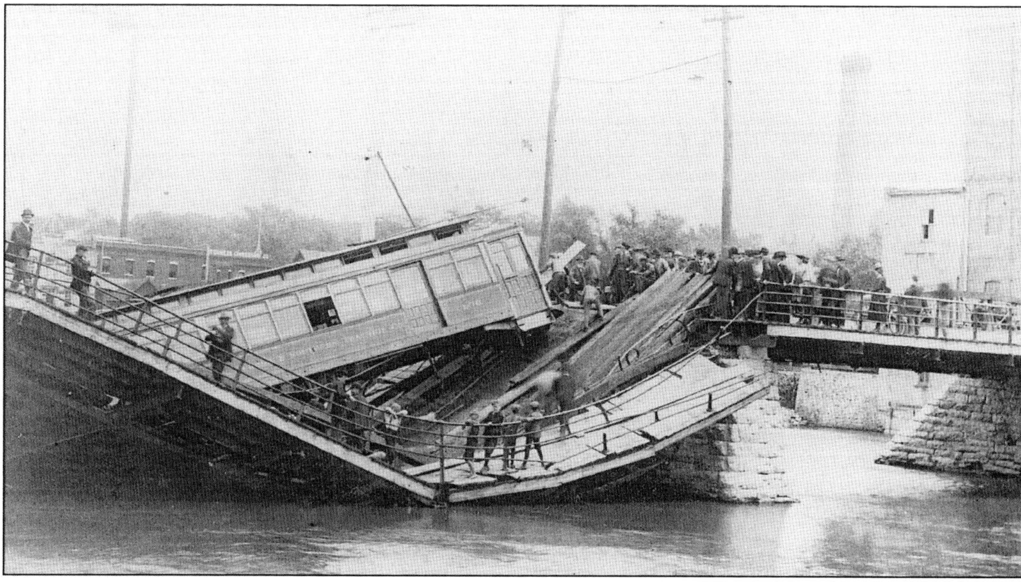

Electric streetcars were put in service between Aurora and Elgin, running through St. Charles, in 1896. The Main Street Bridge collapsed on July 1, 1902, and the streetcar followed it into the river. The fall was a slow, easy one so that there were few injuries and no deaths among the passengers and little damage to the car.

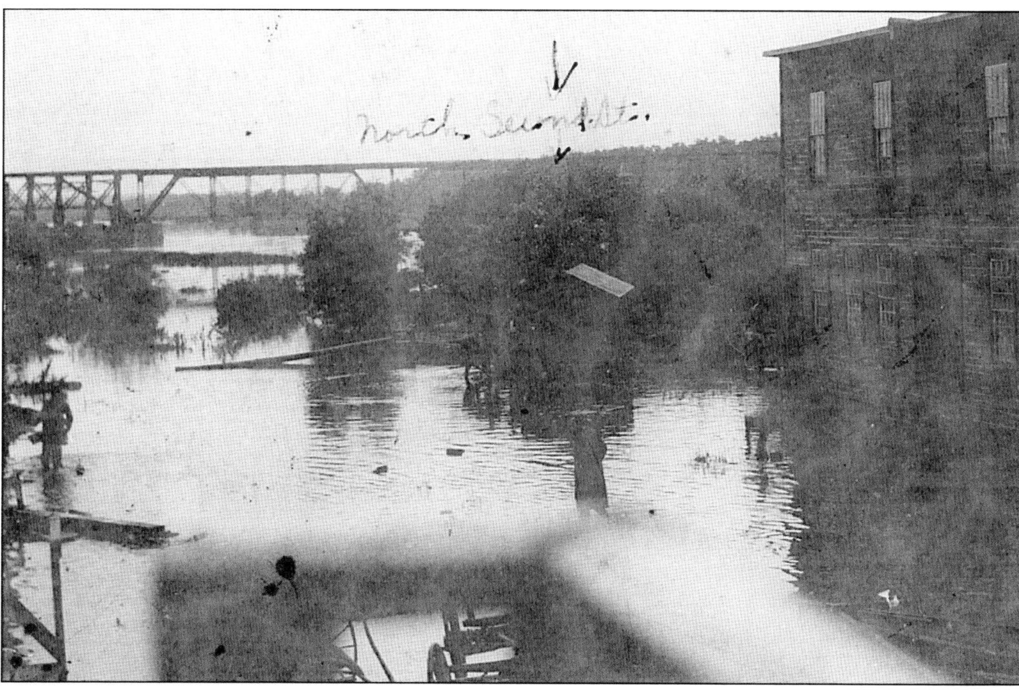

The Fox overflowed its banks in June of 1892. This picture of receding water was taken after the water had fallen 8 inches. Goodhue Windmills is the building on the right, and the person on the left is wading in about a foot of water. Floods were annual events in the early years, but with the building of locks and dams upstream, the floods have become more infrequent.

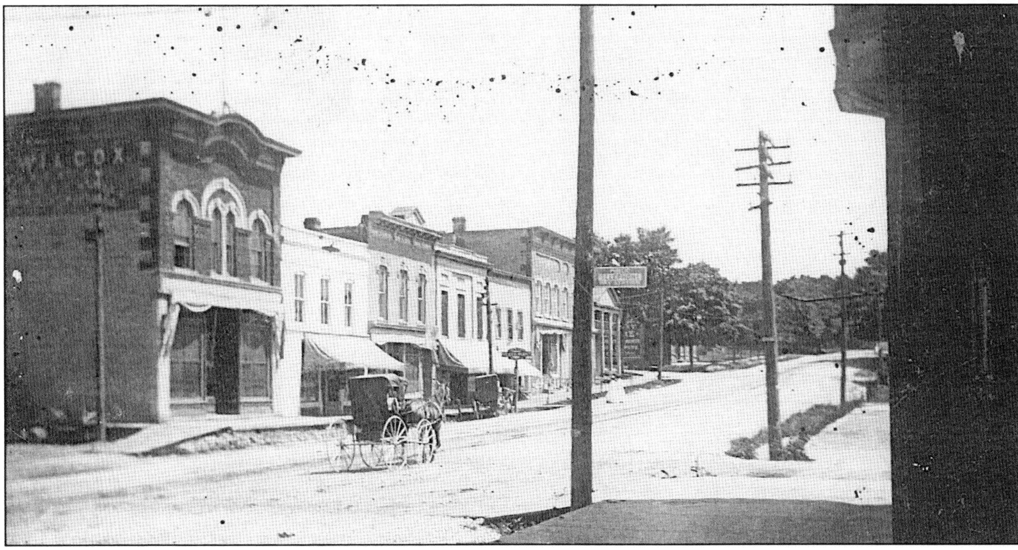

In 1842 the building in left foreground was the location of Franklin Medical Institute directed by Dr. George Richards. In the spring of 1849, a student, Rood, and two others robbed the grave of Mrs. George M. Kinyon of Sycamore. When they were found out, her friends and relatives stormed Dr. Richards's home, demanding the return of the body. Shots were fired at several students. Rood and Dr. Richards were injured. Dr. Richards died a few years later as a result of the incident, and Rood died a couple of weeks after the riot. Mrs. Kinyon's body was not found that day.

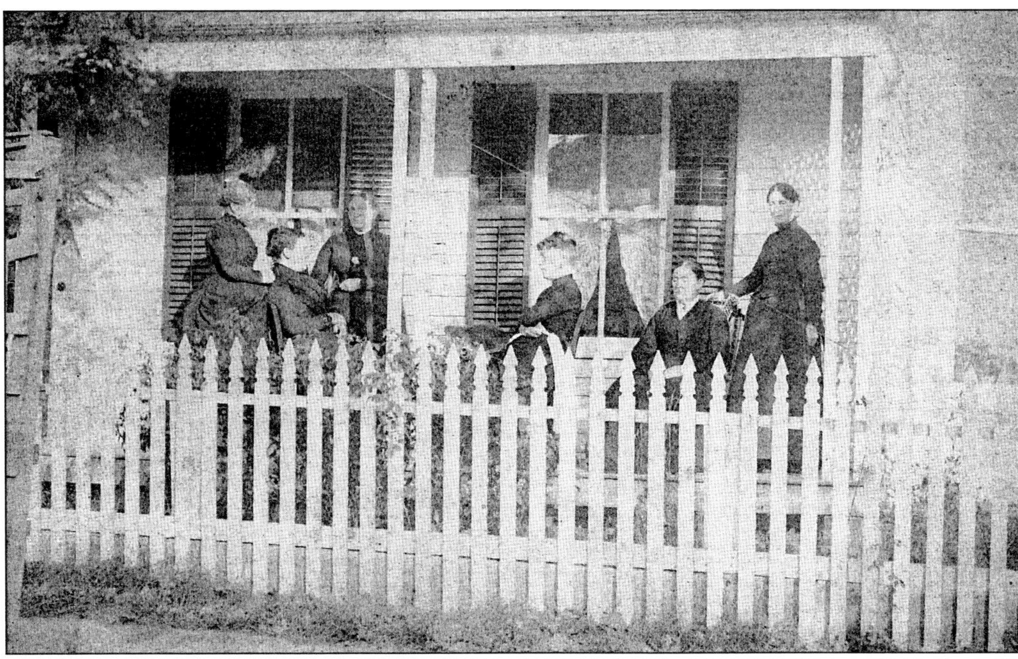

One story goes that with the help of Caroline Howard, a local spiritualist and psychic, the police later found Mrs. Kinyon's body hidden in a shallow grave south of town. This is an 1880 photograph of Caroline Howard, who is second from right. The photographer grouped Miss Howard and her friends to appear as if a seance was underway.

Believe it or not, the spider is mightier than the snake in St. Charles. A small garter snake got caught up in a funnel-shaped black spider web, 5 inches from the floor in Roland Swanberg's basement. It was believed that the snake had been imprisoned for at least 25 days and had attracted nation-wide press before the mayor cut the snake free.

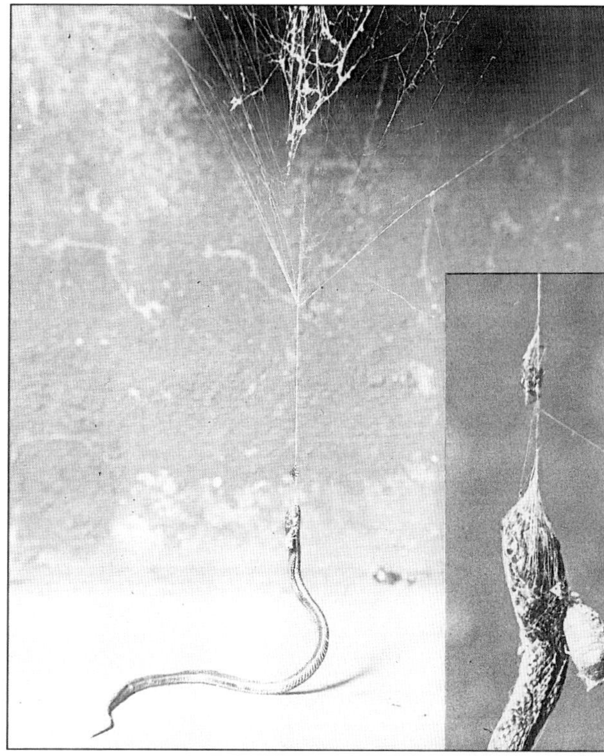

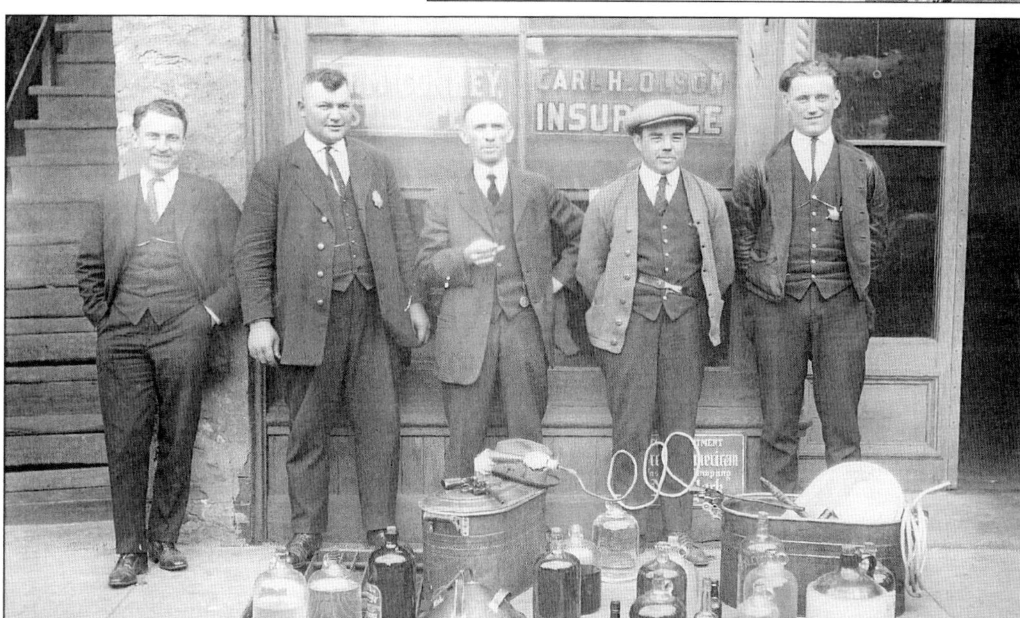


The St. Charles Police Department looks as proud as Izzy and Moe after their capture of a white lightning brew kit. Could it have been found in the back room of the Insurance Office right in the middle of town? This was a disaster to the local drinkers. St. Charles was "dry" for several periods before Prohibition. The second time, in 1917, it was because the U.S. government wanted to conserve grain to feed the troops.

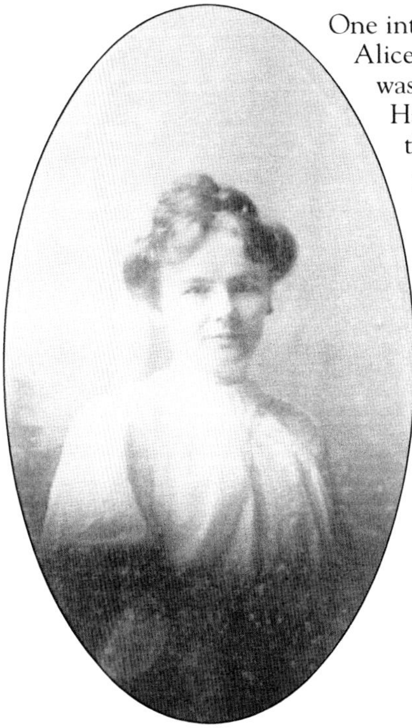

One international disaster had a happy ending for a local family. Alice Berg Johnson, pictured here before her first marriage, was in Finland visiting her sick father with her two children, Harold and Eleanor. They were booked on the *Titanic* for the return home. When the crash occurred, Mrs. Johnson grabbed Eleanor and went to the assigned lifeboat station. A woman she had met on board carried Harold to the deck.

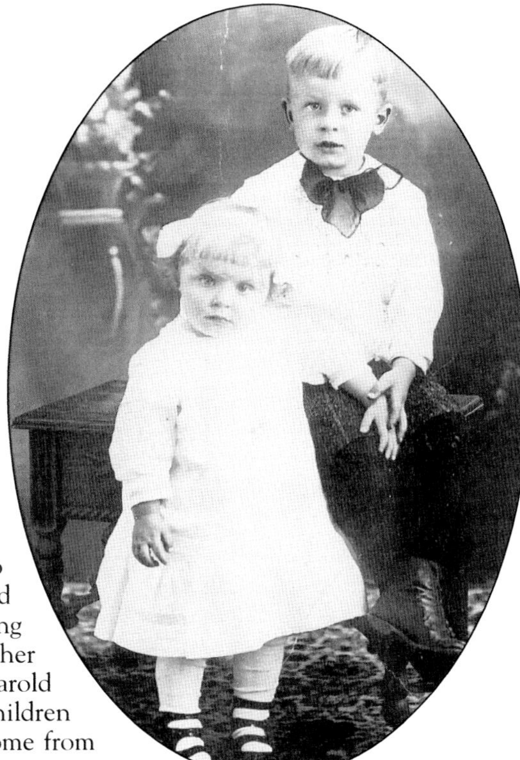

A steward motioned for her to drop Eleanor to him in the life boat. She did, and then jumped into the boat after her child. The woman holding Harold dropped him to Alice, and she put her life belt on him. The woman who dropped Harold perished in the disaster. This portrait of the children was made just after they happily returned home from the *Titanic* disaster.

# *Six*

# ROLLING ON THE RIVER
## *Tents, Camps, and Regattas*

When the first settlers came to the Fox Valley, water and water power were a major attraction. However, the beauty of the land and the rich, black soil were not lost on them. Letters home also commented on the unspoiled cleanliness and potential for healthful living in this spot. St. Charles had been a layover spot for travelers since its beginning and had the hotels to accommodate these travelers. In the early 1900s, the weekly "free" day leisure became big business. Coney Island drew 500,000 visitors a day on weekends. Following that example, entrepreneurs in St. Charles and all up and down the valley began to develop the river banks for leisure activities. Weekend camps, dance halls, and parks were built to provide a place for the weekend and holiday visitors who wanted to enjoy the beauty of St. Charles for even a short time. The city was becoming a resort town, a destination easily reachable by rail.

But before the camps, the local residents were using the river for recreation. One such resident was Frank M. Underwood, who lived on Walnut Street his whole life. Born in 1860 and married in 1883, he later built cabins for the visitors. Underwood roamed the St. Charles area, collected historical artifacts, and later photographed the land as well as family activities. He left a photo album to the St. Charles Heritage Center, depicting a lazy summer long ago. Several of these pictures are included in this chapter.

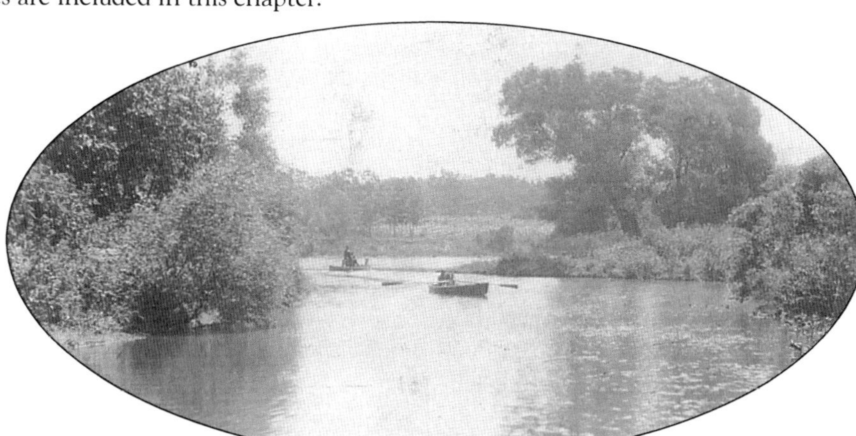

Islands dotting the river were sometimes connected to the bank if the space was not too great. This is one such space that was connected by T.E. Ryan, who spent quite a lot of effort for the betterment of St. Charles. He was sought out by Gates for council when Gates was having patent problems with his barbed wire company.

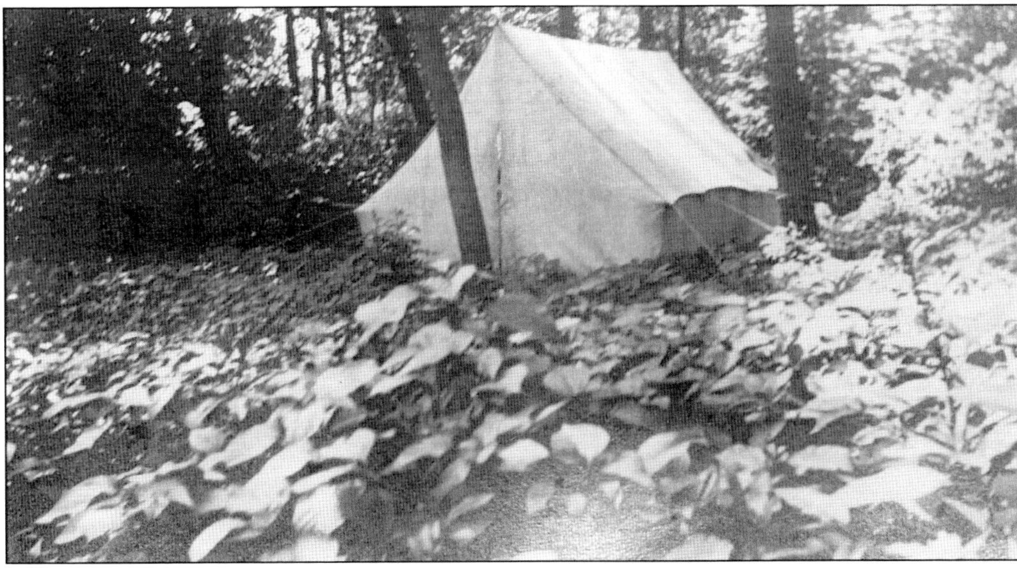

The cook tent was photographed by Frank Underwood. It mostly provided some shelter for the supplies needed to feed the campers. As you can see in a later picture, the actual cooking was done out of doors on nice days. The newly invented thermos kept cold things cold and hot things hot, a great boon to the campers.

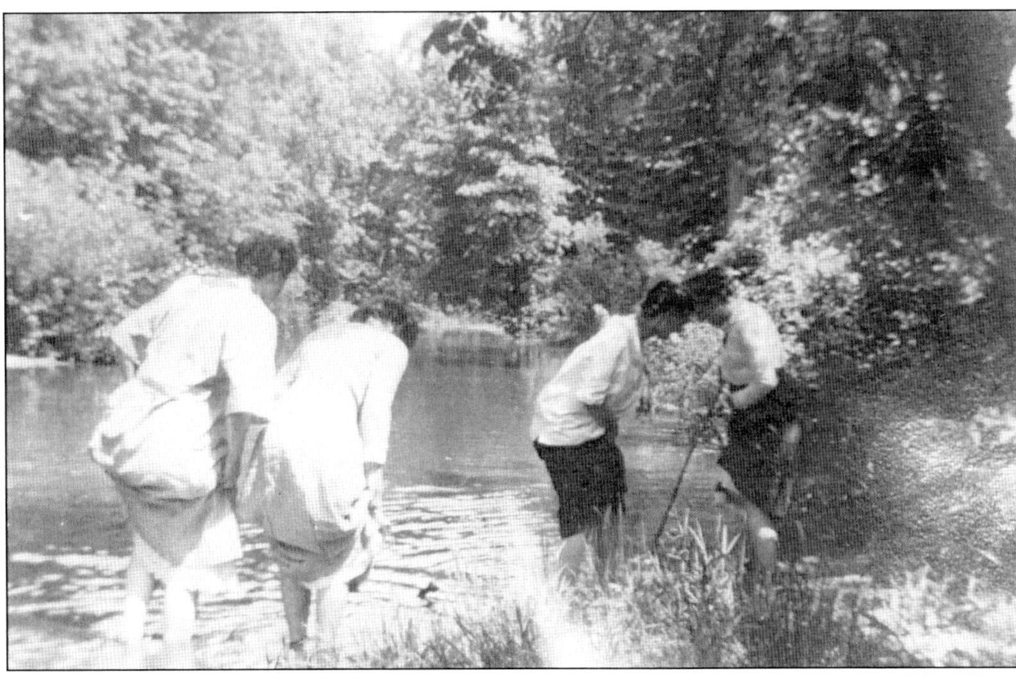

Underwood wrote descriptions of his photographs in white ink on the black paper of the album. This photo was simply described as "wading." Many called this bathing rather than swimming. Swimmers were a more adventurous group. These four women are certainly enjoying the cool water on a warm day.

This more permanent shelter was the bathhouse used for changing from everyday to bathing clothes. The plank walk helped keep wet feet from picking up all that sand on the way back after a dip in the creek and river.

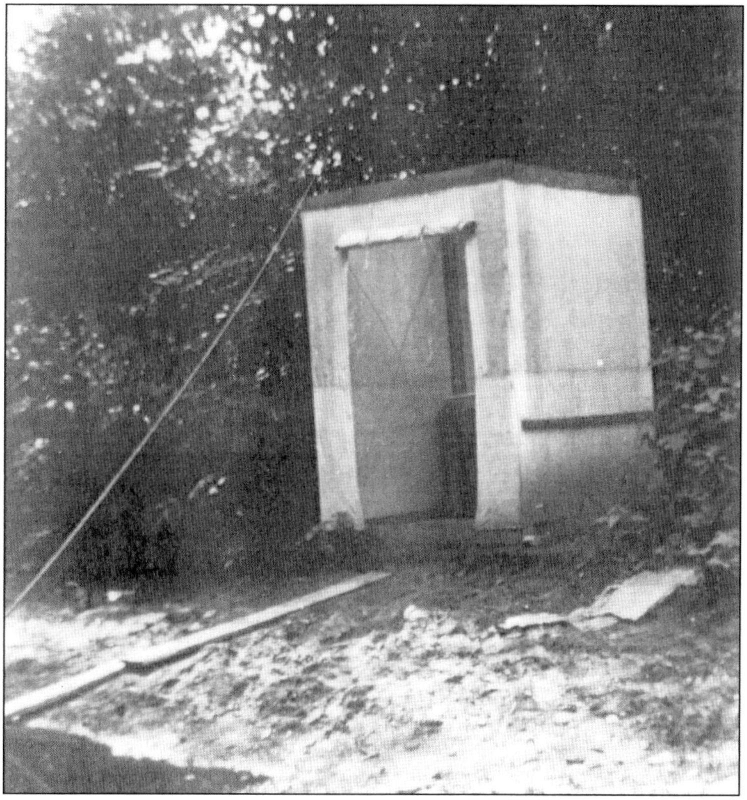

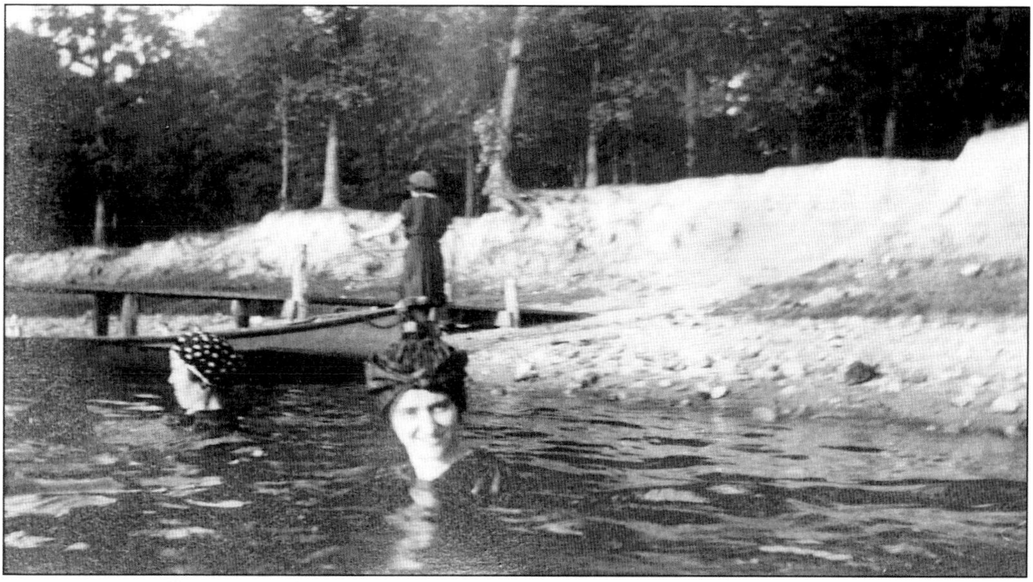

"Very soon we'll swim" is the caption for this photograph. Women had to be strong swimmers to get anywhere wearing these heavy costumes. From looking at the head wraps, one doesn't get the impression that these women were out for a serious swim—cooling off is more likely.

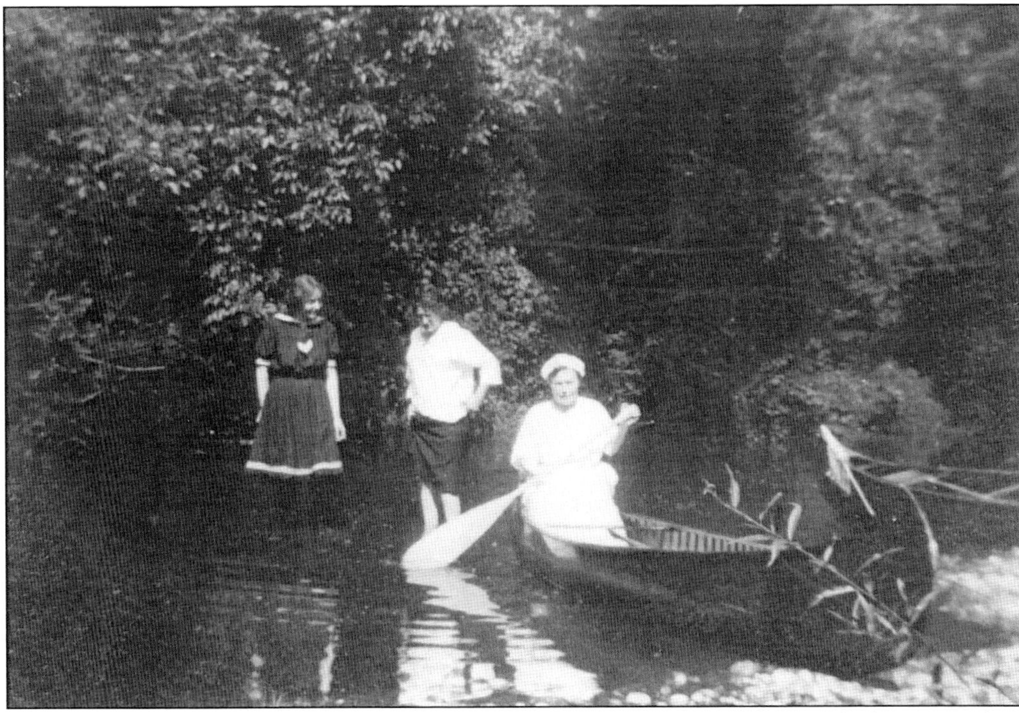

Canoeing was an ever popular activity on the Fox River and the streams that feed into it. These three women have found a secluded cove to cool their feet on what is, evidently, a hot summer day. Very few people in this Underwood family photo album were identified.

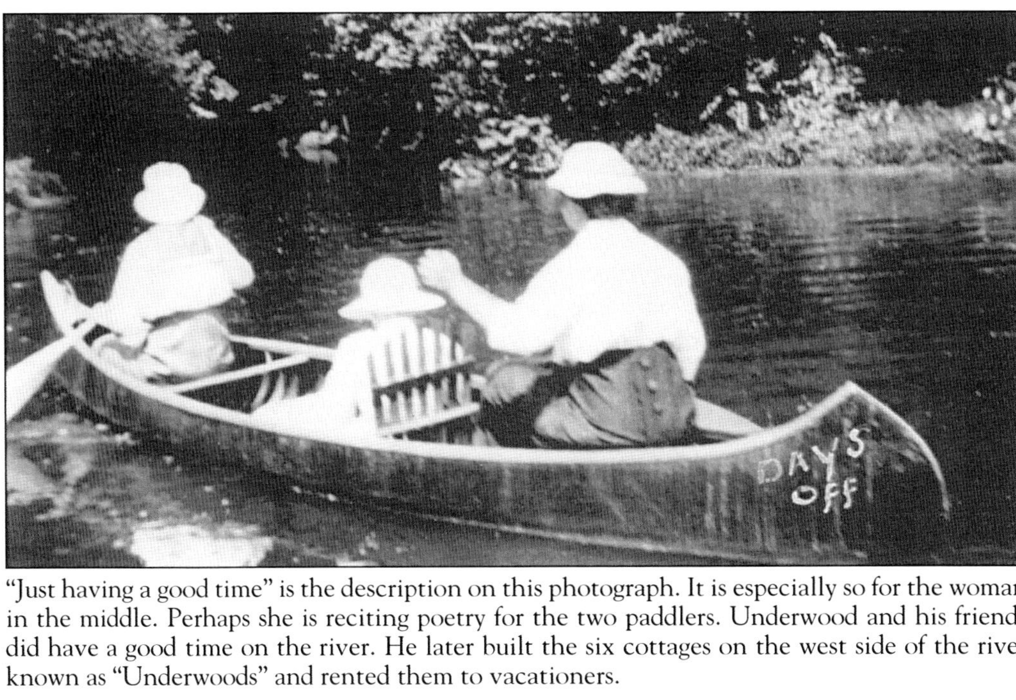


"Just having a good time" is the description on this photograph. It is especially so for the woman in the middle. Perhaps she is reciting poetry for the two paddlers. Underwood and his friends did have a good time on the river. He later built the six cottages on the west side of the river known as "Underwoods" and rented them to vacationers.

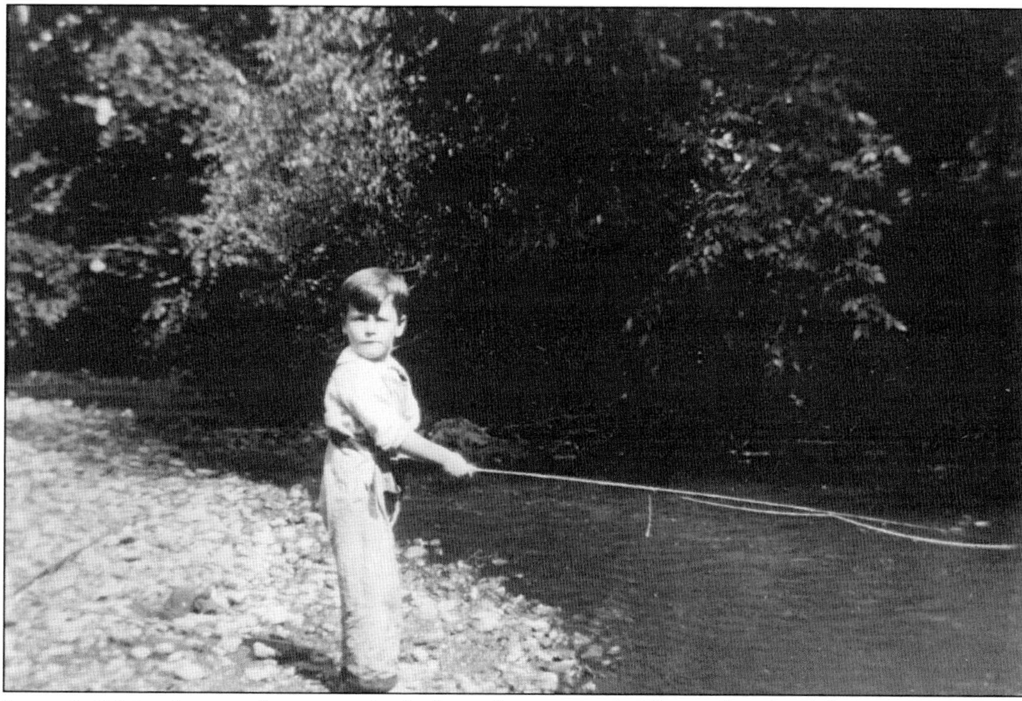

James is fishing here and seems to be looking for approval of his style. The fish are not biting for him today. Note that his line is tied off near the middle of the very long pole. While we don't know who James is, we do know that he isn't the son of Frank Underwood. Frank and Ida's only son was named Lewis.

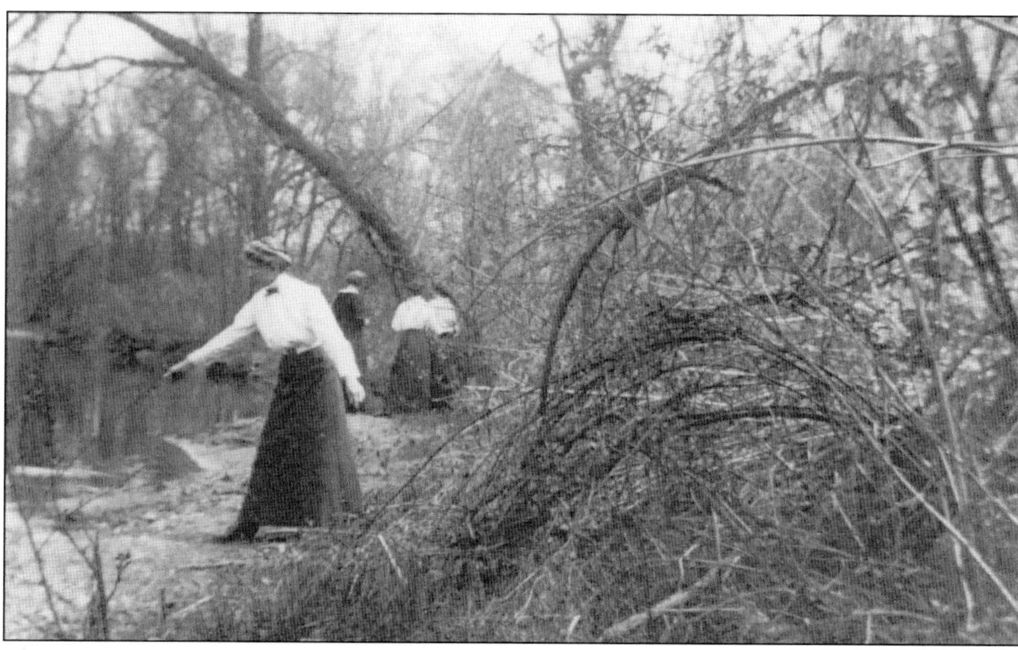

This young woman could take some fishing lessons from James. She doesn't appear to be dressed for the occasion and seems to be very apprehensive about the whole thing since the rod is pointed into the river's edge where few fish can be found.

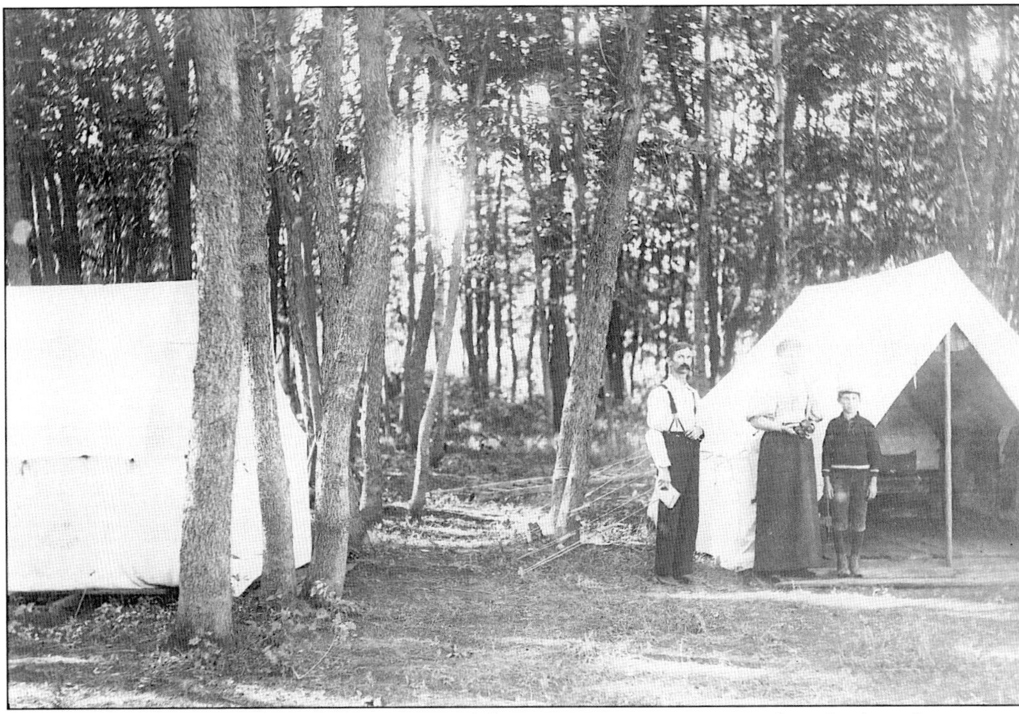

Tenting was a popular activity at the turn of the century. Here we can take a look at the interior of a tent that was used as a sitting space as well as a sleeping space. The flooring kept the inhabitants a little removed from those "creepy crawlys" and any possible rain.

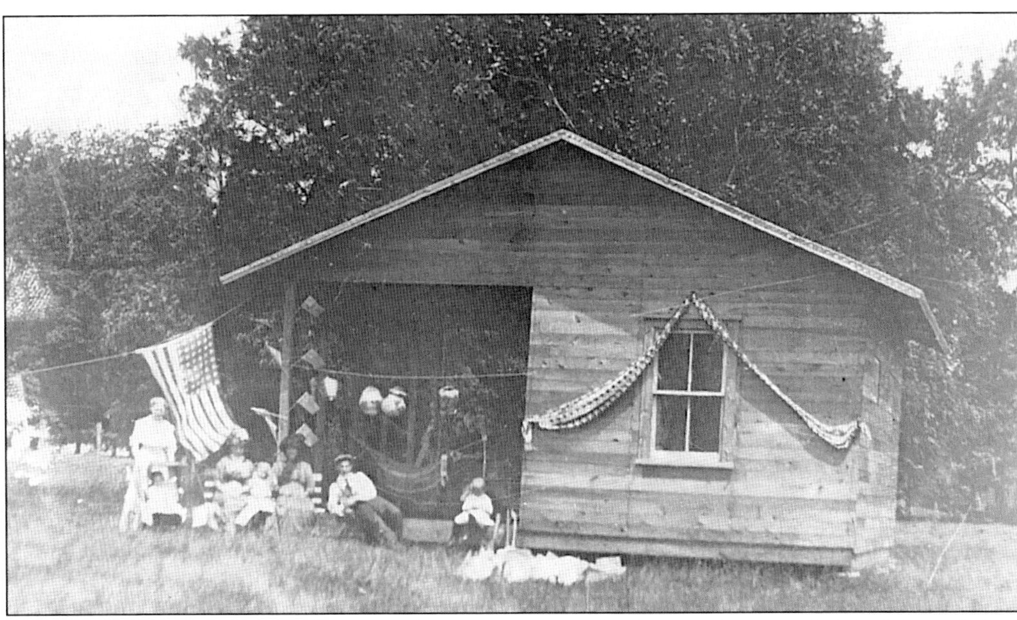

Permanent summer cottages began to dot the shores of the Fox in the early 1900s. Most of these were owned by weekend visitors. This picture of the Charles and Edith Faitz family was taken on the Fourth of July in 1914. Note the colorful bunting and 48-star flag.

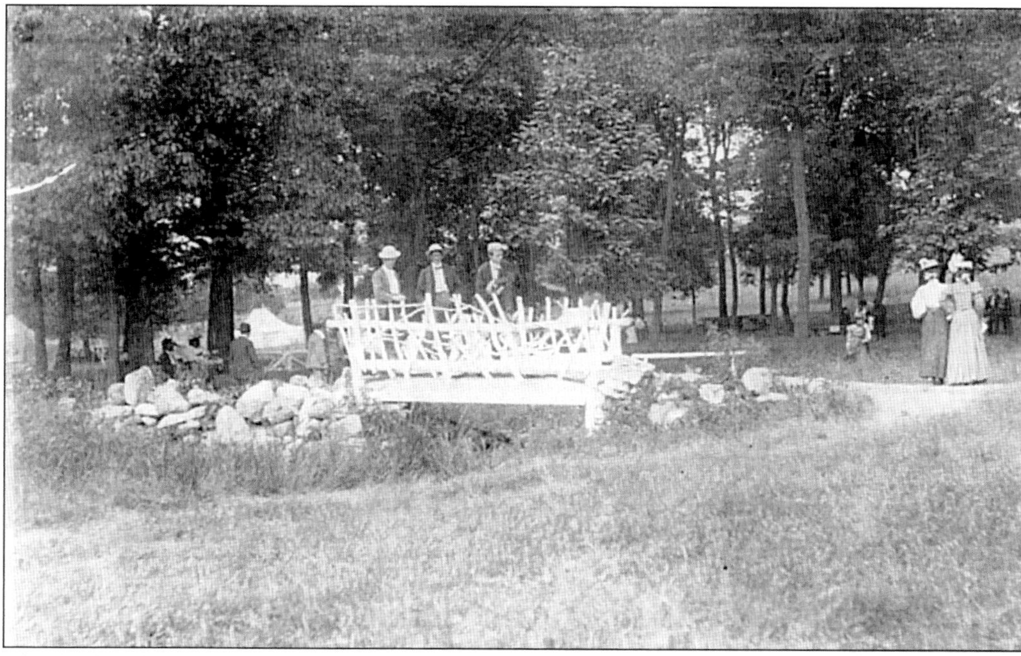

This bridge shows a popular construction method used to provide crossing over the many inlets from the river. The small branches and stones were readily available materials, and construction was rustic to say the least. Tents can be seen in the clearing beyond the grove.

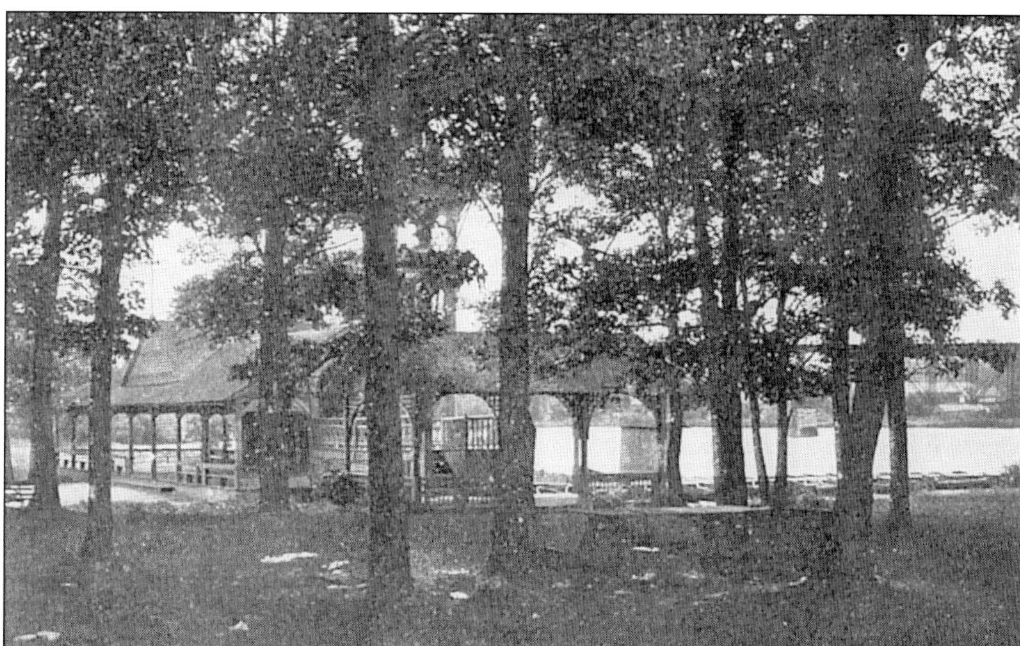

Some summer weekend camps, such as Pinelands and Wing Hammer, featured a dance pavilion. Bands that played regularly at the Trianon and the Aragon ballrooms in Chicago would spend their summers in the Fox Valley playing at the various dance halls in St. Charles. The pavilion pictured above was located in Pottawatomie Park.

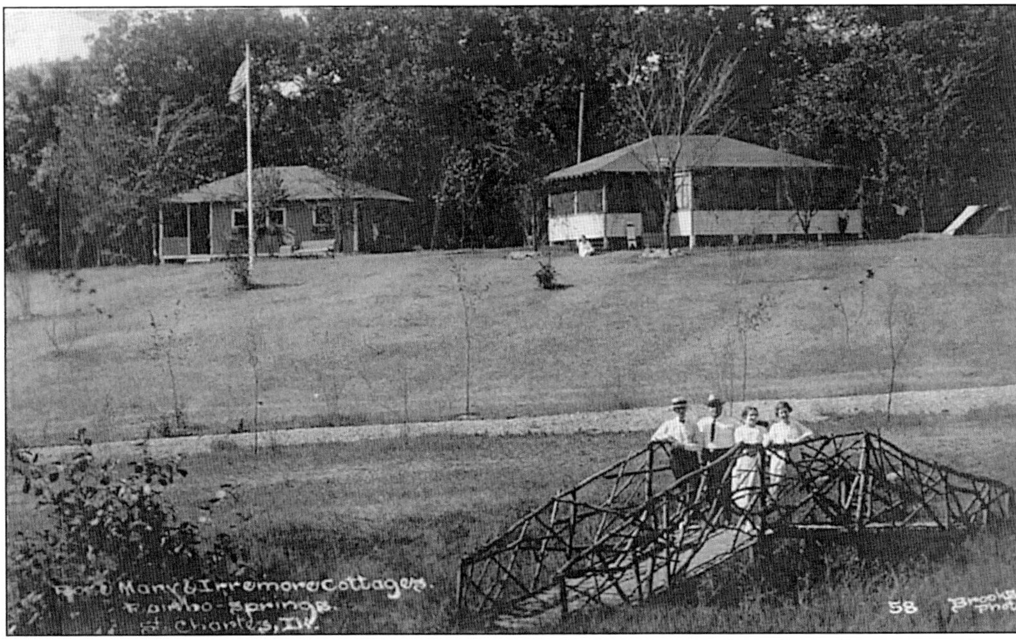


Rainbo Springs advertised commodious cottages with sleeping porches along the river and near the business district of St. Charles. The breezeways helped keep the cabins cool. Their ten cottages were fully booked from the beginning. They later added tents, a concrete swimming pool, and two community houses. The two couples are standing on an excellent example of a spider web natural wood branch bridge, which was a folk art form of its own in the 1890s.

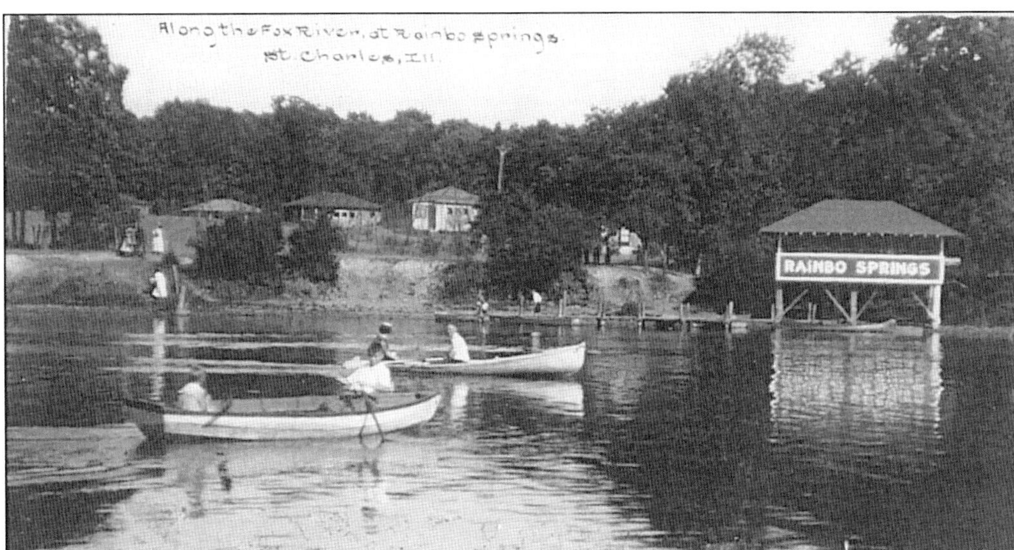


Rainbo Springs was also one of the camps that had dance pavilions featuring bands on Wednesday, Saturday, and Sunday nights. A dining hall meant a holiday for the women too. This camp advertised an addition of a clubhouse for "the womenfolk to spend their spare hours."

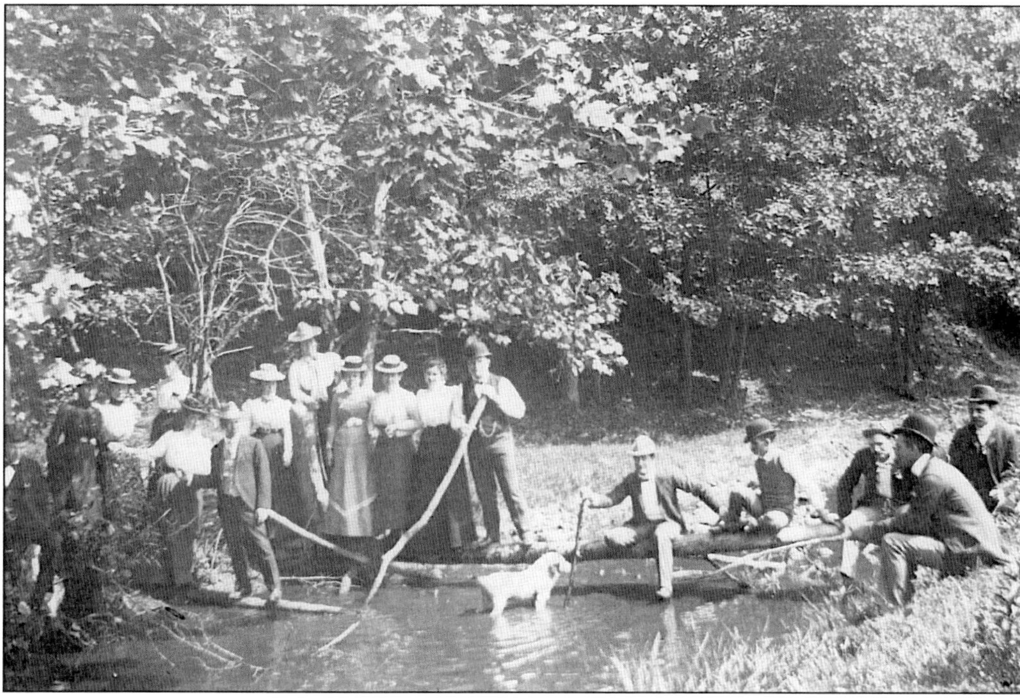

This group of young people, on a weekend exploring venture in June of 1900, includes Miss Haviland, whose family owned farm property near St. Charles. This stream may be on that property. All, even the dog, are having a gay old time.

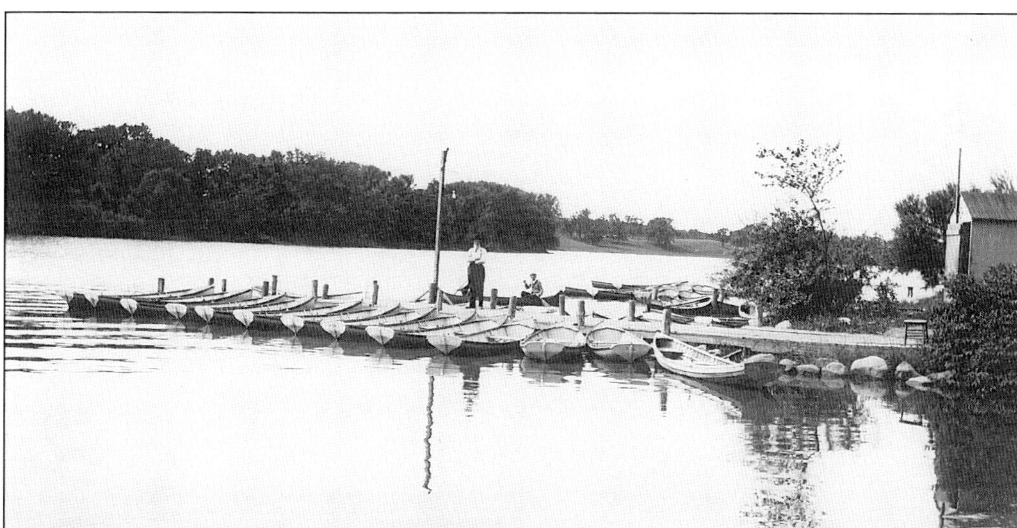

Boating and rivers go together. These gentlemen are ready to rent rowboats or canoes to the many boaters who want to enjoy the water, night or day. Nighttime boating just had to be popular among courting couples who were out to escape the watchful eyes of the female chaperone.

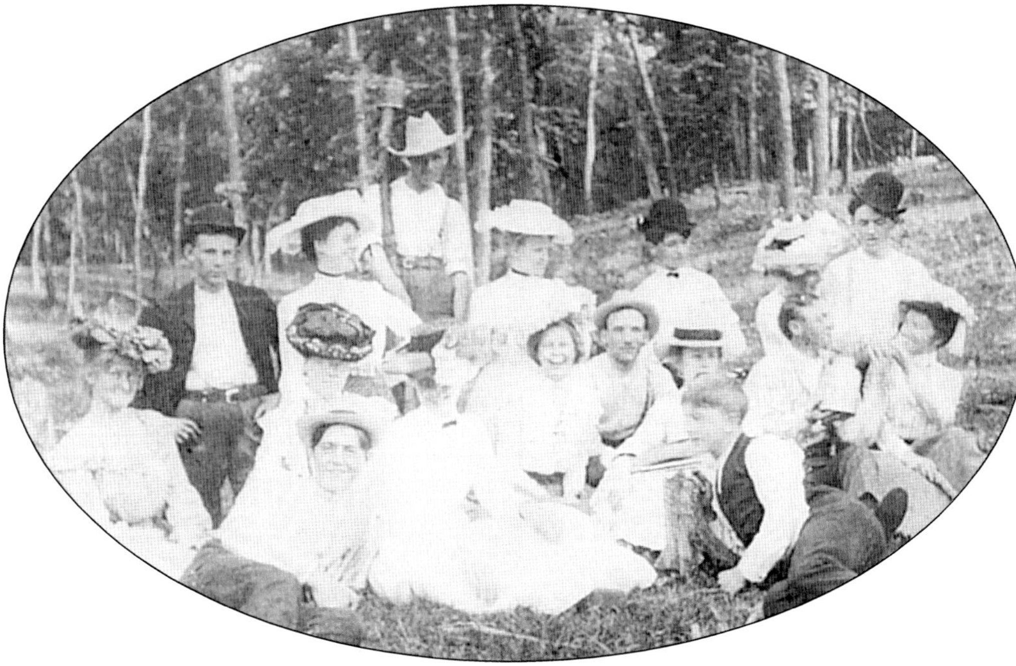

Picnics are always popular summertime activities. These young people have selected their spot, one that has plenty of firewood for a bonfire later. Included in the group are Agnes and Vemina Beoggren, Hilda Modine, Alfred Anderson, Eva Larson, and Elmer and Ellen Dahlstrom. Note the various hat styles worn by both sexes; straws, cokes, and flower patch hats contribute to the spirit of this Edwardian-era picture.

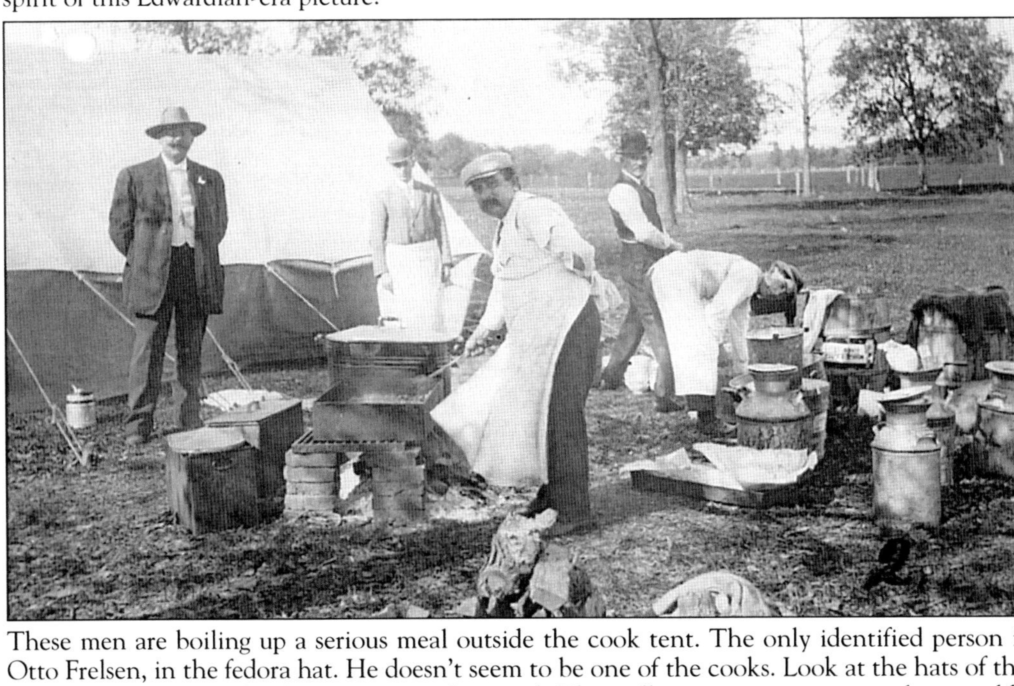

These men are boiling up a serious meal outside the cook tent. The only identified person is Otto Frelsen, in the fedora hat. He doesn't seem to be one of the cooks. Look at the hats of the other gentlemen involved in preparing this meal. The milk containers appear to be portable seating for the cooks as well as vessels for the beverage of the day.

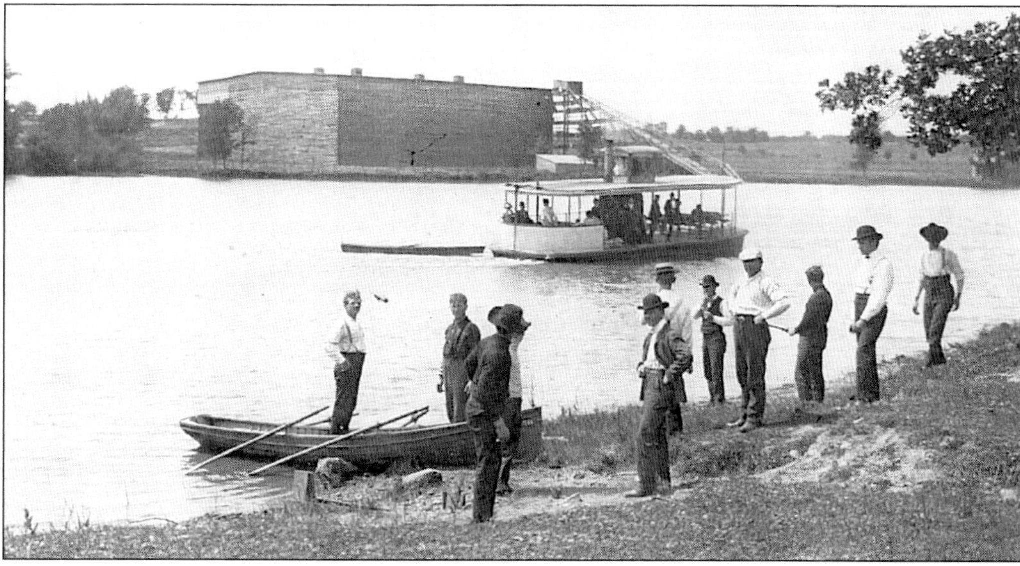

Some of these men are standing on an old bonfire site that is across the river from McBride Brother's Ice House. Vic Rockman's S.S. *Pacific* is on the river, and these men may have been some of it passengers or riverbank strollers.

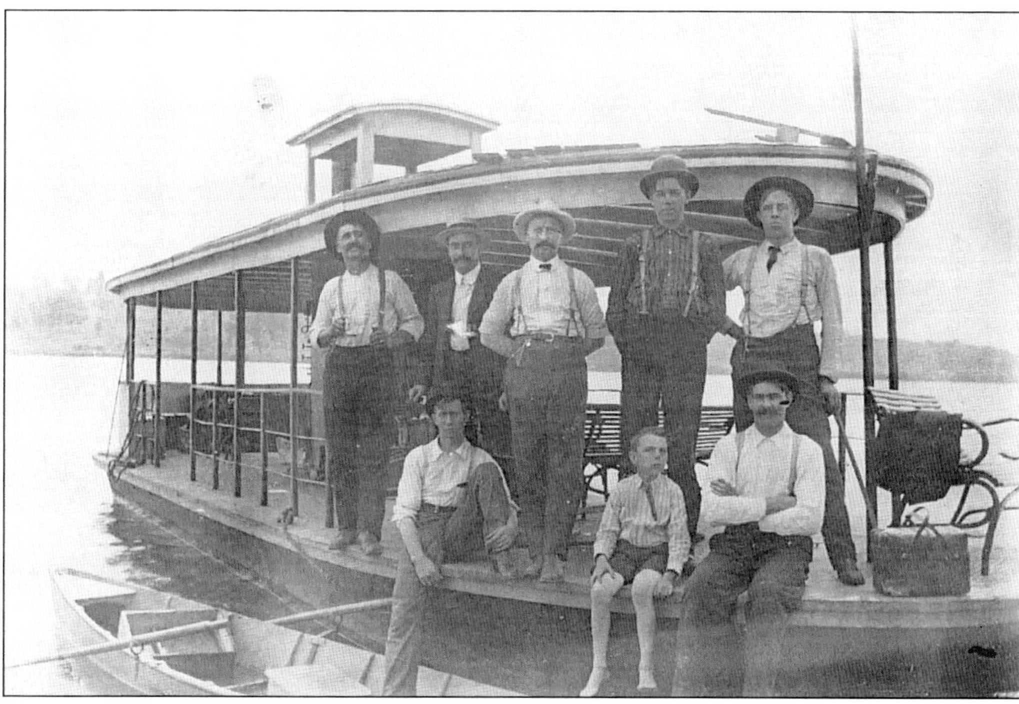

Here is a close-up view of the S.S. *Pacific* and its crew. From left to right are as follows: (standing) Charles and Victor Rockman and Jake Swanson; (seated) Oscar Johnson, Howard Collins, and John Johnson. This steamboat was driven by a coal-fired boiler. On windy days, waves would sometimes flood the deck when the boat was loaded!

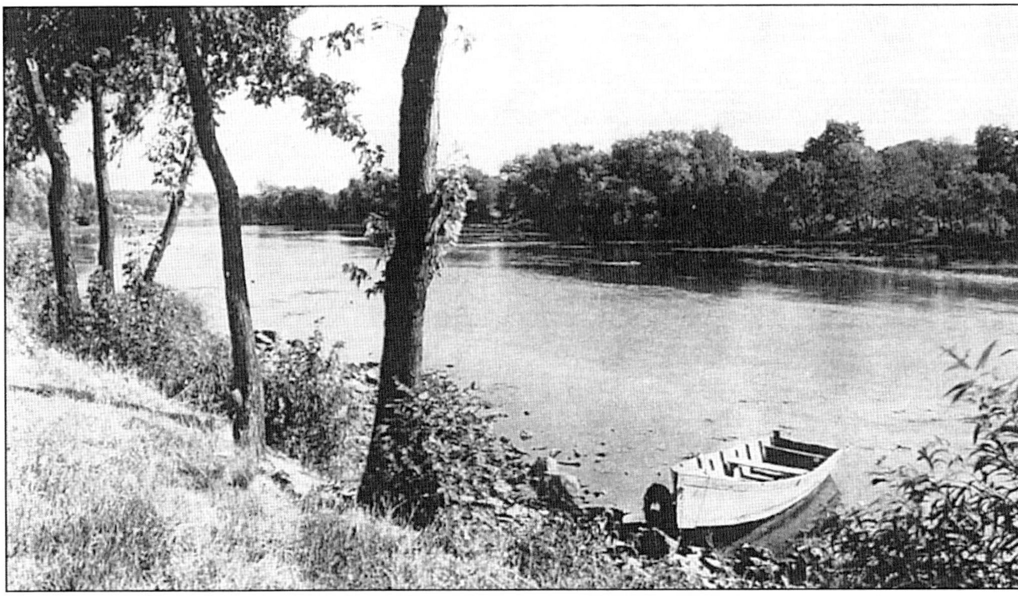

A quiet ride on the river was still the favorite way to enjoy the cool breezes or to fish for supper. Travelling on the water was also often a swifter and more direct way to travel than riding a horse or traveling on rough, plank roads and muddy paths.

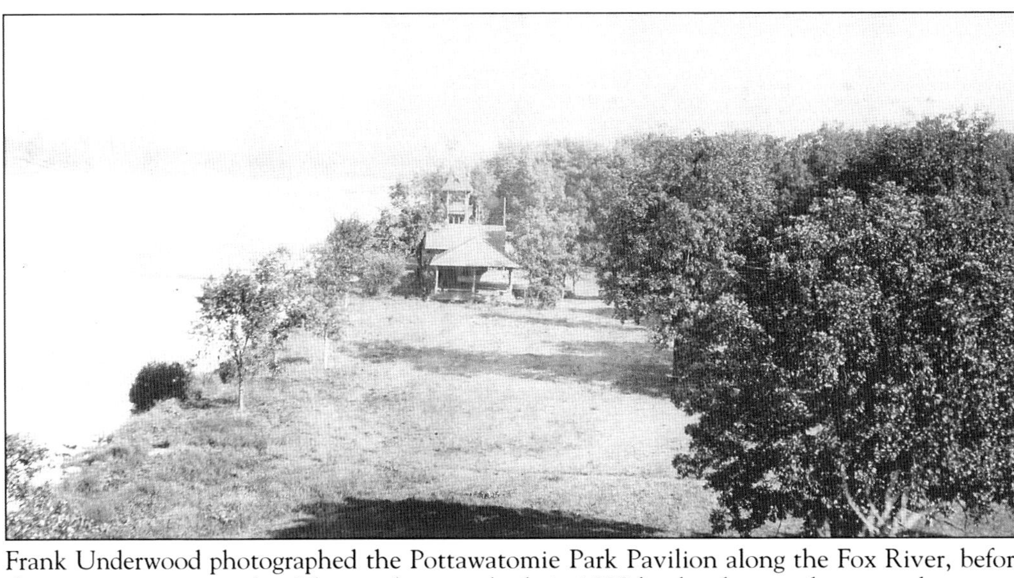

Frank Underwood photographed the Pottawatomie Park Pavilion along the Fox River, before the city grew up around it. The pavilion was built in 1892 by developers who wanted to create a resort hotel and park. In 1912 the park was purchased by the township and became the first public park to be established under the new Illinois Parks Act.

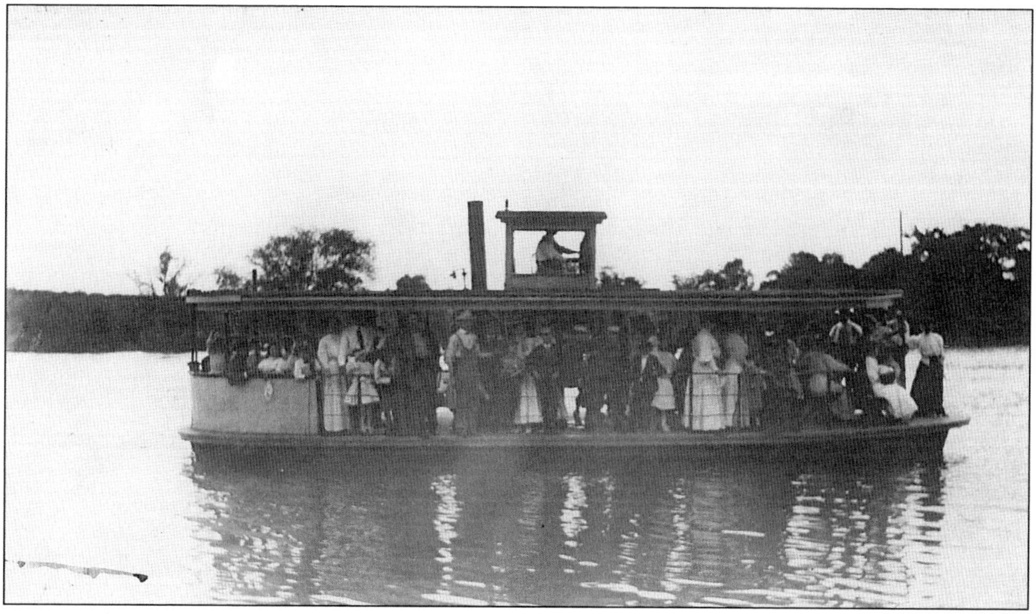

Here is a later riverboat used to take excursionists out on the river with the captain in his cabin on top. The people in the crowd are dressed in the style of the 1900s. This boat is a longer version of the S.S. *Pacific* and appears to have over 50 passengers all crowded along one side of the boat. The deck is still a safe 2 feet off the water line.

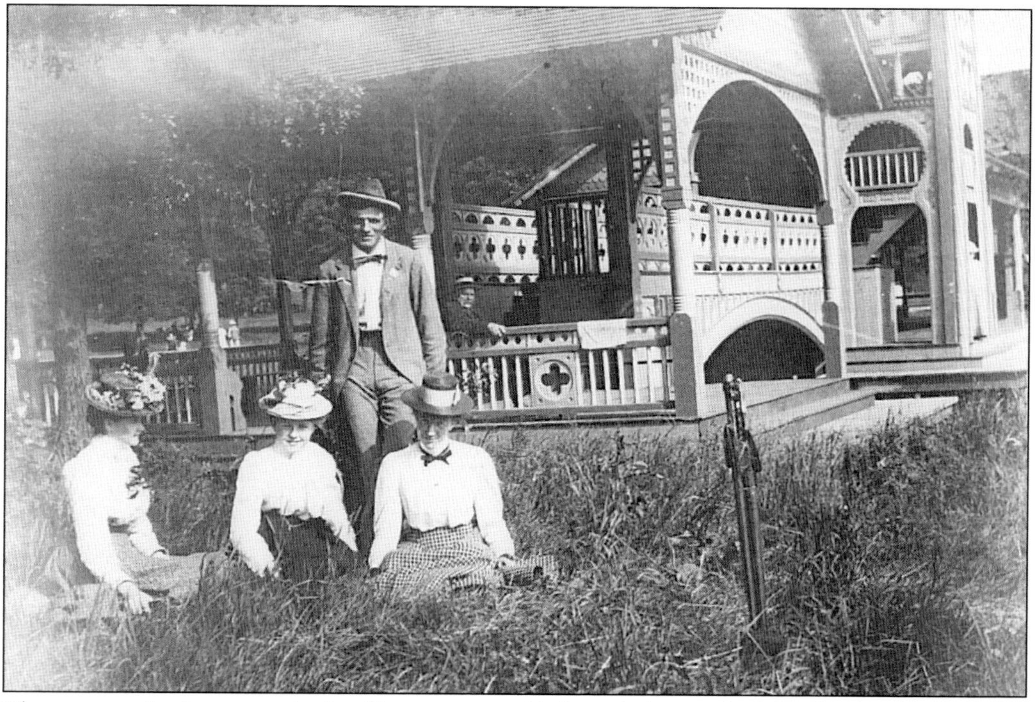

These excursionists are enjoying Pottawatomie Park and the pavilion in the late 1890s. This park was built by developers who wanted to create a resort hotel and park. They built the pavilion along the river in 1892, but the hotel was never built. The architectural style is a combination of Moorish and gingerbread.

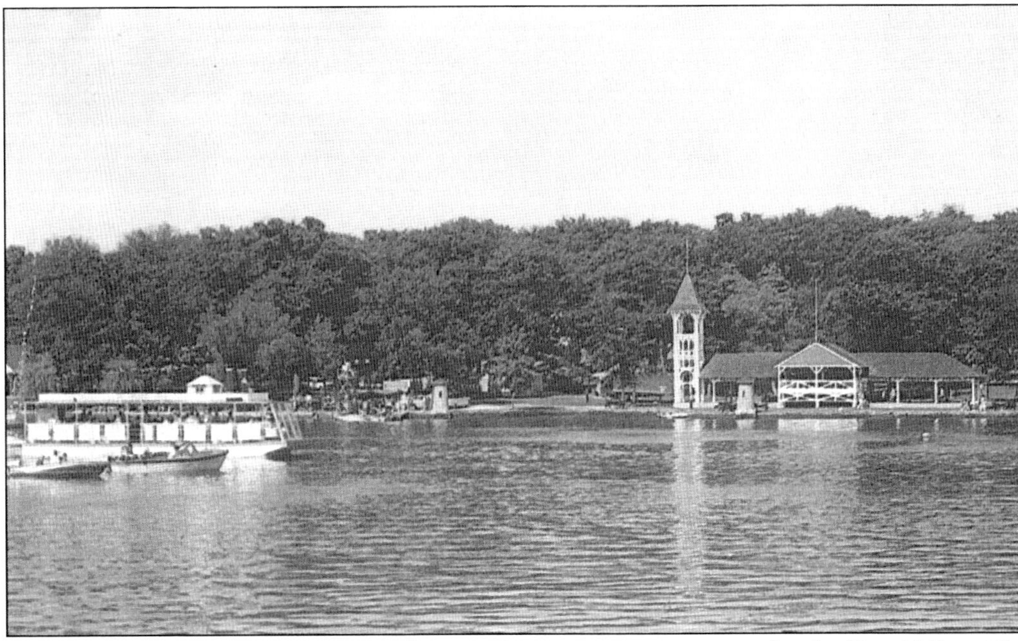

By the late 1920s, Pottawatomie Park was a favorite recreation spot for the Fox Valley. The pavilion was used for dancing, picnicking, and watching boating activity on the river. Notice the presence of gas-powered speed boats and the large excursion boat.

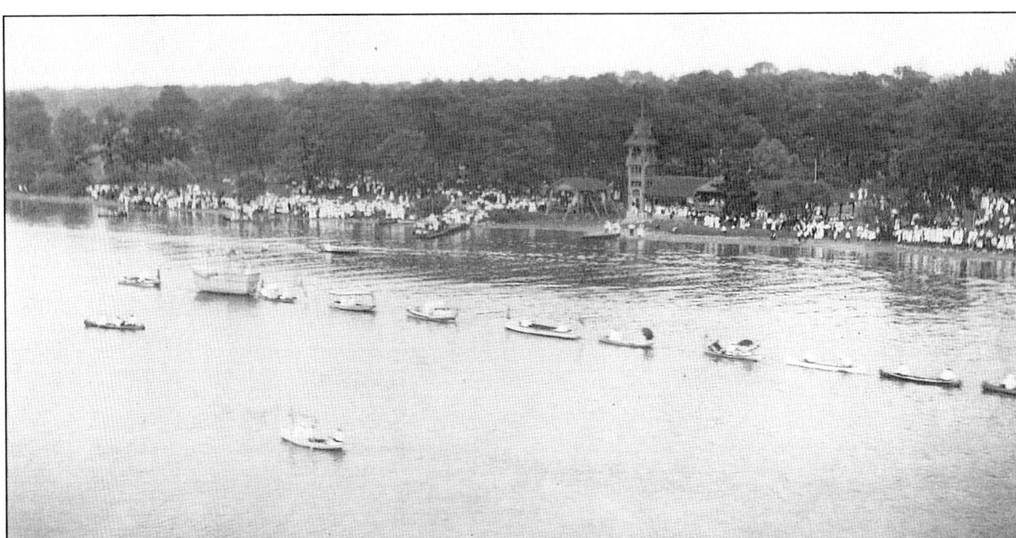

Earling Holmstrom remembered the days when there was a parade up and down the river every Labor Day weekend with boats and canoes, floats, and Japanese-colored lanterns. Hundreds of spectators gathered in Pottawatomie Park and on the other side of the river to watch this regatta, complete with a miniature Spanish galley and a Norse ocean-going vessel.

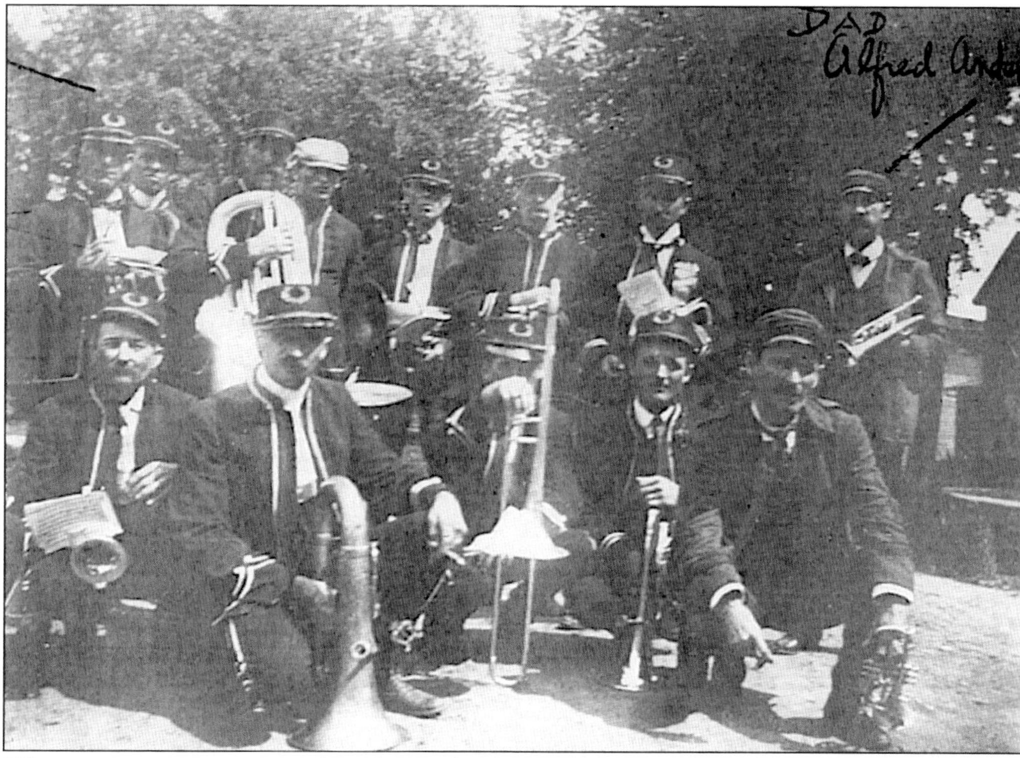


What is summertime in a park without a local oompah band? Here is the St. Charles city band about 1895, uniformed complete with gold braiding. Only Alfred Anderson, in the back row, far right, is identified in the picture. There are summer cottages on the right side of this picture.

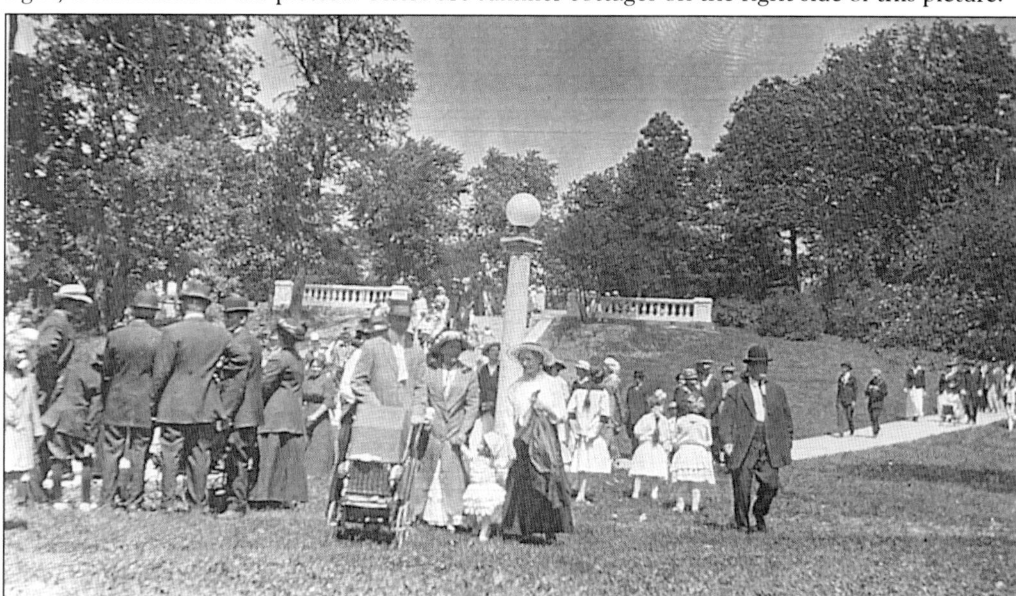

Here are families all dressed up for a Sunday afternoon in Pottawatomie Park. In 1915 the first statue of Pottawatomie was placed in the colonnade area. It was 6 feet tall but didn't resemble a real Native American very much. This statue was later vandalized and removed.

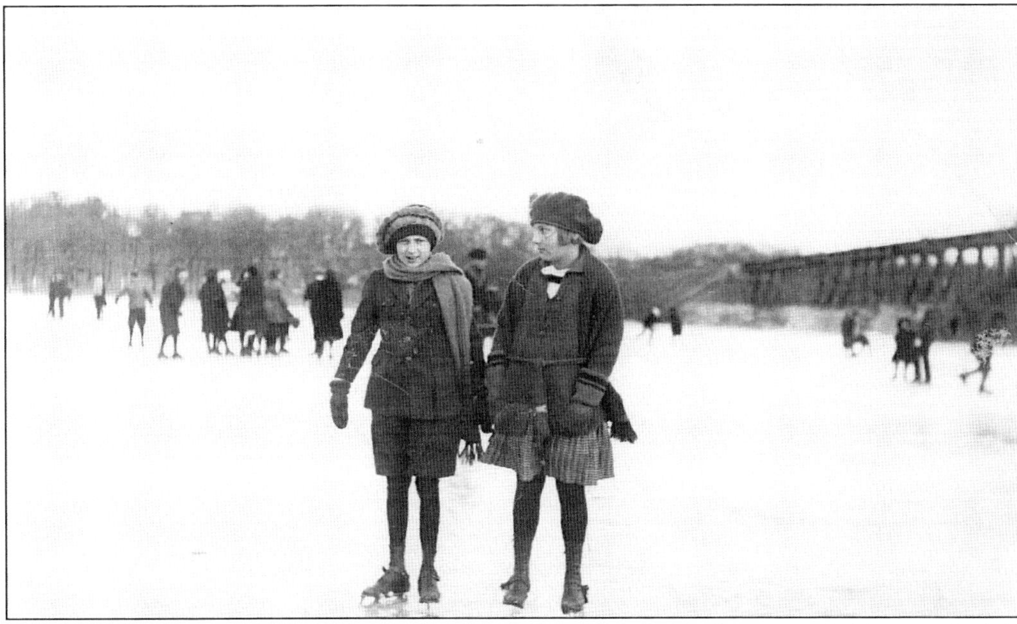

The river was popular in winter months also. All up and down the river, children and adults alike skated on the ice. Shoe skates were not yet the fashion. Blades were put on expandable platforms, which were strapped onto the shoes.

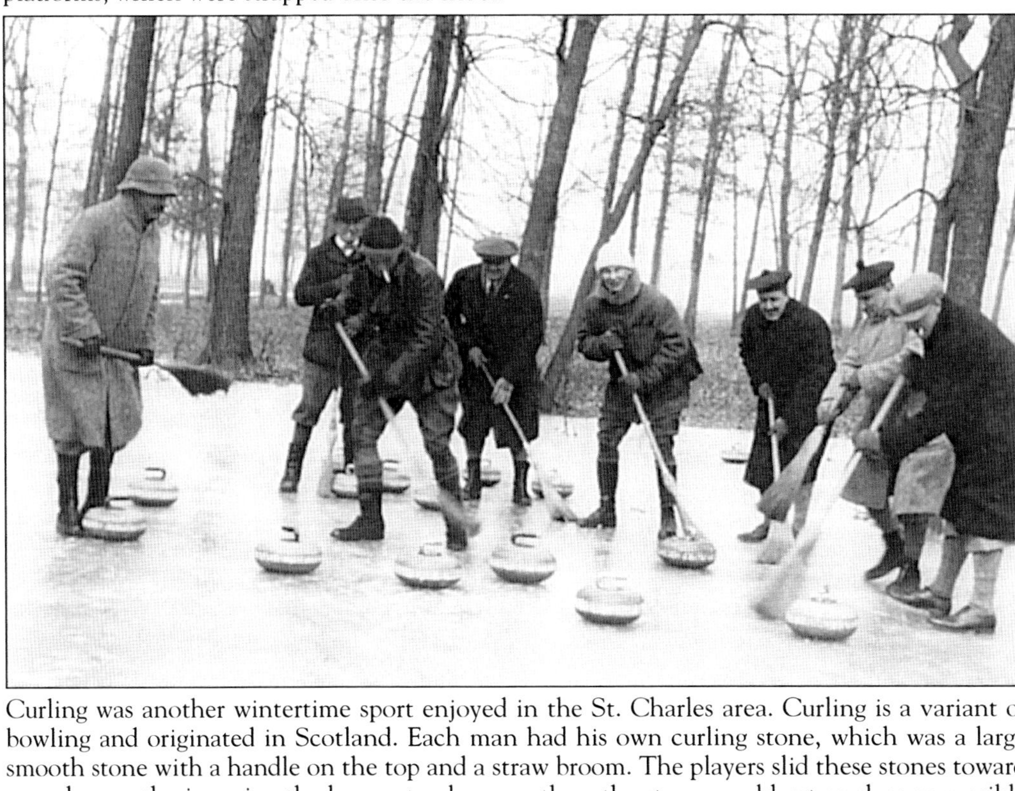

Curling was another wintertime sport enjoyed in the St. Charles area. Curling is a variant of bowling and originated in Scotland. Each man had his own curling stone, which was a large smooth stone with a handle on the top and a straw broom. The players slid these stones toward a marker on the ice using the broom to clear a path so the stone would get as close as possible to the marker.

# *Seven*

# Home & Garden
## *The Beautiful Lifestyle Emerges*

When the new and prosperous middle class emerged in America during the height of the boom days of the Industrial Revolution, they attained a lifestyle not unlike the ruling class as defined by the Vanderbilts, Eastmans, Goulds, and Fields. Soon, many of these middle-class entrepreneurs would be regarded as full-fledged barons of wealth.

Books were written to teach this new middle-class America how to talk, how to read the language of flowers, how to eat at the table, and hundreds of other social refinements of the day. Mansions with many tiny rooms were being built, and the front parlors were repositories of countless bric-a-brac from all over the world. One's home truly was one's castle, and even the garden was expected to be picture perfect.

The fashions of Paris or New York were eagerly sought and found in local stores. Clothing was becoming available from local stores and from catalogues, and even small town stores were developing into department stores.

The dogs of war interrupted the general euphoria that had swept the land and the people of the valley. Following World War I in the mid-1920s, prosperity and bathtub gin were back. Upward-bound St. Charles boomed with a new palace of entertainment, the Arcada, and for the traveler, Hotel Baker.

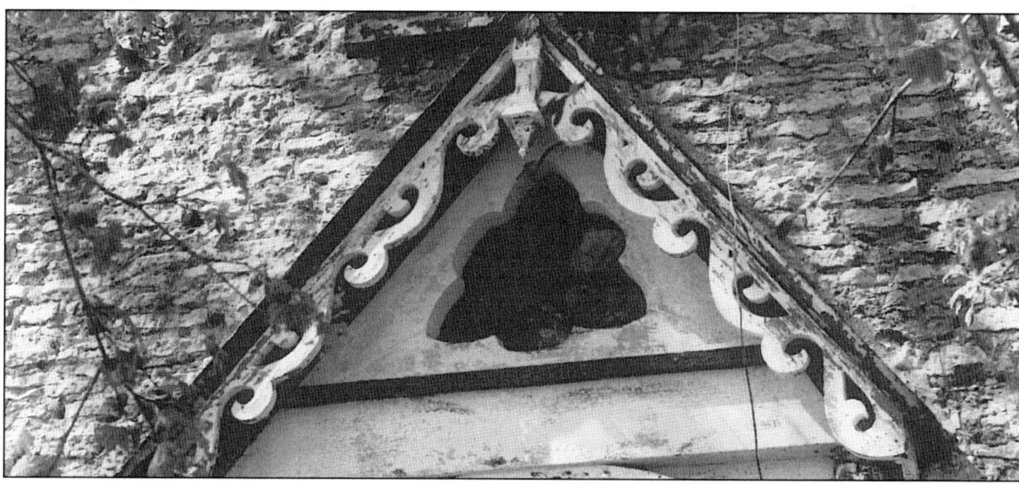

European architectural traditions can be found scattered all over the city of St. Charles. Local limestone was used to build the Dearborn House. There is an element of Victorian gingerbread with a Scandinavian influence in the trim used for the house.

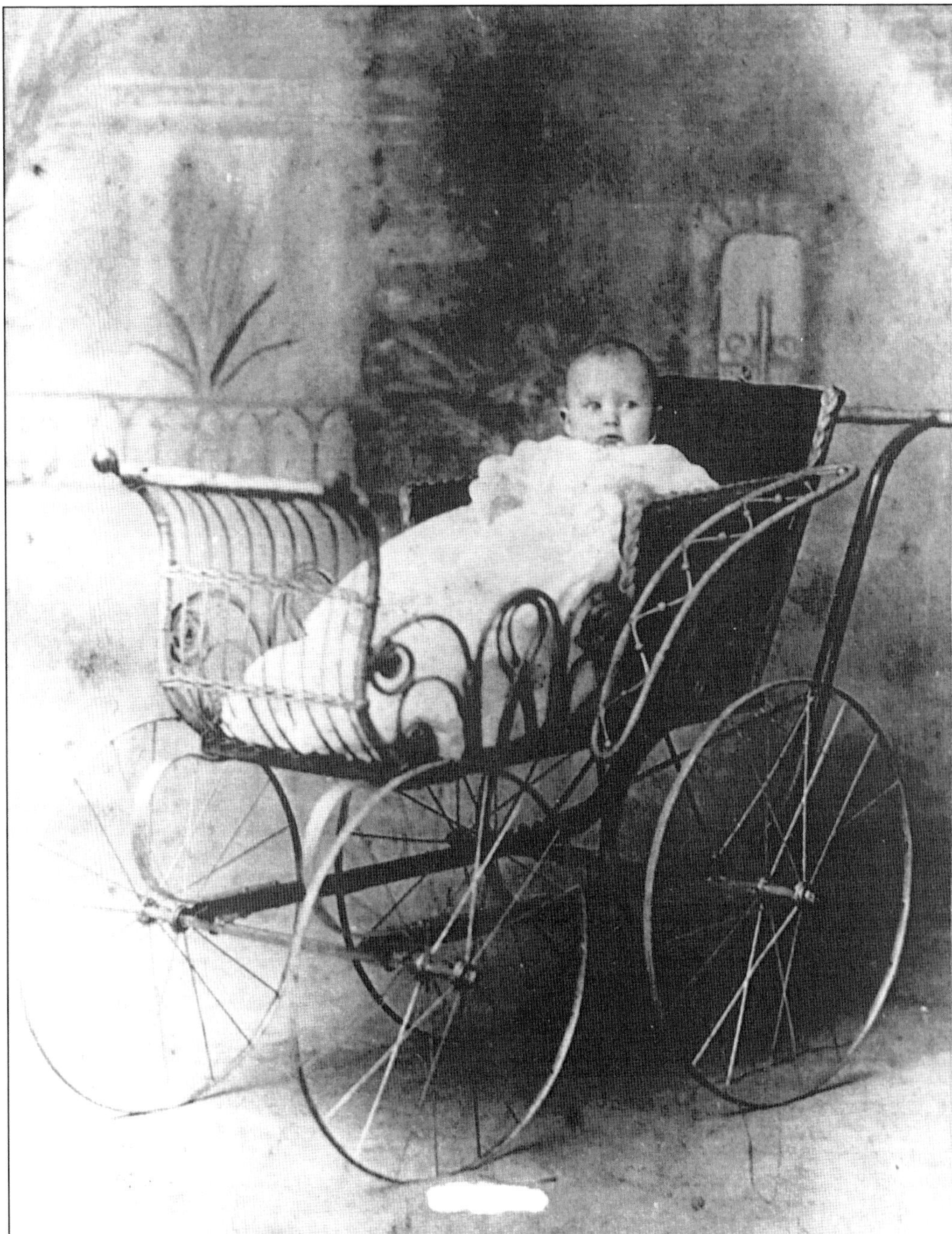

Baby Walter Hahn is sitting in a buggy that was the height of fashion. This baby carriage may look like a photographer's expensive prop, but for $6 or so, anyone could purchase a carriage like this with a lace-covered umbrella made of silesia. The carriage was made of a reed body, hand woven and shellacked. There were steel wheels and axles, springs, and an automatic brake. If rubber-tired wheels were wanted, they could be had for an additional 75¢. The upholstery came in a variety of colors. In chapter one, in the S Veale & Sons picture, the front of a carriage like this can be seen to the left. A painted mural was used as a backdrop.

Marion Reilly, cousin of James Brennan, is dressed in the style of little girls around the turn of the century, complete with a blousy, layered dress, a locket, and an oversized hair bow. When she posed for this picture, little girls wore high, buttoned shoes. Children of the time were well dressed and well behaved, speaking only when spoken to in the presence of adults. This basic dress was shown in the 1908 Sears catalogue.

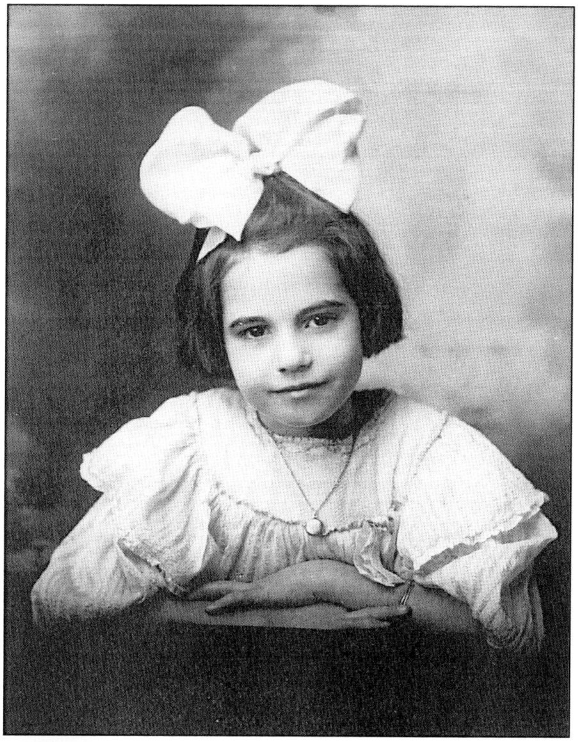

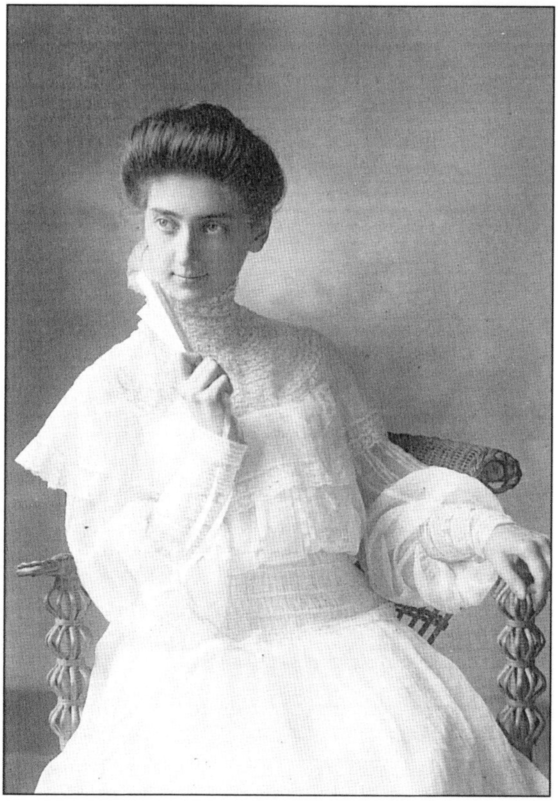

Belle Alexander married her engineer husband in 1904. According to the notation on the picture, this was her high school graduation picture of the same year. Either she or her dressmaker had quite a talent with tucks and laces. Heavy eyebrows like hers were fashionable at this time. With the brows and the beautiful hair, Belle would have made a wonderful candidate for the society painter Sargent.

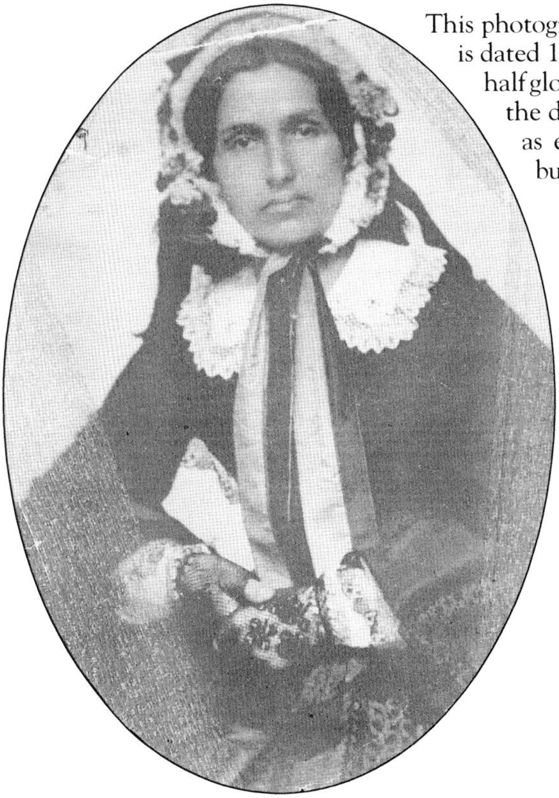

This photograph of Mary Lee Burr, wife of James Burr, is dated 1843. Lace adorns her hat, collar, cuffs, and half gloves. Flowers, ribbons, and ruffles help soften the dark material of her smock. She is every bit as elegant and beautiful as Belle Alexander, but dress for women was very austere.

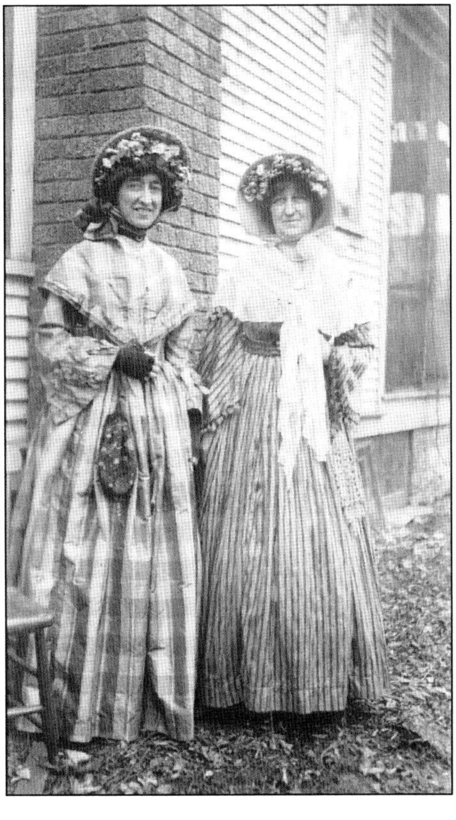

Both Hattie Glos (left) and Myrtle Gray were from pioneer St. Charles farming families. Flowers adorn their bonnets, and both are wearing shawls. Myrtle's is more likely a Spanish or Mexican mantilla. Their small waists were formed by steel corsets.

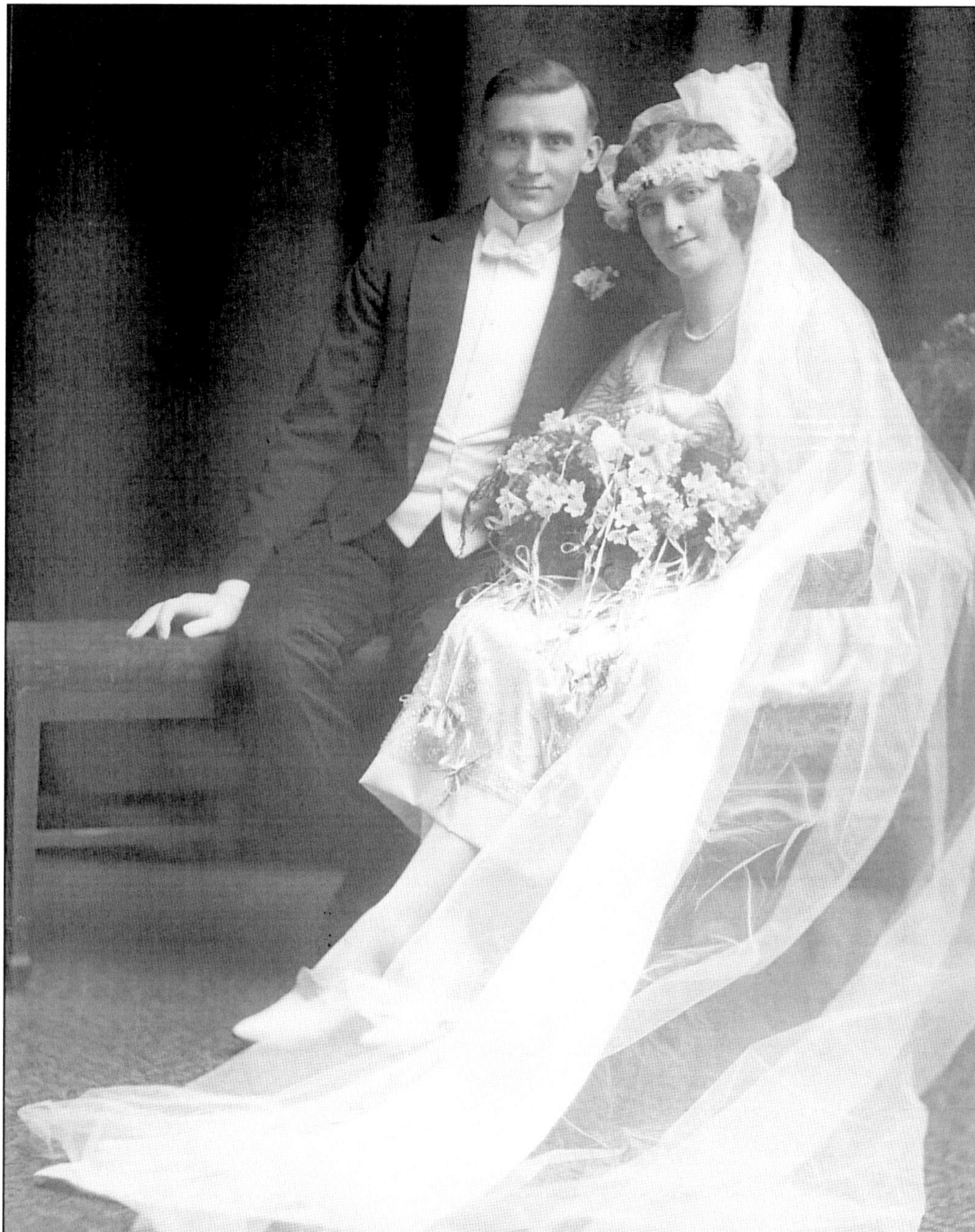

It is hard to imagine a more elegant wedding couple than these two. This early 1900s wedding photograph is from an album donated by a member of the Anderson family. It is thought that the bride is Myrtle Anderson. The groom's tuxedo, with the high collar, and the bride's dress, with its shortened skirt, were very fashionable for the period. The beads on the dress could have been cultured pearls made from clams in the Fox River. The bride's bouquet has ribbon streamers with "love knots" tied at the end, most with blossoms in them. The bride is seated in a chair, and the groom is on a piano bench drawn up to the chair. Later pictures in the album show this couple as still retaining their looks.

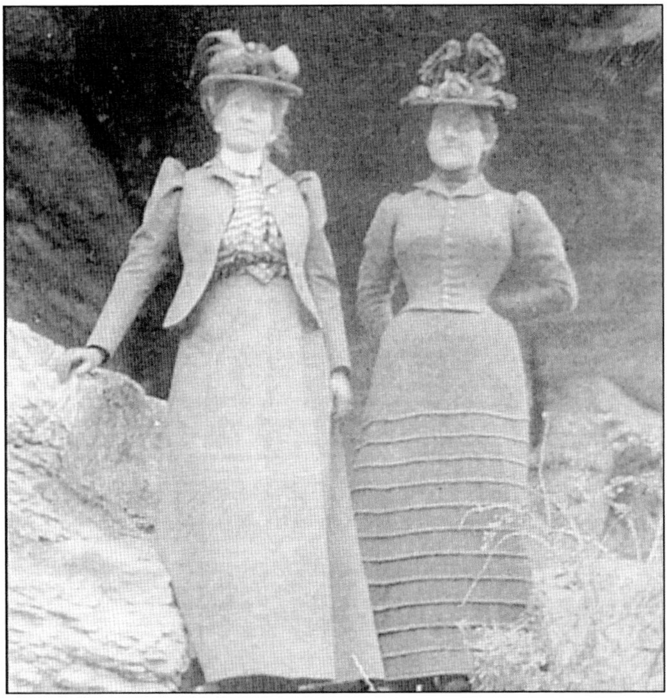

Not all entrepreneurs were men as the new century gained momentum. Hattie Wing, on the right, is enjoying the outdoors with an unidentified friend. Hattie and Anna H. Hammer operated the Pinelands resort north of St. Charles. In 1918 they bought 10 acres south of Pinelands and developed Oak Ridge Camp. Hattie was the daughter of Clinton Wing, the second mayor of St. Charles.

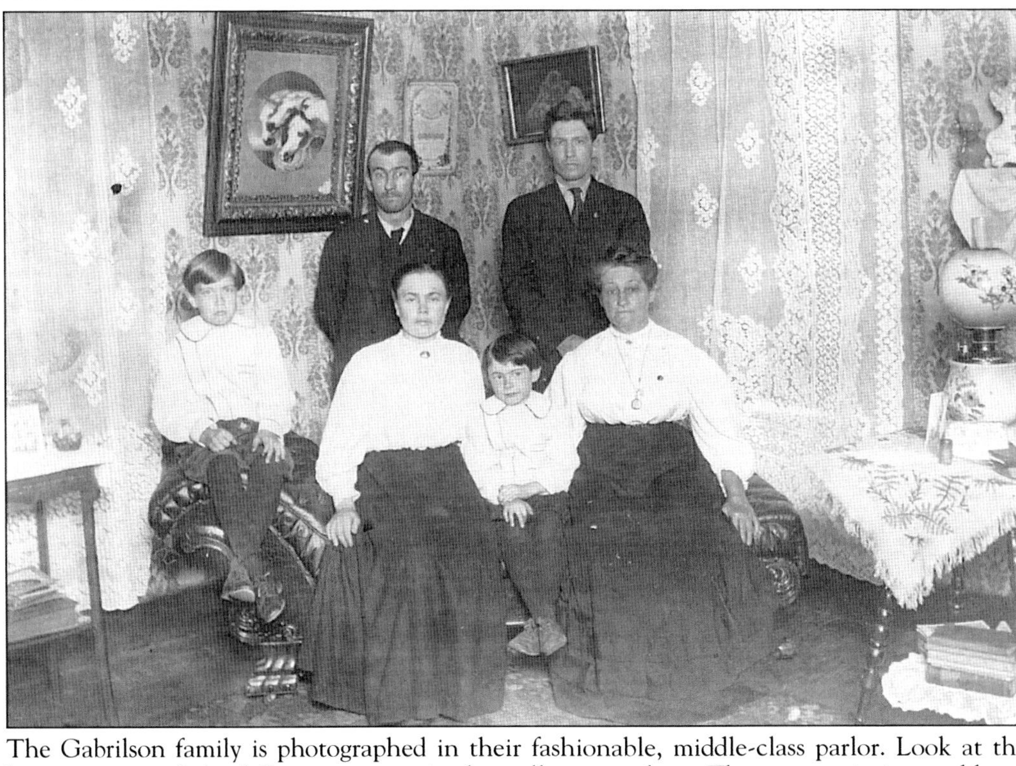

The Gabrilson family is photographed in their fashionable, middle-class parlor. Look at the lace curtains and the different patterns in the wallpaper and rug. The many paintings, tabletop objects, lamps, and clocks were typical in the over-done Victorian period. The family is posed on a heavily carved fainting couch.

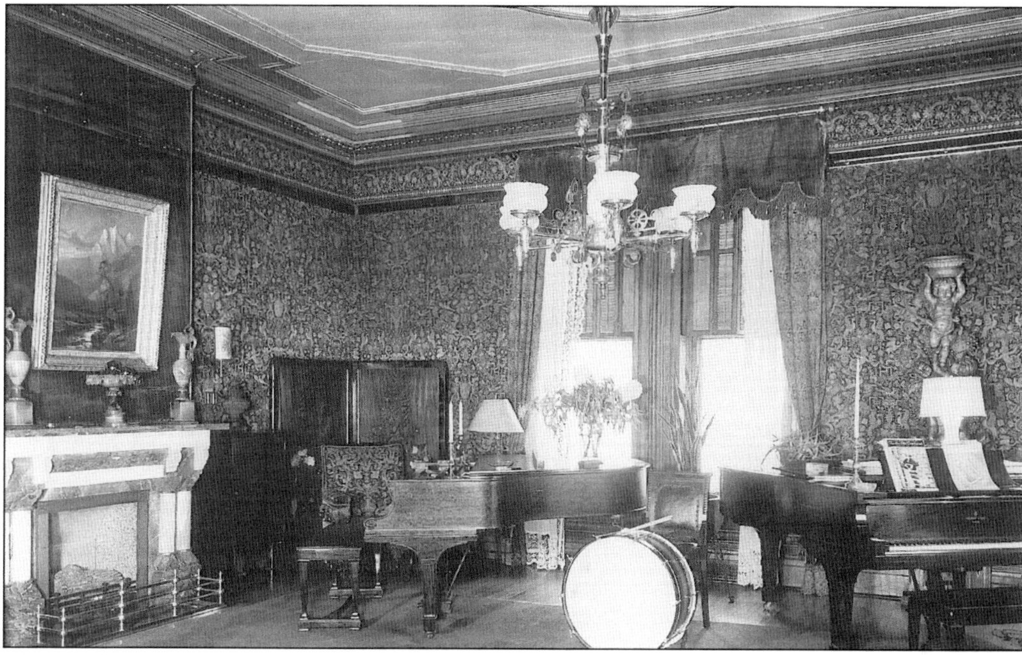

The Dunham castle parlor was remade into a music room but the tapestries on the walls and the tapestry-covered furniture were kept. The wallpaper in the Dunham Hunt Museum was chosen to resemble this tapestry. Live music in the home was the norm at the turn of the century, and many homes had a piano. This music room is set up for music combos and could be used for dancing as well.

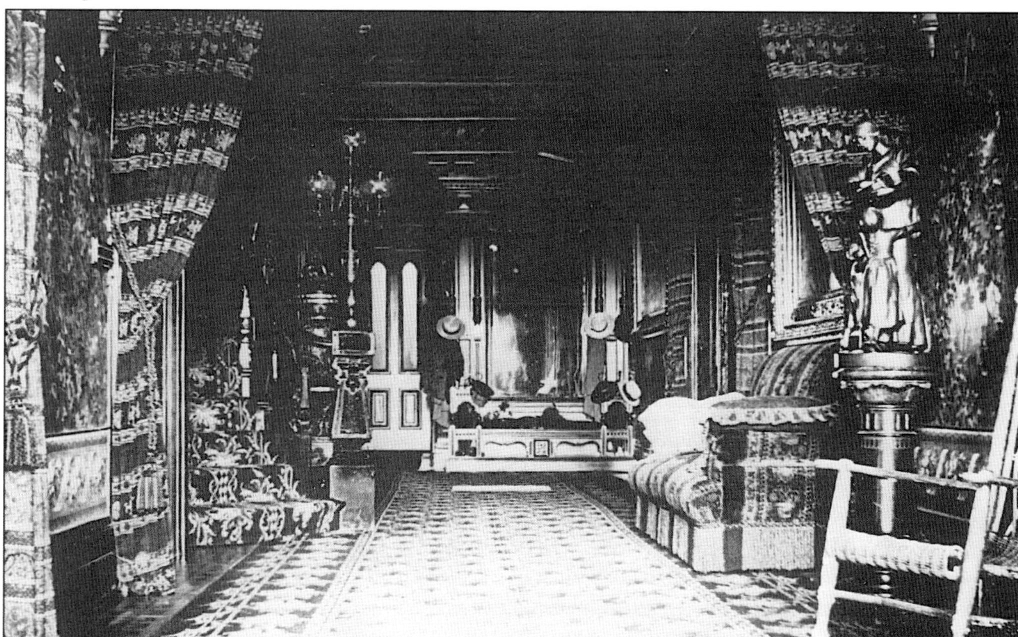

When the Dunham castle was built, pine, black walnut, and butternut woods were used inside, and the floors were laid in white ash and black walnut. Rich tapestries were imported to cover the walls, and rugs covered the floors. This photograph is of one of the hallways in the castle.

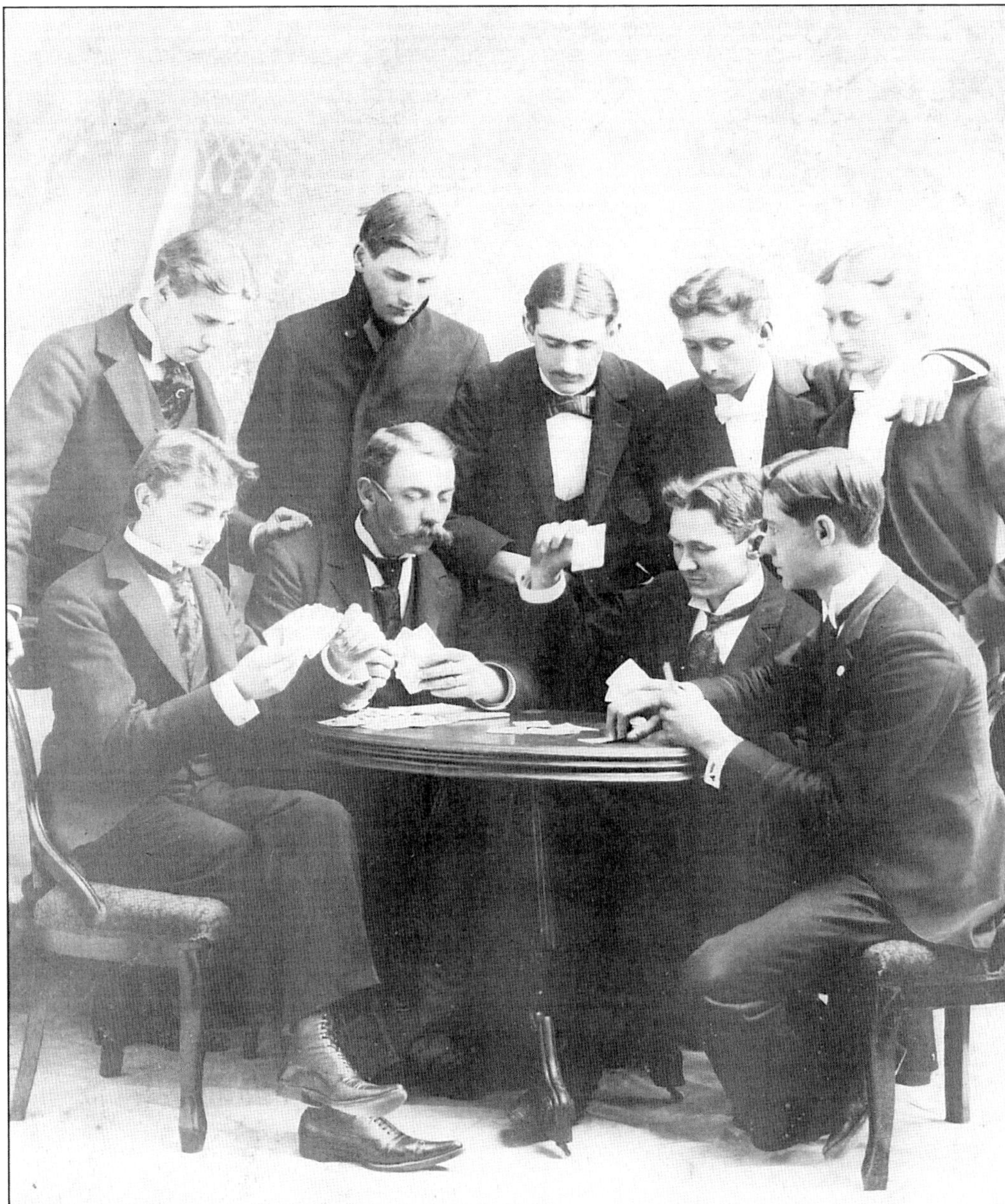

These intent young men are, from left to right, as follows: (standing) Charles Hunt, Fred Matoon, Fred Miller, Fred Pools, and Louis (Doc) Andrews; (sitting) Frank Jorney, Spencer Smith Huls, Bert Huls, and Tom Fisher. These young men posed for this photograph in 1896, dressed in their finest. From the 1910 City Directory, we find that Charles Hunt, grandson of Bela, was an attorney who also made real estate loans and sold fire insurance. Fred Miller was a dentist, while Fred Poole was a clerk at Thatcher's Grocery Store. Louis Andrews clerked at Moline Malleable Iron Company, and S.S. Huls was in business with his father as a merchant. Tom Fisher was a machinist at Crown Electric. The four at the table are probably playing whist, a predecessor to bridge. Stylish young men were usually clean shaven, and high-laced shoes were fashionable.

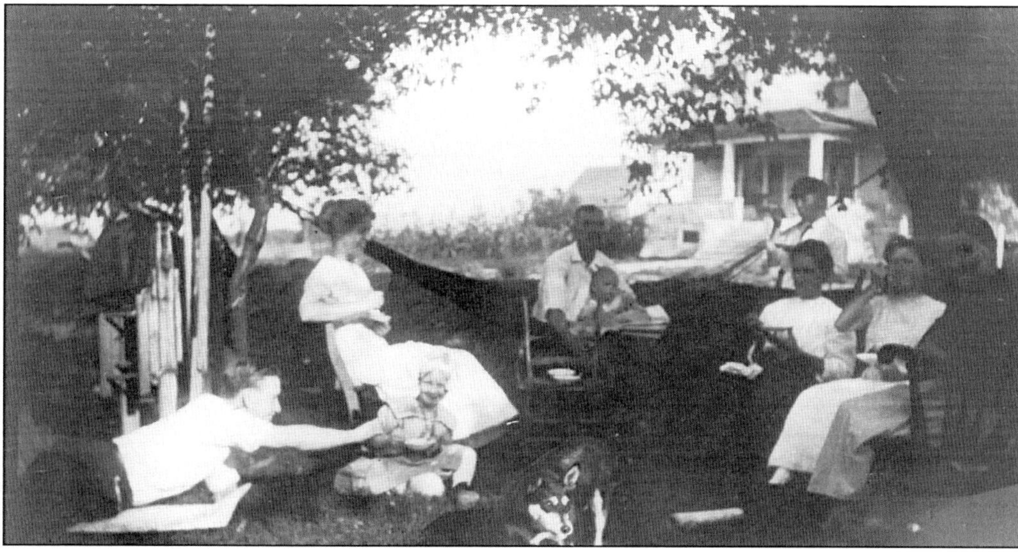

This picture of unidentified people, under the shady trees on a nearby farm with their bowls of freshly made ice cream, is captioned by one of the children, "a real treat ceeping cool." The misspelled caption reminds us that many children at the turn of the century were not so well educated. They read and wrote phonetically.

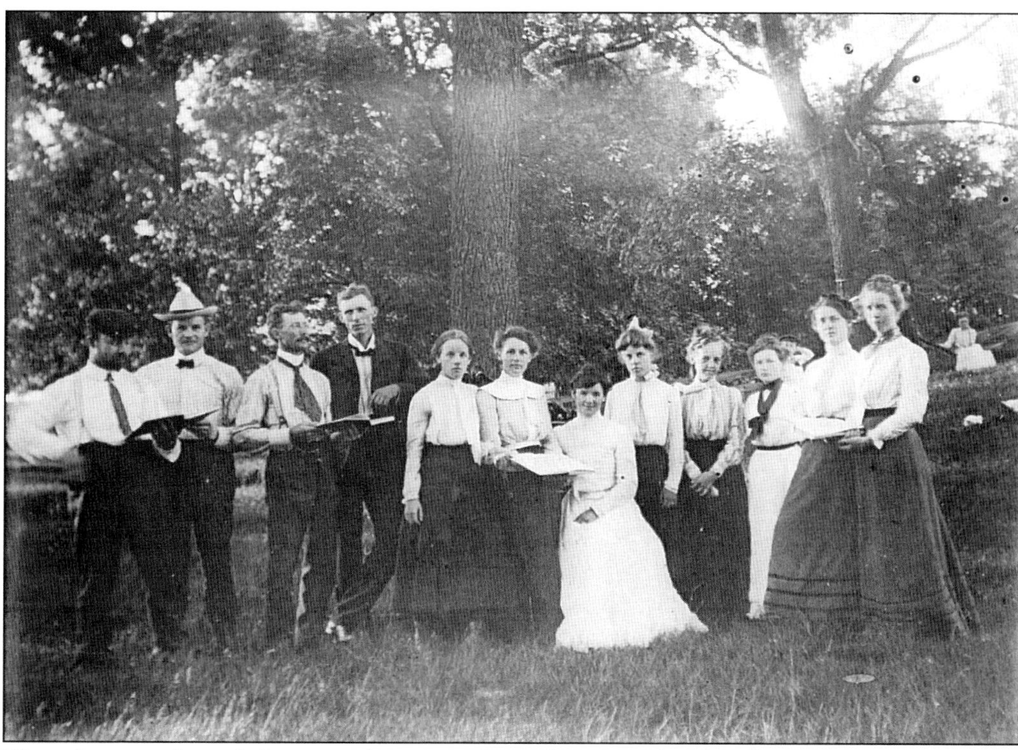

This photograph and the one above are from the same family album, one of the several unidentified family albums in the St. Charles Heritage Center's collection. This group is the Bethlehem Lutheran Choir. The only identified person is Fritz, second from the right.

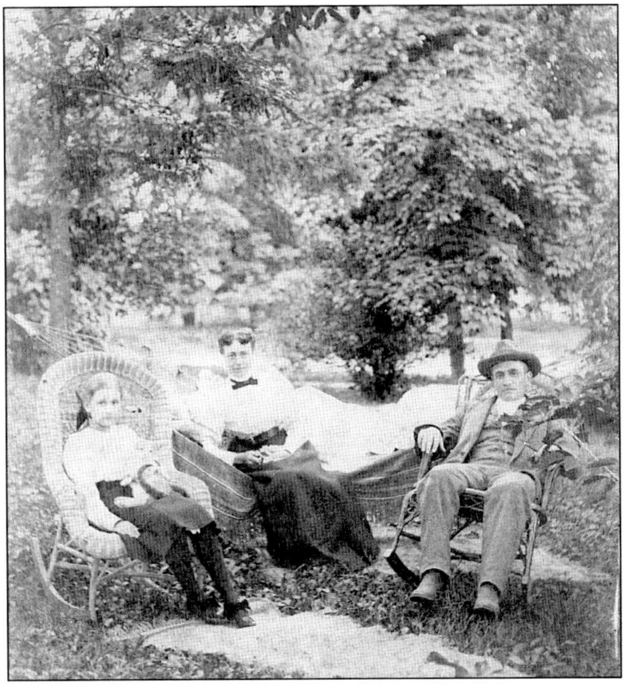

William Morse and his brother Levi had a meat market at the west end of the Main Street Bridge. William and his wife, Jennie, are enjoying a summer day outside with their daughter Norma. Norma was known for her beauty and, in later years, continued this family tradition of spending happy hours outside with her friends. Norma's cat is at attention in her lap, with her dark tail caught frozen in action.

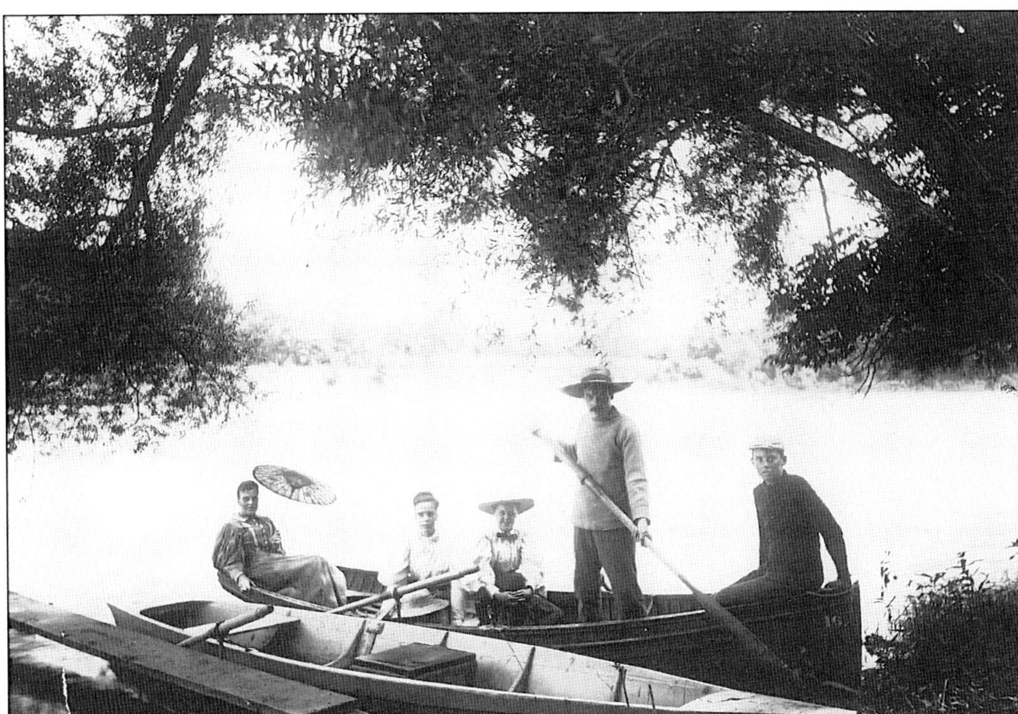

The Underwood family enjoyed being outdoors in the beautiful Fox River environment. Here, one woman keeps to the shade with her Japanese parasol as the family keeps cool on the Fox River. Underwood was a master photographer to have caught such intensity of enjoyment.

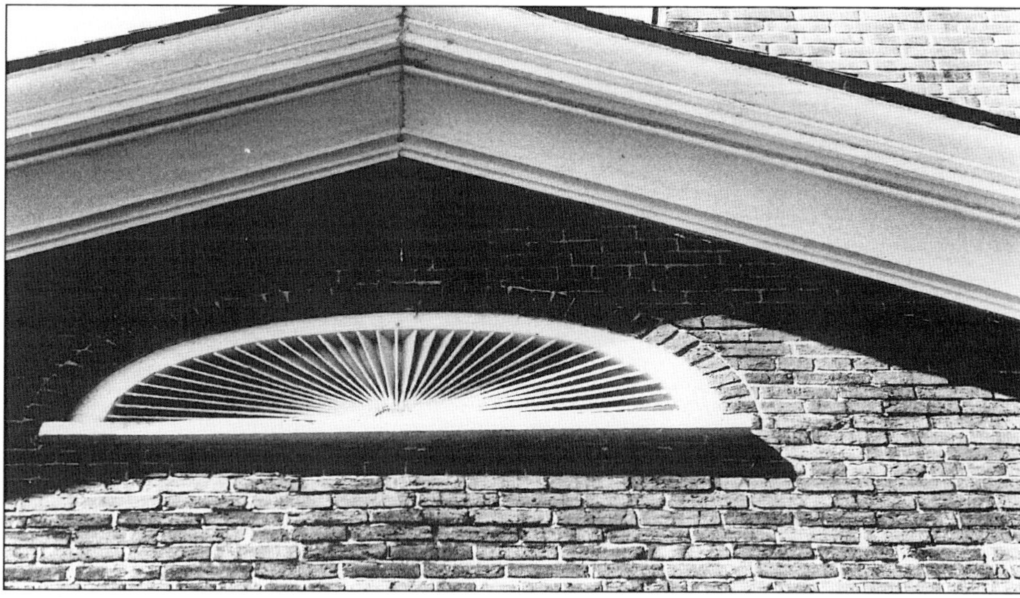

Residents of St. Charles adorned their houses with details to give aesthetic appeal to their dwellings. This fan-shaped grill ventilated the attic and kept the birds and hot air out of the Hunt house.

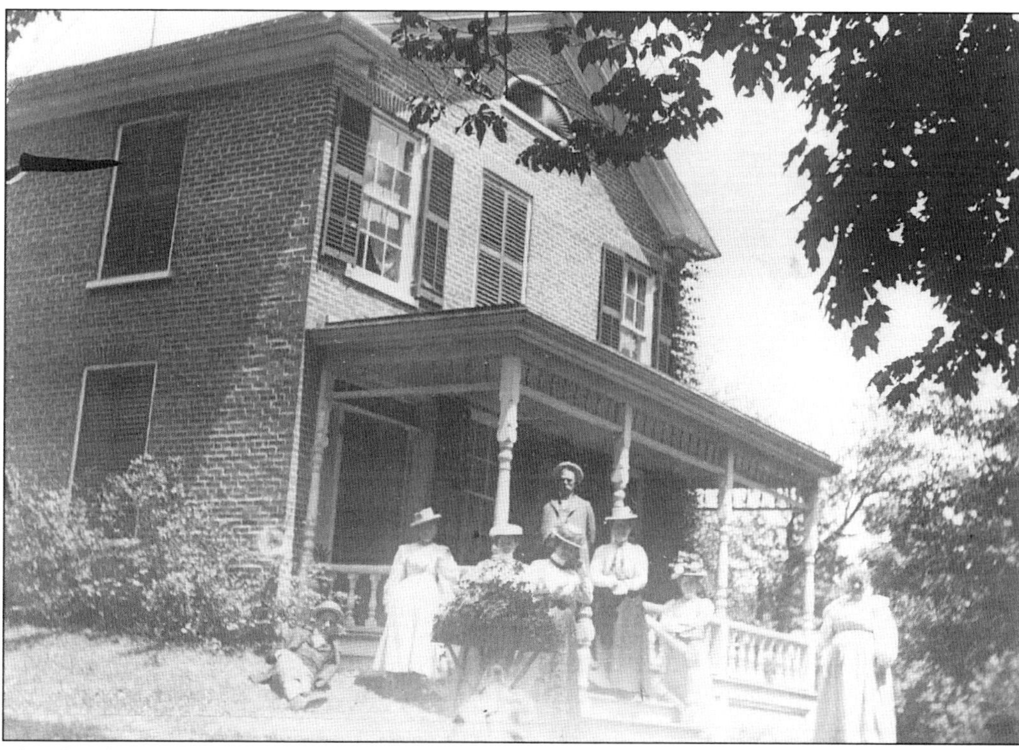

The family of Frank B. Hunt and their employees are standing in front of their house at 304 Cedar. Frank, the son of Bela T. Hunt, is on the front porch. Frank Hunt served as mayor in three separate terms: 1880 to 1895, 1899 to 1905, and 1907 to 1911. Note the matching fan-shaped attic ventilator as well as the working shutters on the windows.

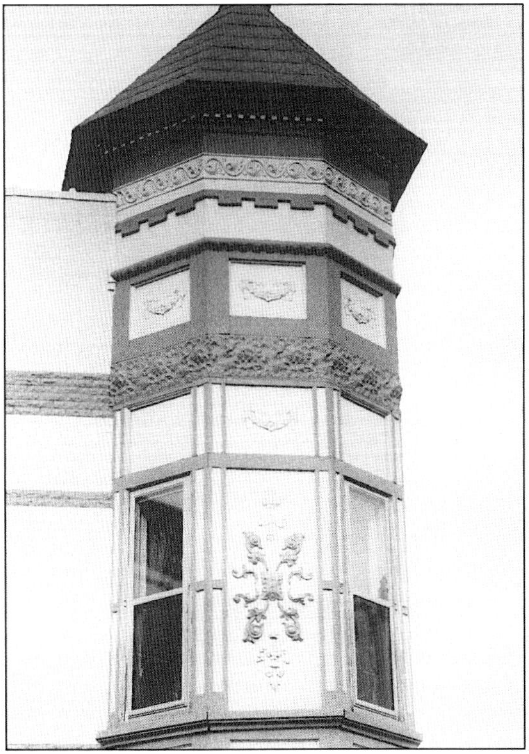

The Osgood Building reflected a resurgence in the commerce of St. Charles at the turn of the century. When the building was rebuilt, the architect didn't just design a plain block building but added features such as this turret, with the ornate metal strip and curved wooden details. You can see this detail at the corner of Main and First Streets.

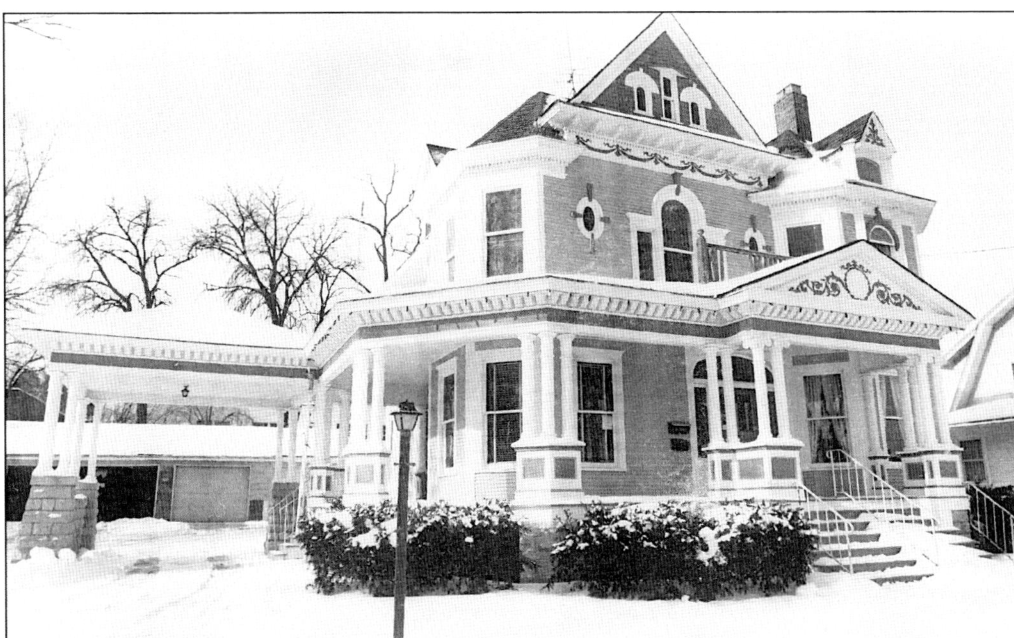

The James B. Horne House, at 411 South Second Street, was built in 1898 for $8,000. Horne and F.J. Mosedale owned the Crown Electric Manufacturing Company. Later, Horne formed the St. Charles Fixture Manufacturing Company. This Queen Anne wedding cake delight reflected his standing in the community.

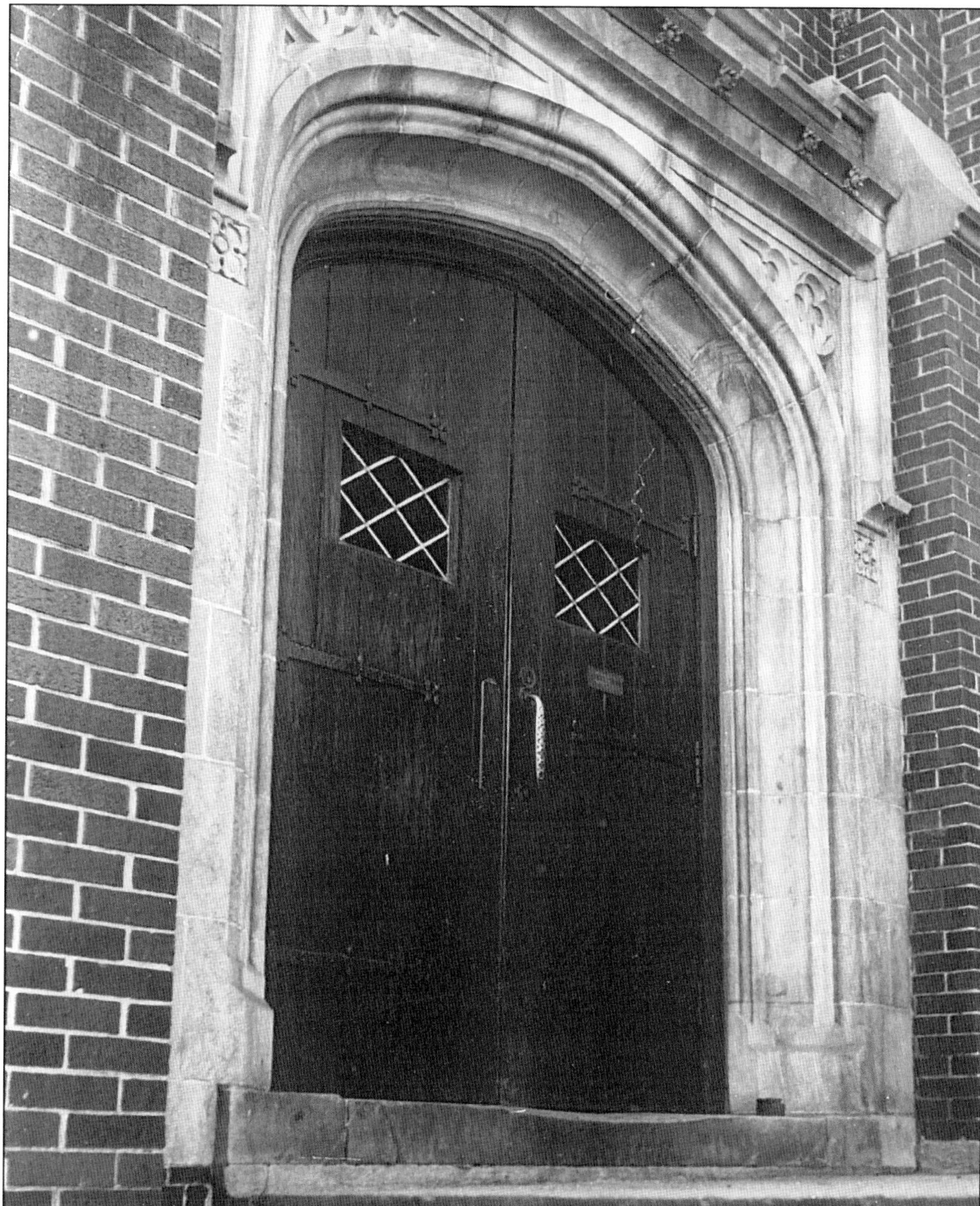

This is one of the entrances to the Henry Rockwell Baker Memorial Community Center. Architects Wolf, Sexton, Harper, & Truex blended the Medieval styles of Gothic and Tudor to give the feeling of permanence to the Community Center. In the spirit of these styles, local craftsmen were used to craft the leaded windows, half-timbered, stucco walls, the slate roof, and ashlar stone and brick work. Much attention was paid to the details of the building as evidenced by this doorway. The heavily detailed entrance is inviting and friendly in appearance. The surrounding grounds were landscaped under the supervision of the Garden Club of St. Charles.

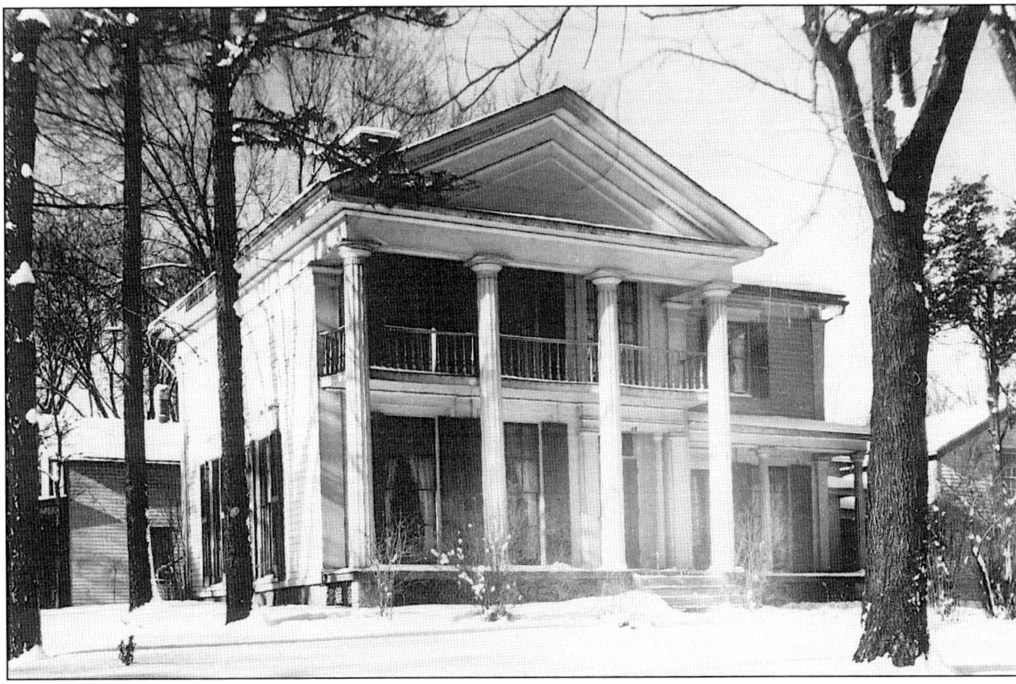

Dr. James K. Lewis built this mansion in 1859. It is an excellent example of the early Greek Revival style of architecture with its two-story portico and Ionic-style columns. The floor-to-ceiling windows were typical of Southern houses, where capturing the available breeze was essential to comfort. Lewis was both the first and third mayor of St. Charles.

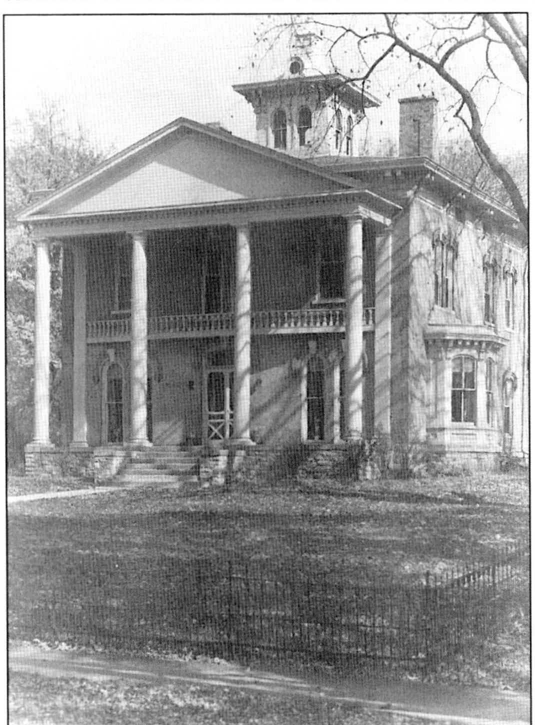

The Homer Gillette Mansion, at 416 N. Second Avenue, is a northern adaptation of an antebellum style. The front is similar to the Horne residence, but the brickwork extends to the ground instead of leaving room for circulating air. Rounded stone arches top the windows, and the sleeping porch on the second floor is for show only. No doors lead out to it.

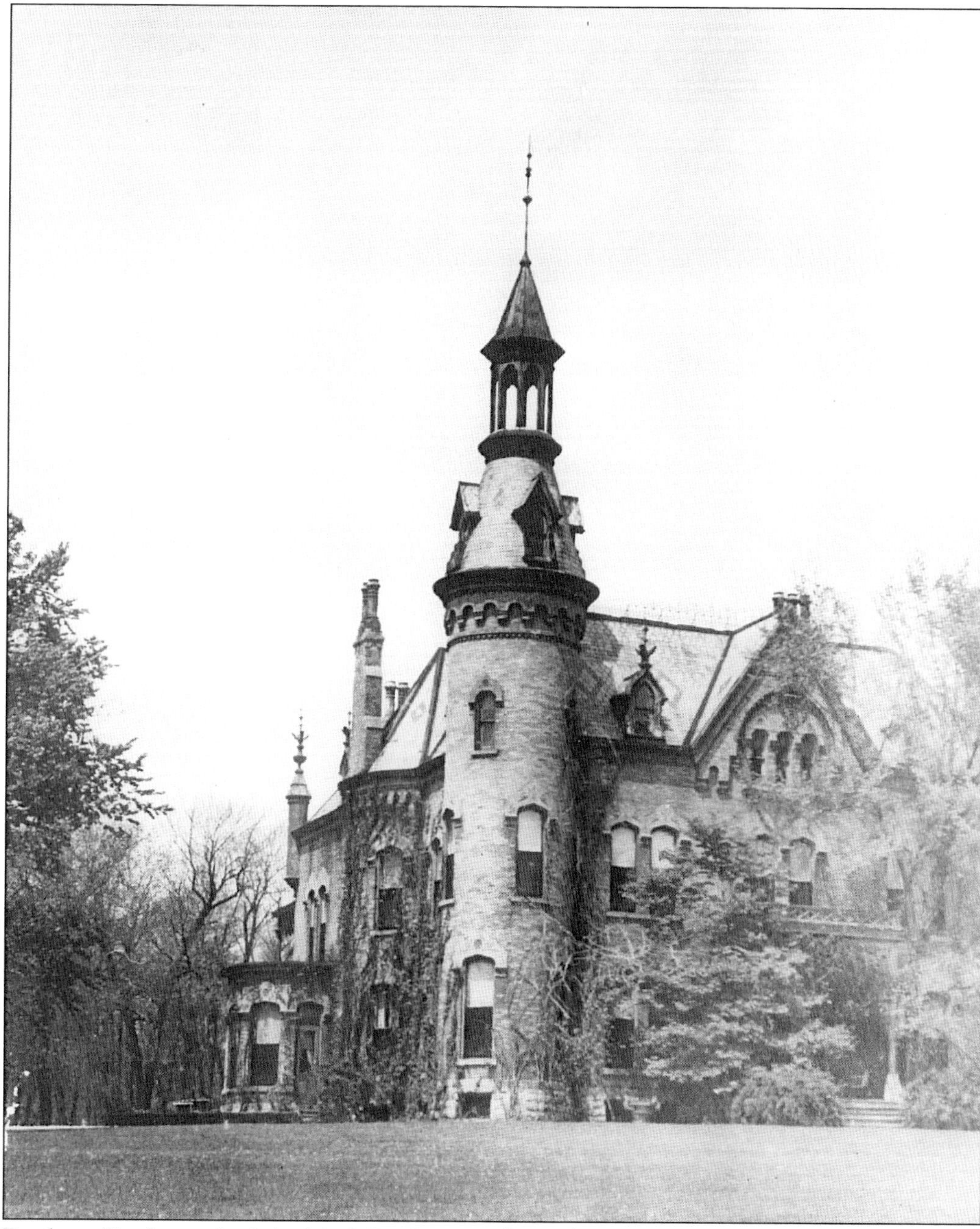

Dunham Castle was built by Mark Dunham in the early 1880s. The castle was patterned after a French chateau he had seen on one of his trips to Normandy while he was purchasing horses. The style is a modification of the Norman and Gothic styles of architecture, with some French modifications. The 70-by-100-foot building is three stories tall with a mansard roof and two different style towers. Shown on the southeast corner is an impressive circular tower with a Gothic spire and finial. The northeast corner has an octagonal tower in the Norman style topped with a crenelated battlement appearance. The foundation was laid with Batavia stone, and the bricks were manufactured in Wisconsin. There are 25 to 30 rooms, which were, at the time of construction, fitted with the most advanced amenities of the day.

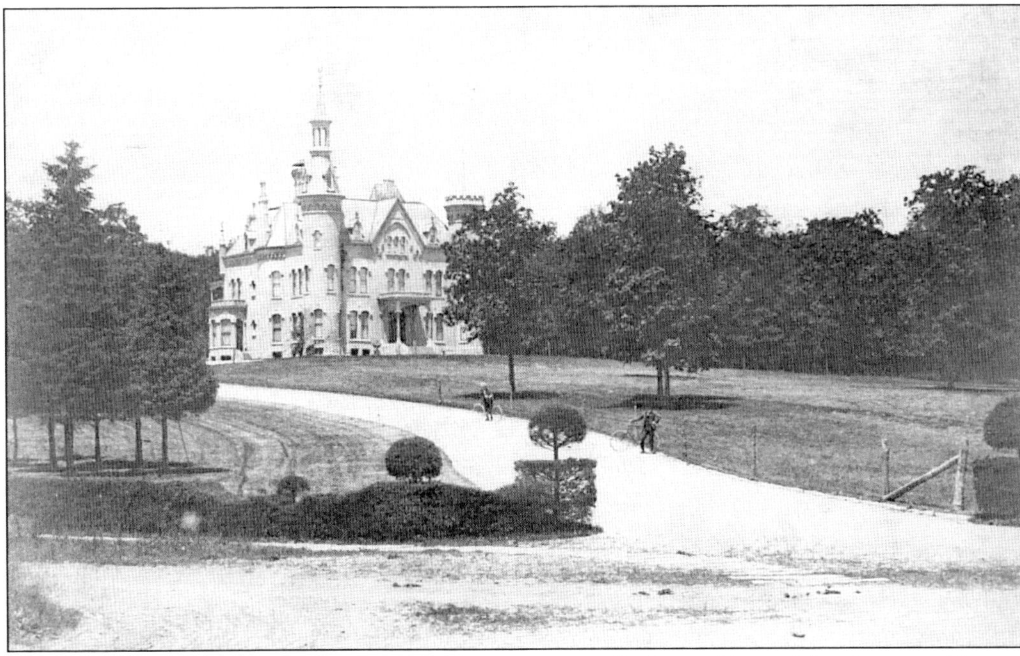

The Dunham Castle was set in a park-like setting in Oaklawn Farm. The farm itself was a showcase with five barns and 660 feet of stables. Horsemen travelled great distances to purchase Dunham's famous Percherons and to see the buildings on the farm. Bicycles, which were all the rage in the early 1900s, are more in evidence than horses in this photograph.

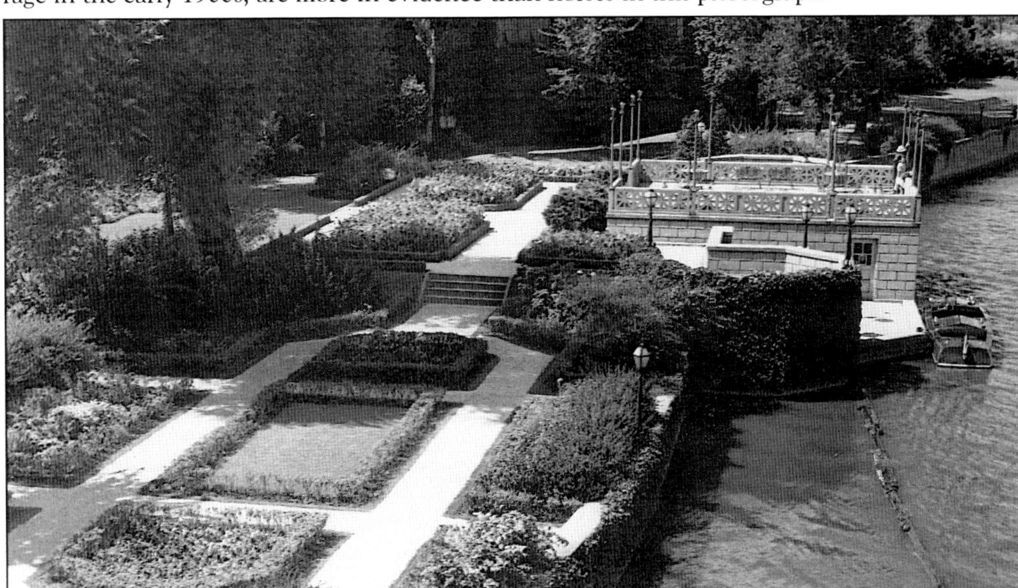

This photograph shows the Hotel Baker gardens as they were once planted. In the beginning, there was a rose garden with over 150 rose bushes in ten varieties surrounded by manicured privet hedges. Later, gardens featured masses of tulip bulbs in the spring and annuals later in the summer. There was once a rock garden as well as a goldfish pool. The observation deck building also served as a boat dock and storage area. The logs were used to keep boats from docking so people could climb into the garden.

# *Eight*

# PEOPLE
## *Haines, Texaco, and the Oldest Boy Scout*

The unwritten code of behavior for the wealthy was exemplified by Andrew Carnegie, the Scotsman who built a great fortune in steel. He gave all of his fortune away to worthy causes. He felt that a man who died wealthy was a disgrace because he had not given a major measure of his bounty to his community, state, or nation. He practiced what he preached for the most part by establishing dozens of endowments, hundreds of libraries (including the St. Charles Public Library) and church pipe organs, and building that great New York center of culture, Carnegie Hall.

St. Charles is lucky to have philanthropic people who lived by that code and provided for the city's current and future success. Very few communities can point to so many gifts of time, money, and talent as St. Charles. Rich, not so rich, and outright poor have all done their part to make the city of St. Charles the "Pride of the Fox."

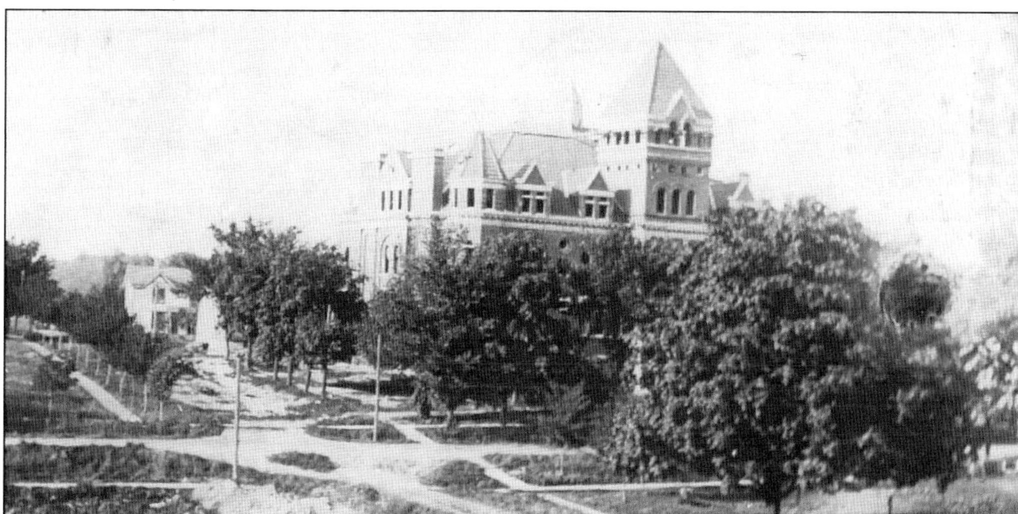

This photograph is of the school, completed in 1899, that united the east-side and west-side school systems. Once there were two school districts in St. Charles with the accompanying rivalry. After the districts consolidated in 1897, Charles H. Haines gave part of his family farm for the site of a future high school for the whole community.

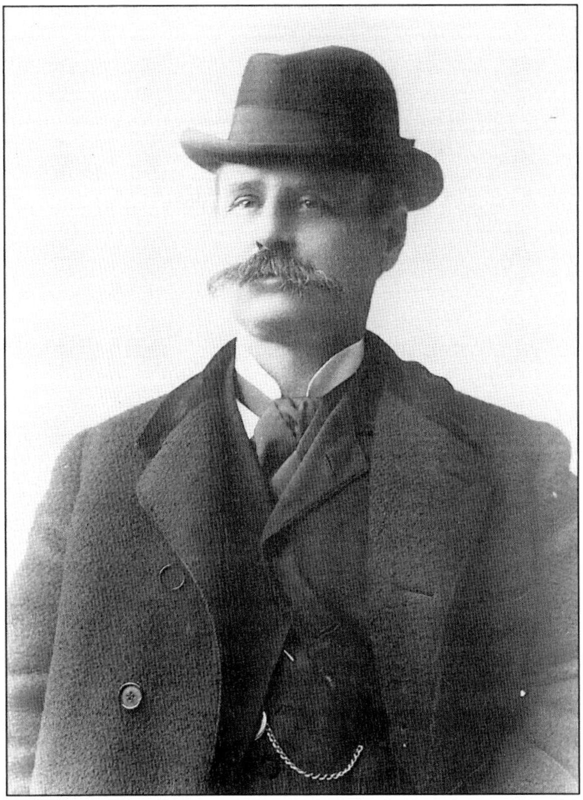

Charles H. Haines was born March 3, 1844, and lived in St. Charles his entire life. Education and community service were the focus of his life. He was president of the board of education from its consolidation until his death in 1914. He also served as mayor from 1889 to 1891.

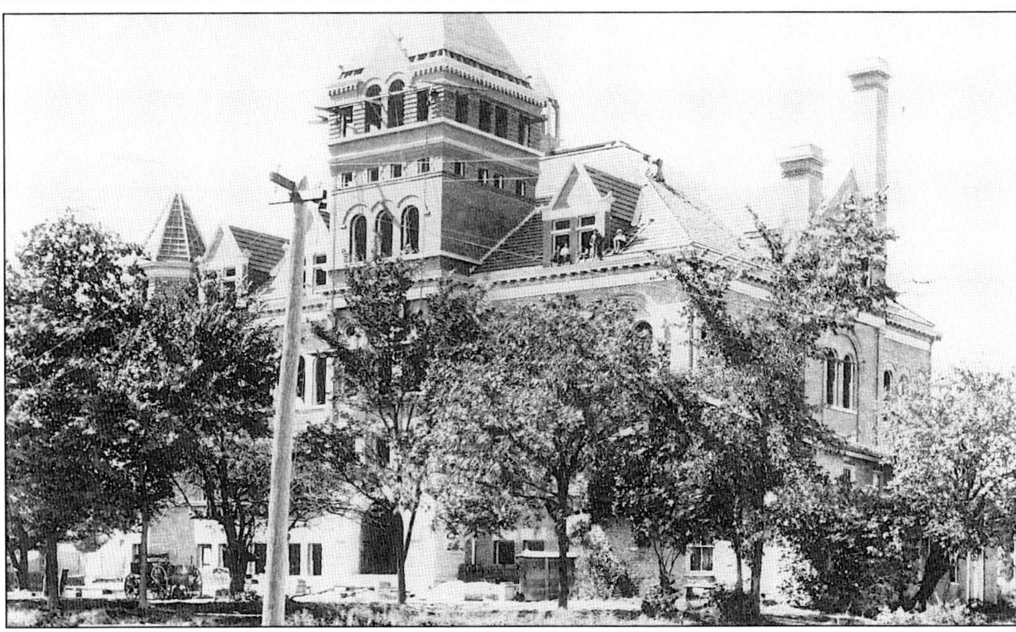

The school built on the Haines property featured skylights, gables, and towers. It served first as a high school and later as a junior high school. When he died, Haines bequeathed to the school district several additional acres of land in the area and in Chicago and $100,000 to benefit future generations of St. Charles students.

The influence of teacher Alice Davis overlaps that of community leader Charles Haines. Miss Davis graduated from St. Charles High School in 1901. After graduating from DeKalb's teachers college, she taught fourth and later, seventh and eighth grades. After further education, she returned and again taught junior high school before becoming the principal of that school. One of the later elementary schools is named for her.

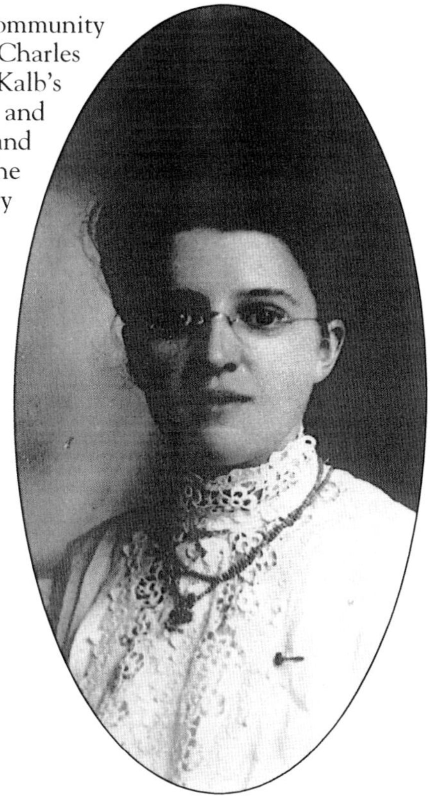

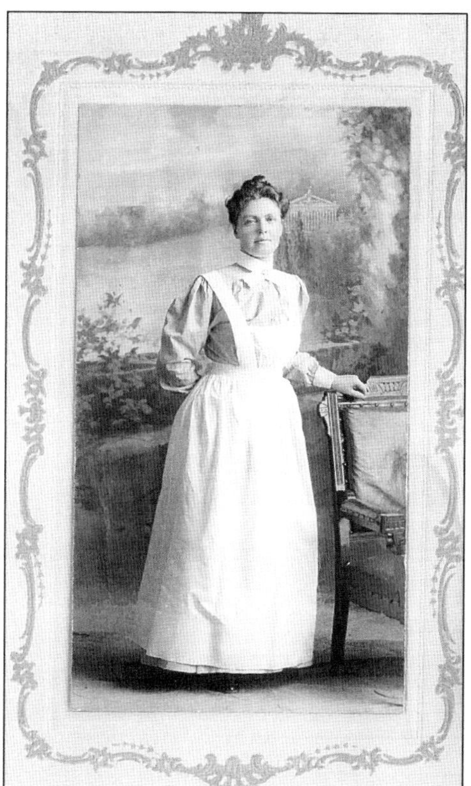

Amelia Anderson was the first nurse assigned to the schools. She is remembered not only for the care she gave during school hours, but also for the home visits to sick children. She also made sure that children and indigent adults received adequate health care, food, and clothing and often found resources for those in need.

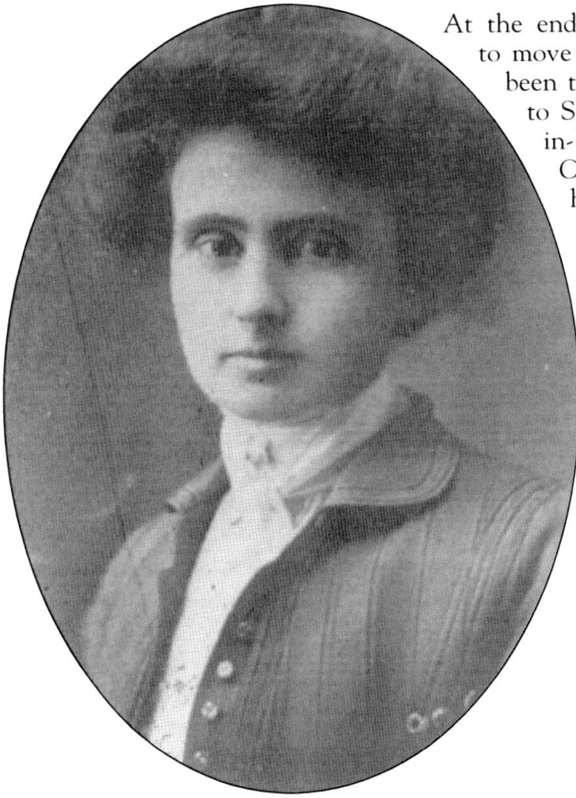

At the end of the 1800s, women were beginning to move into jobs and businesses that had once been the domain of men. Lina Paschal moved to St. Charles at the urging of her brother-in-law, who was editor of the *St. Charles Chronicle*. She purchased the paper from him and became the first area female editor. She was later honored for sending the hometown newspaper to service men overseas.

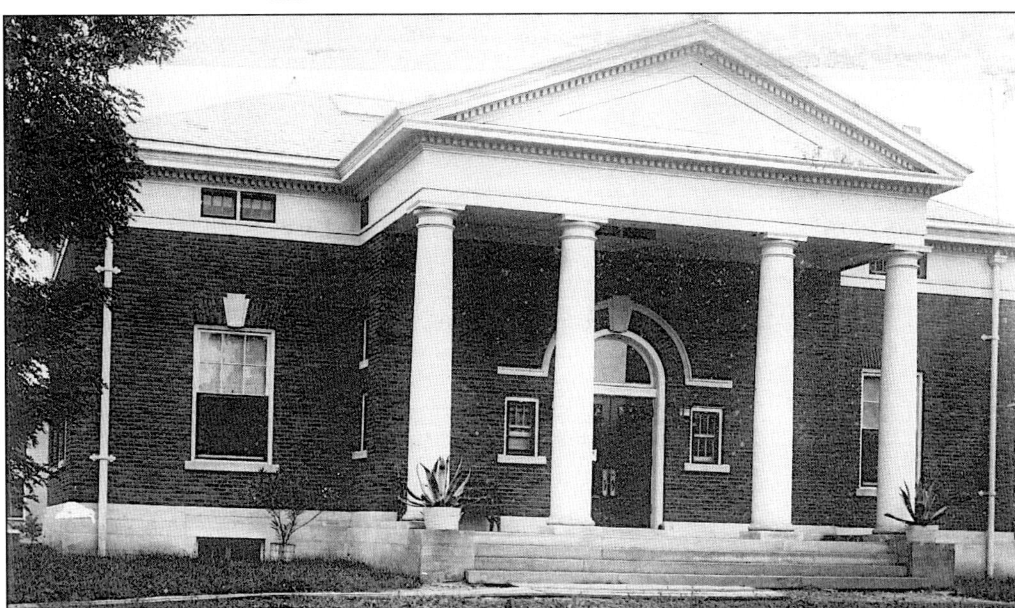

The St. Charles Library was one of the hundreds of Carnegie libraries. Andrew Carnegie, the steel king, donated $12,500 toward the $15,000 needed to build the St. Charles Library. The public library system began in 1906. Before that, the city had a subscription library, which required an annual $2 fee to join.

Karl Asplund moved to St. Charles in 1896 to work at Moline Malleable as a carpenter. In 1912 he founded Boy Scout Troop 1 and spent the rest of his life teaching boys not only the skills of knot-tying, camping, and building fires, but also those of succeeding in life. At the time of his death, he was known as "the world's oldest Scout."

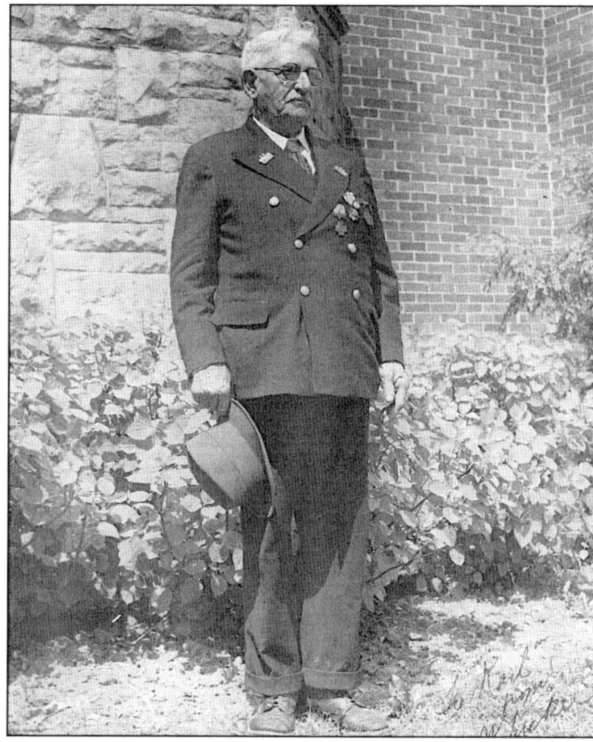

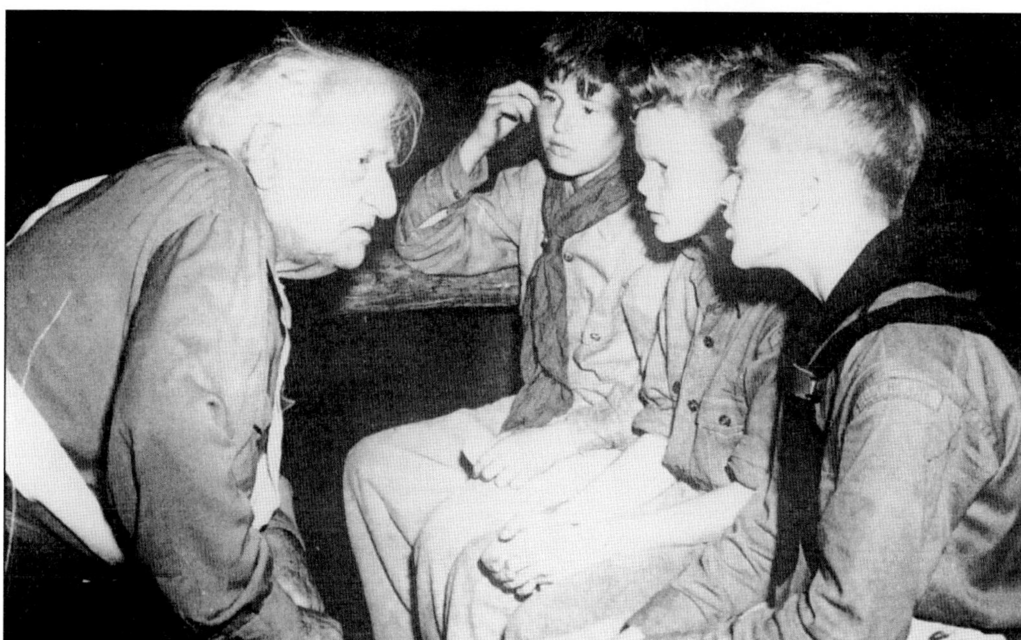

It was reported that from day one, Karl Asplund captured the Scouts' attention and won their affection. It was said that there wasn't anything he wouldn't do for the youth of St. Charles. In his later life, the city repaid their debt to this humanitarian by giving him a kitchenette on the second floor of the old city hall to use until the day he died. It was said that he lived in the community, for the community, and with the help of the community.

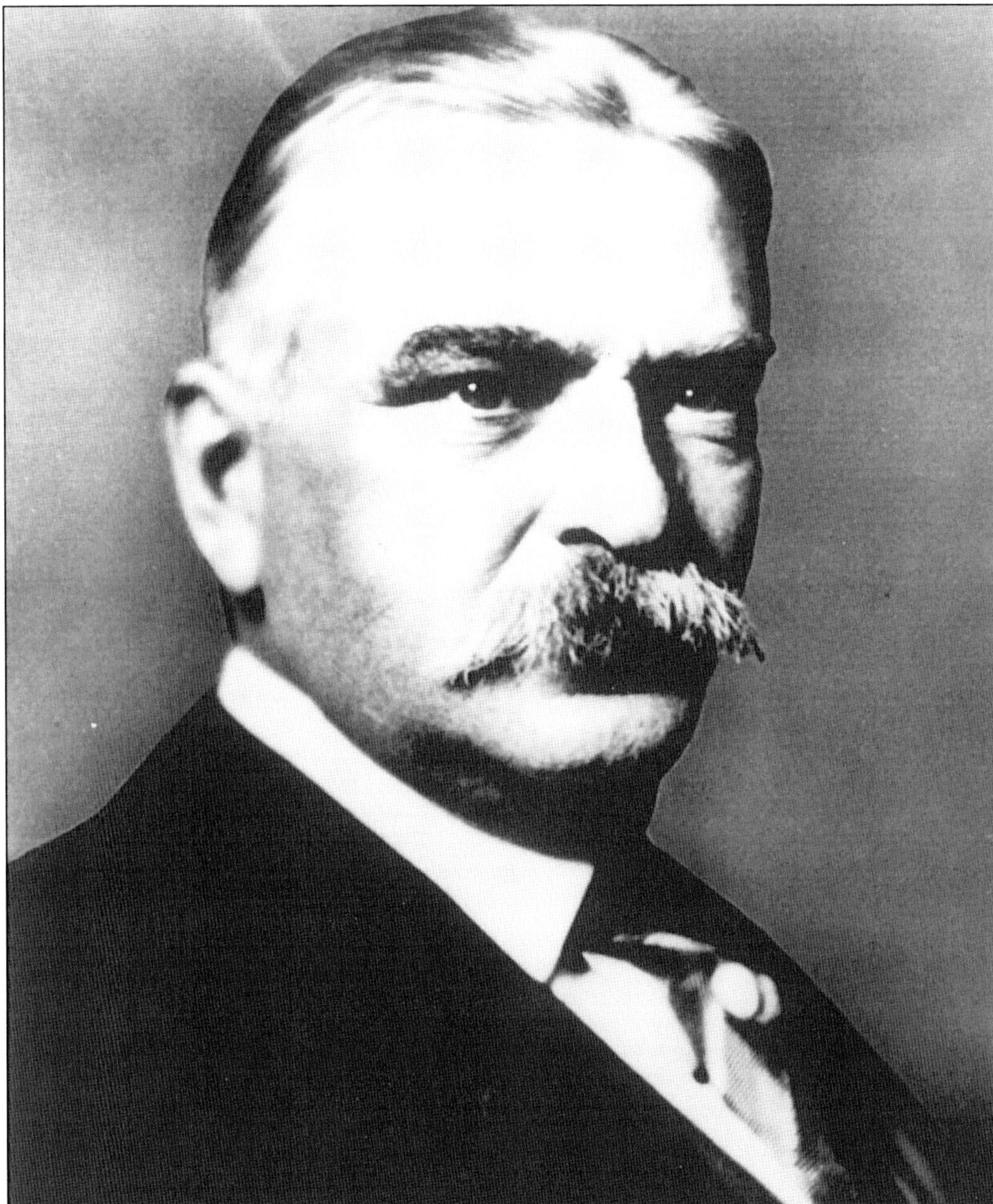

John W. Gates was one of the more picturesque figures of the business and financial life of this country. In 1874 he married Dellora Baker of St. Charles and opened a hardware store. He later found his calling in sales and as an entrepreneur. Early on, Gates saw the benefits of barbed wire and demonstrated its properties to the ranchers of Texas with great success. In 1907 he formed the Texas Company, later to be known as Texaco. While he lived, Gates was generous with his fortunes both in St. Charles, Illinois, and in Port Arthur, Texas. He left the bulk of his estate in trust to his wife and son, who only lived on a few more years. After Dellora Gates's death, the family fortune was left to her brother, Edward Baker, and to her niece, Dellora Angell, who later married Lester Norris. All these were St. Charles residents. Through his heirs and their St. Charles charities, the Gates fortune continues to have a profound influence on St. Charles.

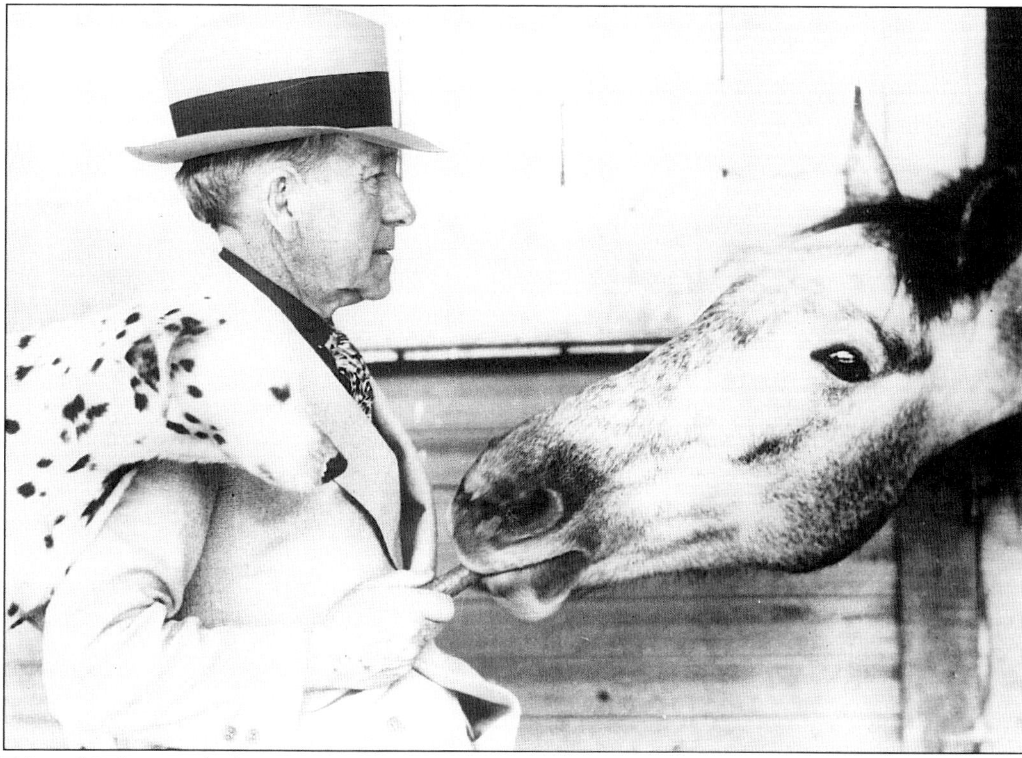

Edward Baker worked as a grain inspector in Chicago, but he and his wife, the former Harriet Rockwell, lived in St. Charles. Local charities such as Boy and Girl Scouts, American Legion, and VFW all also benefited from their charity. Here, Baker is seen as benefactor to Greyhound, world champion trotter and Baker's favorite horse, as the dog Fritter looks on in envy.

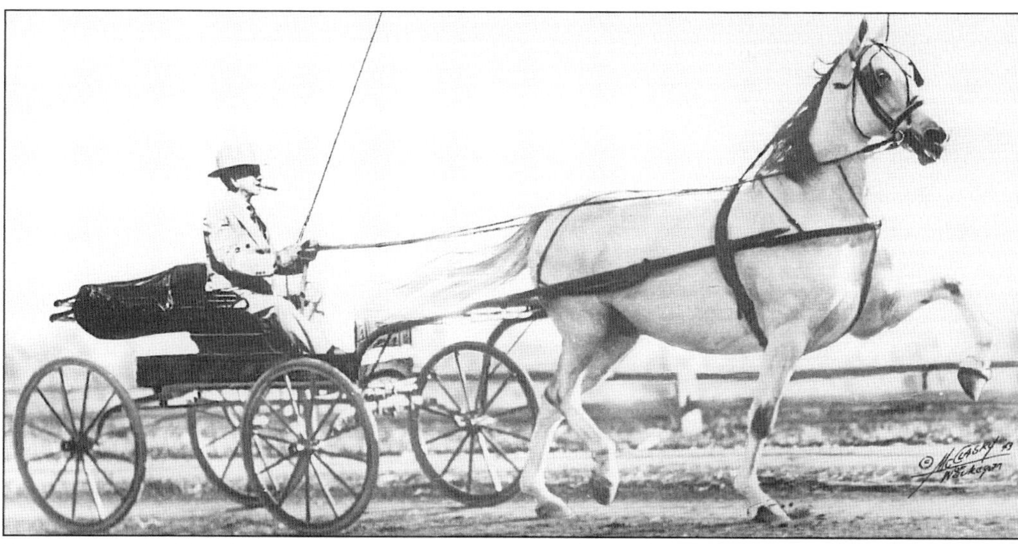

Baker expanded his farm holdings to 1,500 acres with 300 head of cattle. When his interests turned to harness racing, he bought a trotter named Greyhound. Before this horse retired, he had won 17 international records and 33 race victories. The governor of Kentucky gave Baker the title of Colonel for his role in developing and popularizing harness racing in America.

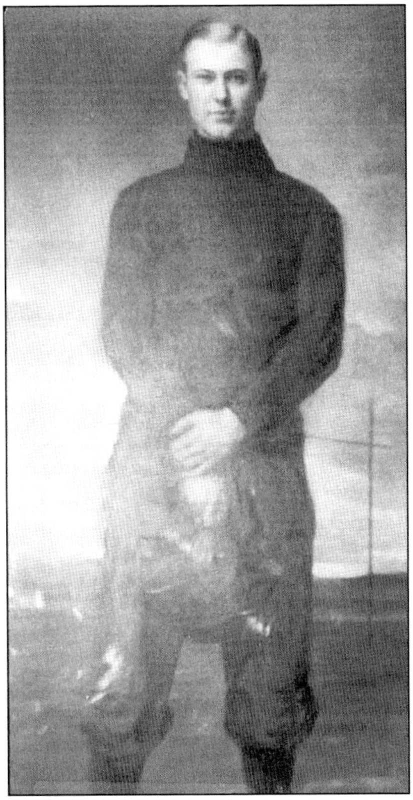

Henry Rockwell Baker, the only son of Edward and Harriet Baker, died in 1914 at the age of 23 from tuberculosis. This was the year that World War I began. His parents wanted to honor him and the young men who died in World War I with a memorial in his city. He is shown here with his football helmet in front of the goal posts.

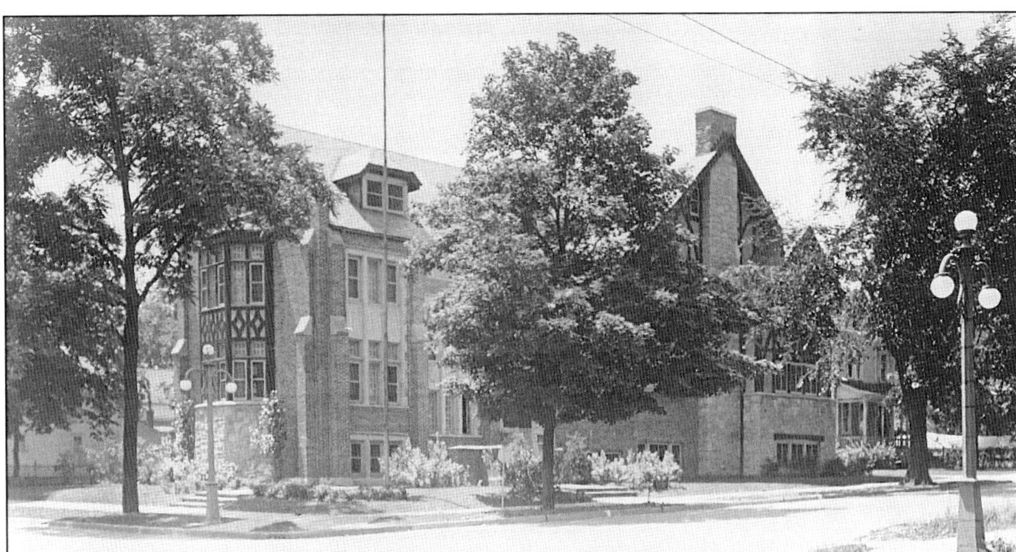

The Henry Rockwell Baker Community Center was given to the City of St. Charles in Baker's honor and in honor of the youth who died in World War I by Col. and Mrs. Baker. The building was to be used as a community meeting place, a site for civic activities, and for recreational, educational, and artistic activities for the whole community. The Baker Community Center was the hub of recreational activities before the formation of the park district.

Dellora Angell was born in 1902. She was once described as an unspoiled child, even though she had everything, including a playhouse with furniture made to scale where she and her friends played each summer when the family resided in Wisconsin. Here she is posing in a "Morton salt girl" attitude.

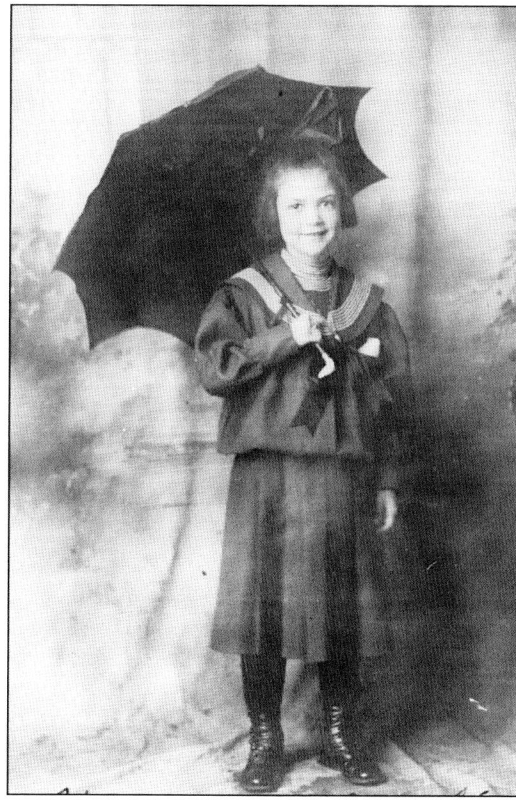

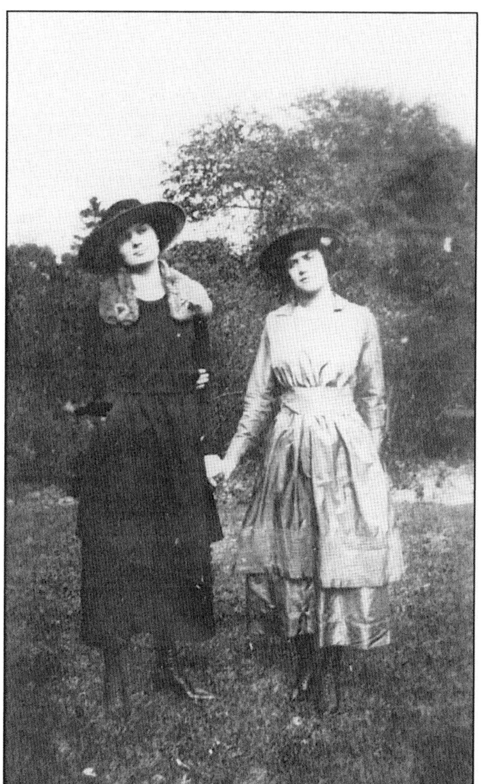

Dellora Angell was 15 years old when she was named as one of the two beneficiaries of the huge Gates fortune. Family and community were always important to Dellora Angell. When she was just 22, she, along with her husband and uncle, founded and contributed to the St. Charles Charities. We see her on the right with her friend Wilda Blanchard on the left.

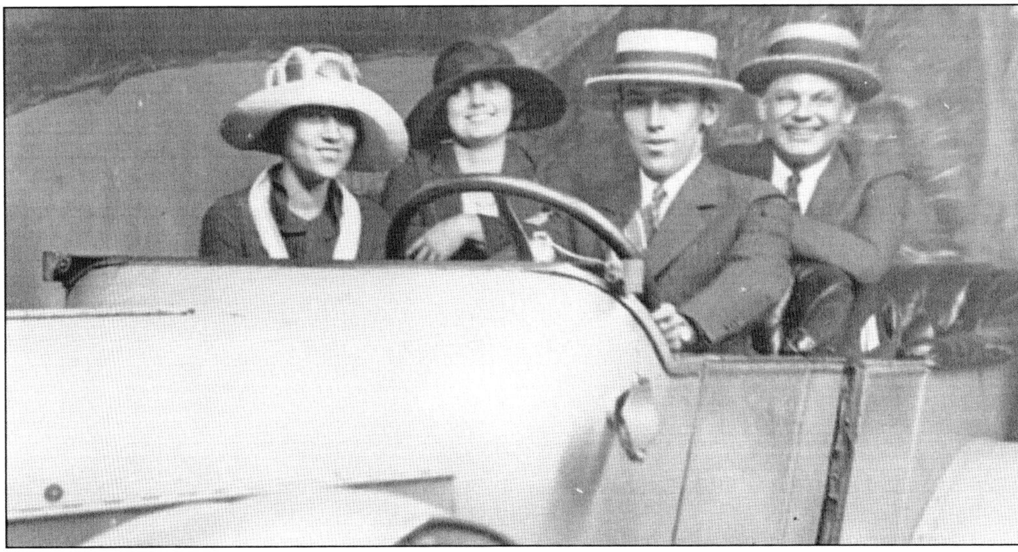

Dellora Angell and Lester Norris were childhood sweethearts who married in 1923. Through their efforts, the city of St. Charles continued to benefit from the family's philanthropy. It has been written that the building of the Arcada showed the Norris' confidence in the future of St. Charles as an entertainment destination. Dellora and Lester Norris are in the front seat while Wilda Blanchard and Mr. Howard are in the rear.

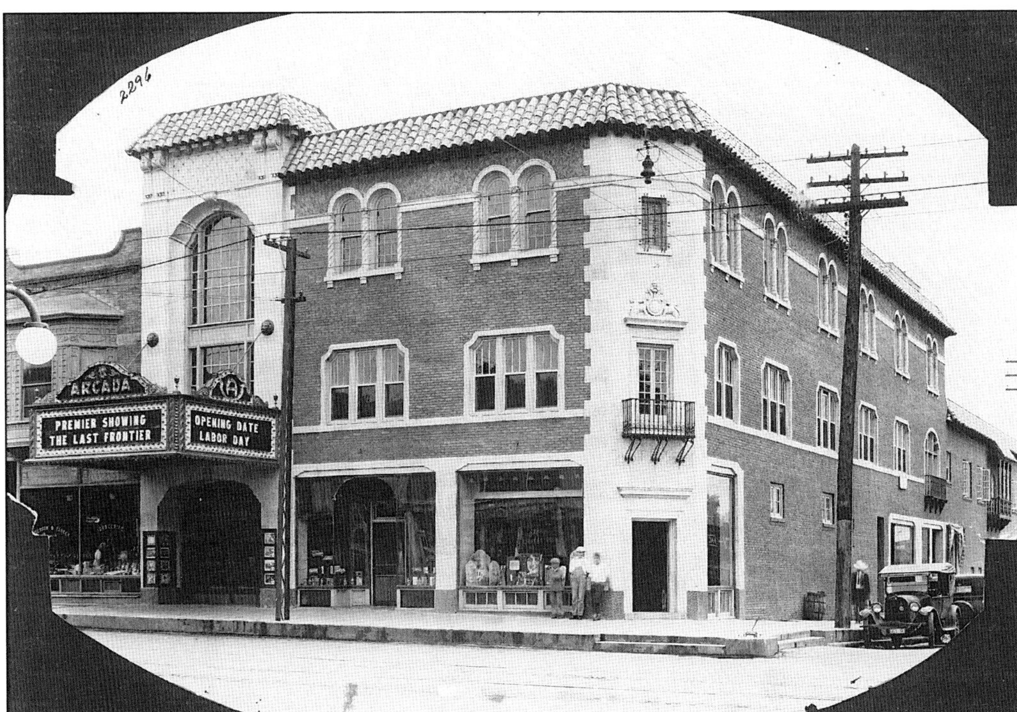


The Arcada Theatre was built at First Avenue and Main Street in 1926. Elmer Behrens was selected as the architect. Behrens used a style called Venetian-Spanish. The building provided for three floors of shop and office spaces and a theater, seating over 1,000 people, that was entered through a long arcade.

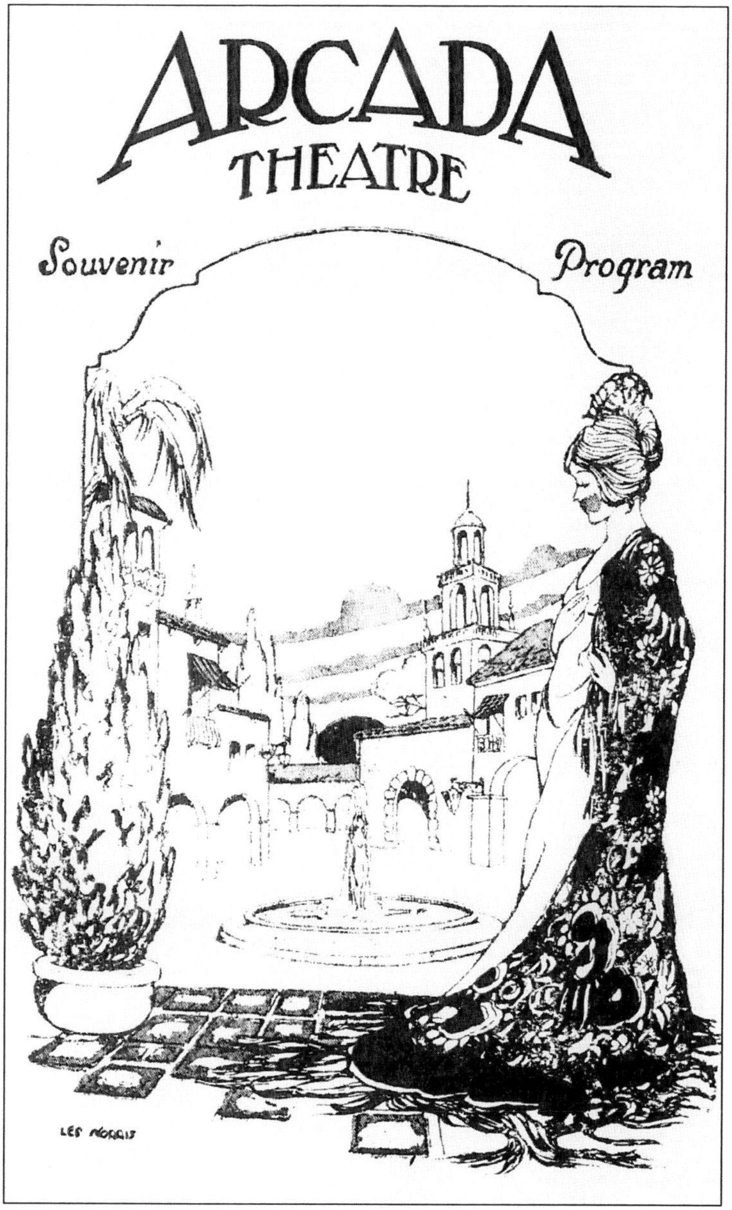


Spain and Venice came to St. Charles on September 6, 1926, when the Arcada Theatre opened with a gala event. People came from all over to see the plush and elegant theater with floating curtains, chandeliers, and expensive art works. Lester Norris put his artistic talent to work and drew the illustration for the cover of the premier program. Earling Holmstrom remembers the opening weekend offering the movie "The Last Frontier" and the "Our Gang Comedy Group," complete with newsreel and vaudeville line up of the Ross and Louise Dance Troupe, the famous Fibber McGee and Molly, and a live orchestra. The Arcada became a regular on the "circuit" until the last days of vaudeville and was one of the few theaters in the Chicago area to remain open throughout the Depression. At the time the Arcada was built, it was noted as the finest 1,000-seat theater in the region at a time when the population of St. Charles was only 5,000.

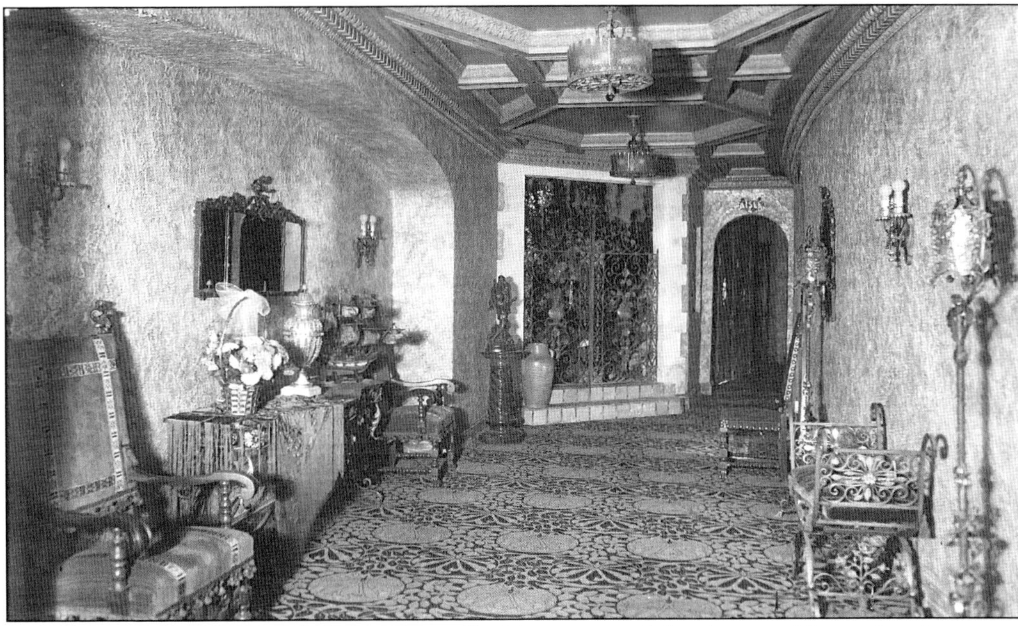

The Spanish influence is felt throughout all of the spaces of the theater. The ceiling beams are ornamented with carved Indian heads that had been designed by Lester Norris, who studied at the Academy of Fine Arts in Chicago. Huge ornate Spanish-influenced chairs, tall torch lights, and rough stucco walls completed the theme of the theater.

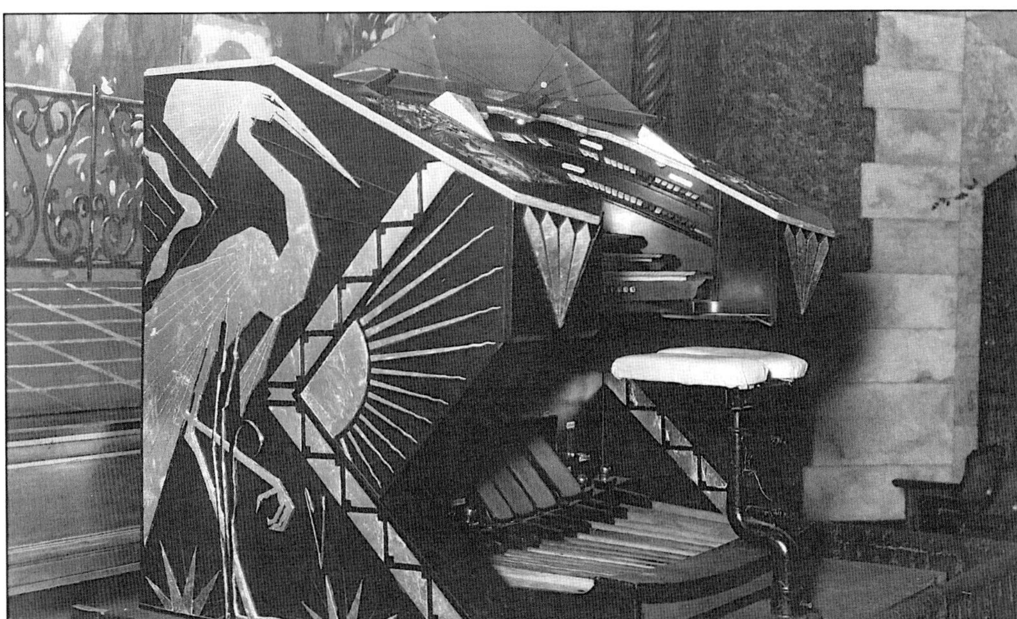

Andalusian jars bathed in blue lights are featured in the theater. There are also mission bells coupled to the pipe organ. The organ is a three manual Mar & Colton organ that rises from the floor to be played. The style of the organ is European Art Deco rather than Spanish.

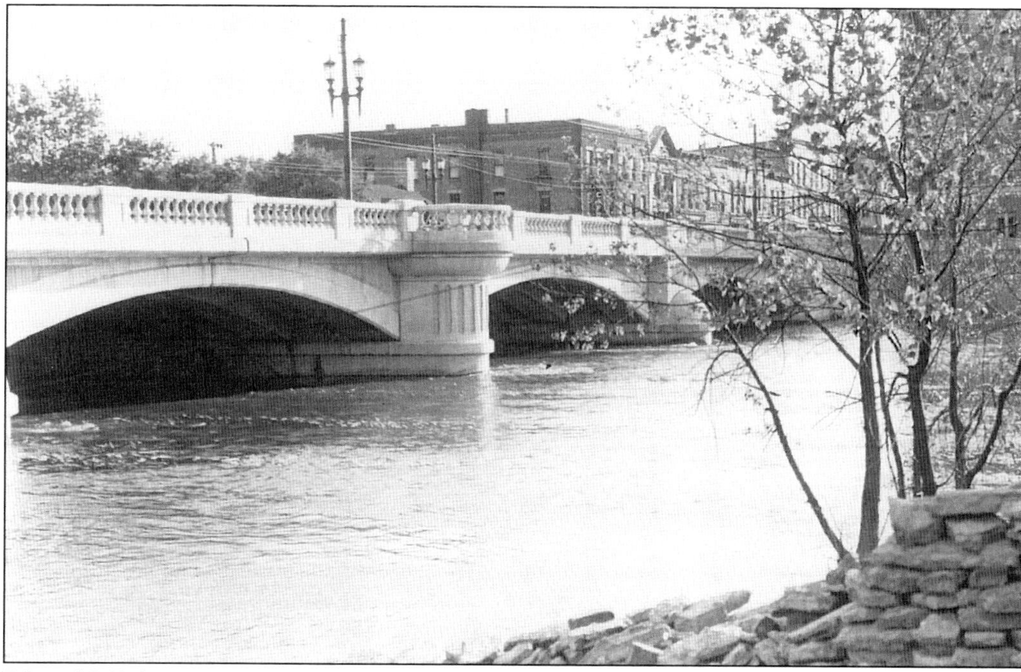

Edward J. Baker was responsible for the reconstruction of the bridge linking the Hotel Baker to the Arcada and widening Route 64 all the way to Chicago. Lester Norris designed the bridge. Baker believed that a way to encourage business in St. Charles, then with a population of almost 5,000, would be to build the finest small hotel in the United States. Work began on the Baker Hotel in 1926 and was completed on June 2, 1928. The whole town experienced a business boom as the area became a vacation getaway.

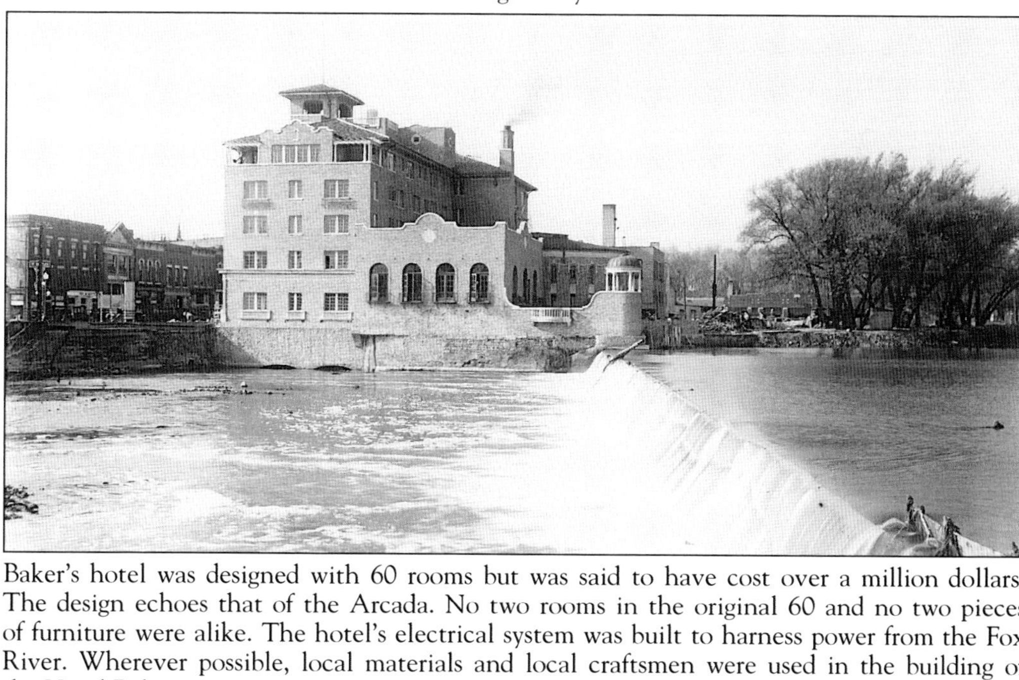

Baker's hotel was designed with 60 rooms but was said to have cost over a million dollars. The design echoes that of the Arcada. No two rooms in the original 60 and no two pieces of furniture were alike. The hotel's electrical system was built to harness power from the Fox River. Wherever possible, local materials and local craftsmen were used in the building of the Hotel Baker.

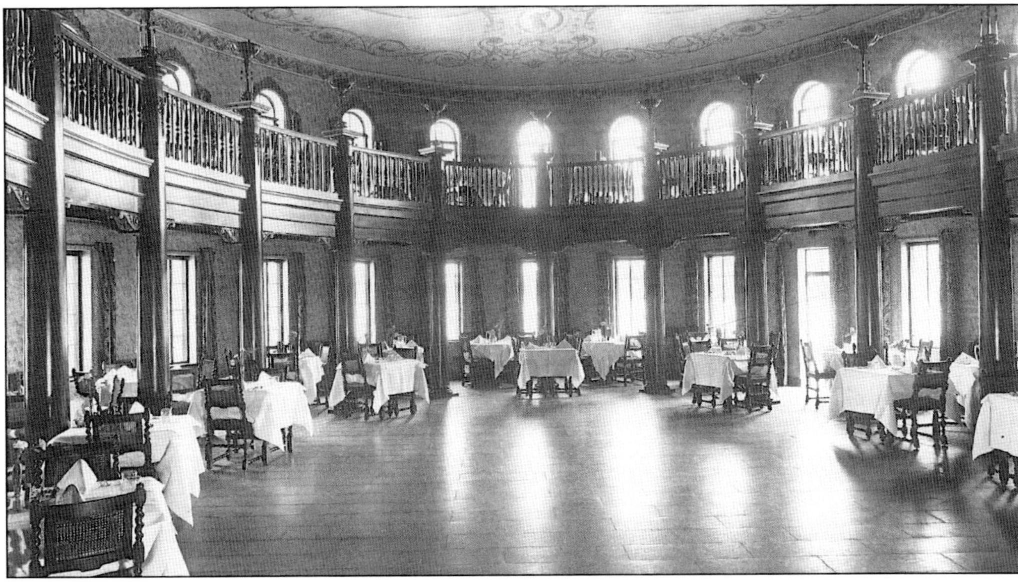

The rainbow room was a two-story, oval dining room with 2,600 colored lights that could shine through a glass block floor. The lights could be controlled to provide a kaleidoscope of colored patterns for the Saturday night dinner-dances and floor shows. The punched paper roll technology used in player piano was the same as that used to control the lights.

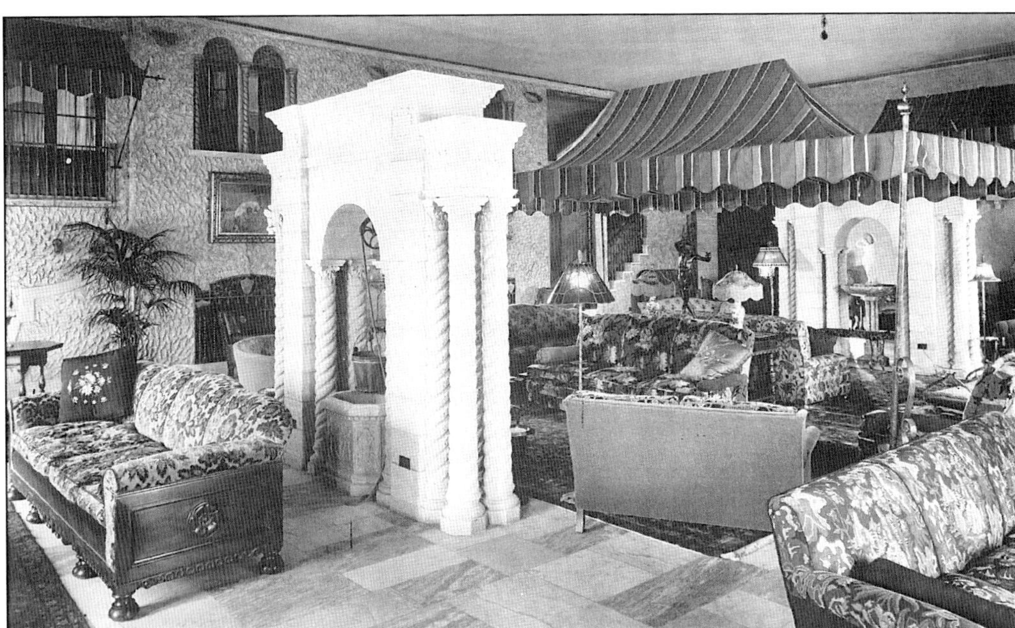

The Trophy Room was designed to represent the courtyard of an old Spanish mansion. The walls resemble the exterior of buildings surrounding the courtyard, with small scale eaves and balconies overlooking it. Seven French doors provided an excellent view of the river. The ceiling was decorated like the sky with the unique effect of clouds floating across it. The Trophy Room, with its victory arches, contained numerous trophies that were won by Colonel Baker's horses.